THE SPIRITUAL CRISIS OF MAN

BY PAUL BRUNTON

A HERMIT IN THE HIMALAYAS

DISCOVER YOURSELF

THE SECRET PATH

THE HIDDEN TEACHING BEYOND YOGA

A MESSAGE FROM ARUNACHALA

THE QUEST OF THE OVERSELF

A SEARCH IN SECRET EGYPT

A SEARCH IN SECRET INDIA

THE WISDOM OF THE OVERSELF

THE SPIRITUAL CRISIS OF MAN

THE
SPIRITUAL CRISIS
OF MAN

BY PAUL BRUNTON

E S T · 1 8 5 2

New York

E. P. DUTTON & CO., INC.

1953

Distributed by
DeVorss & Co.
520 W. Ninth
Los Angeles 15

To
Dr. E. C. Wilson
from
Miss Laura Scherer.

Library of Congress Catalog Card Number: 52-12961

CONTENTS

THE SPIRITUAL CRISIS OF MAN

CHAPTER I

THE CRISIS IN SOCIETY

THE PREWAR WORLD eagerly sought and avidly swallowed an overdose of pleasure to titillate the senses and of progress to gratify the mind. Before long it was also forced to swallow an unsought overdose of suffering and loss. At the very moment of its grandest triumph, when it had won the supreme conquest over material things and subtle forces, world civilization turned into a tragedy.

So many people hoped and supposed that the close of war and the opening of peace would also open a period where trouble would steadily grow less and normality would steadily grow more. So many people hoped and supposed that the nations would make a fresh start in friendship and understanding. But the history of the postwar world, which was to have been a history of this triumphant movement from bad to good, has become instead a history of lamented movement from bad to worse. The peace that was to follow war turns out to be no peace.

Postwar times are noteworthy for their supreme suspense, for the unpleasant chaos and insecurity which grips whole countries or even continents, and for their state of continued crisis. But for a score of years crisis has succeeded crisis without any end in sight. Never before were so many people plunged in so much uncertainty, so much perplexity and unsettlement. Signs of this condition are plenty and plain for all to read. The confusions come with the morning's breakfast.

They move with terrific speed. A week without a world sensation hardly exists. Our newspapers give us in a single issue what was once the history of a whole month. Their pages dismay and distract us with reports of new crises that follow each other rhythmically; they tense and strain our nerves with pictures of depressed markets or oppressed mankind; they narrow our eyes with stories of swift changes. The situation is already dramatic enough and would be fantastic were it not so tragic.

Exposed to the agitations of our age as we are, it is harder to keep a serene mind than ever before. Discouraging news is heard too often and distracting fears have become too insidious to allow us to keep serenity without earning it the hard way. Without inward peace, without outward security, modern man who for so long pitied his ancient and medieval fathers is now himself to be pitied. There are alarming features in the growth of his emotional disequilibrium and mental instability. There are neurotic excitements and pathological turmoils, vehement passions and dangerous indecisions in his mind and life.

A dismal undertone runs beneath the world's everyday talk. Men's brows are intermittently wrinkled with worries as their hopes rise and fall alternately. They live in long-drawn suspense and anxious expectation. They look to each other for strength but find it not. Fear replaces faith, and perplexity shuttles to and fro with confidence. There is foreboding in their hearts and bewilderment in their minds. They begin to ask, "Is this the inglorious end to which our vaunted modern civilization leads?"

The wars and crises have exposed the terrible potentiality for evil which still lurks in man despite his civilized appearance. Not so long ago he thought he had left savagery far behind, but his recent and contemporary activities show quite definitely that he has not. The real tragedy of our time lies not so much in the unprecedented external events themselves as in the unprecedented ethical destitution and spiritual infirmity which they glaringly reveal. When we remember the impressive efforts and institutional legacies of religious prophets, and when we add to this the vast amount of hortatory literature which has been left for the guidance of posterity by the philosophic sages and renowned thinkers of so many past periods in so many parts of the world, we might reasonably expect to see less of the veiled barbarism, the unintuitive materialism and the violent selfishness which have been so rampant in our own time. Does each age have to learn its ethics afresh? Shall the wandering soul of man never come to rest? The world is heavy with experience but it does not seem to avail us in our hour of need.

The sorry confusion of our epoch seems complete. It is unnecessary to paint a vivid picture of conditions which are so obvious to most of the weary inhabitants of this harassed planet. The scientist at work in his laboratory, the politician declaiming from the benches, the historian with eyes glued to the records of vanished centuries, the economist with his serried ranks of figures, the clergyman puzzling over apocalyptic pages of the scriptures, and the soldier watchful over national passions—all alike offer us their opinions, their strongly held convictions and their pet panaceas. We need not doubt that what they have to offer possesses a greater or lesser degree of truth, but when we listen to all their voices together it is as though we were transplanted to some modern tower of Babel, so conflicting and contradictory are their descriptive explanations and prescriptive suggestions. The dark problems of our age are not easy for professors to solve and send mankind's well-wishers out into the night to take counsel with the stars. If the crisis has clarified much for a few minds, it has confused everything for many minds. They do not know where to turn for truth, nor what to believe in the present, nor what to expect in the future. They are bewildered by the paralyzing uncertainties and despondent over the staggering headlines which stare at them daily from the tops of newspapers. Such events make most of them feel they are being carried along, they do not know where. The result is that they do also not know how to deal with the doubts that infect their consciousness or the obstacles that interfere with their conduct.

The terrible physical shocks of war had their repercussions in the succeeding mental shocks. Men have thus been forced to examine, and consequently to find out, the values and the truths as well as the errors and the delusions in their views. The course of events has forced them to question whether their attitudes are worth holding and whether their beliefs are true or false. The answers may have been totally wrong but the questions could not easily have been evaded.

Wartime shocks and peacetime anxieties have influenced character both for worse and for better. Whoever has lived through them and remained the same unchanged man, holding the same unchanged views, is either a sage or a fool—and sages, who take the trouble to plumb depths and not stop at surfaces, are rare. Of course there are those who sincerely believe they are no different from what they were before. They are mistaken. They may seem to have changed little, but the subconscious has registered more. The bodily wounds of war may be quickly healed, but the deepest effects of war are slowly manifested.

A curious effect of both war and crisis upon people everywhere is their division into three distinct and different groups —so widely different that the picture is paradoxical. For, although having identically the same experience of wartime misery and peacetime chaos, people have drawn divergent conclusions from it! The same world distress or personal woe which has broken the religious faith of a number of people, has actually strengthened it for others; while it has left a third group indifferent and apathetic toward religion, preoccupied with a wholly political or economic view of life that is based on fierce class or national hatred. The same catastrophe which has damaged the brittle faith of some has fortified and revived the ebbing faith of others, or brought it for the first time into the minds of still others; yet there are many who have lost interest in either acceptance or denial and turned aside to more mundane questions altogether. Of those who have reacted by accepting religion, not a few did so because they urgently needed some kind of refuge, not because they investigated whether it be a certain or a durable refuge. For precisely the same reasons others have turned to drink or to sensuality or to political violence.

All humanity's crisis has brought some nearer to a good life but it has also taken others further away from it. It is a truism that men are complex beings. The good and evil in them are mixed together, the exalted aims and low motives are intertwined. Hence, their conduct in the circumstances now prevailing is equally complex. If many have succumbed to the unleashed lures of short-lived sensualism, others have risen to the higher call of spiritual seeking; still others find their satisfaction in enthusiastic adherence to political parties or economic doctrines bearing the flag of altruistic slogans but leading in the end to demonic violence.

Humanity, shocked in its nerves and wounded in its feelings, passed through the ordeal of world war either to fall morally through a negative reading of its experiences or to rise spiritually through a positive understanding of their true meaning. The one reaction increased egoism and stimulated animality. The other lessened egoism and subdued animality. One aroused men through the distresses of war and the anxieties of crisis to spiritual seeking. The other led by the same events, either into spiritual carelessness and degradation or into fiercely destructive social hatred.

The violence of war has been succeeded by the tumult of peace. The sacrifice and idealism of the first have been followed by a relapse into the selfishness and cynicism of the second. The influences of moral disintegration and social disruption are menacingly active. Despite the miseries and lessons of life in battle-scarred lands, the old error and the old spirit are once more in our midst. The moral effects of what humanity has passed through do not show enough of the advance in character and aims needed to carry it through this dangerous period. Although some residue remains, some definite mark on the character, the public inspiration and individual unselfishness so often generated during these critical war years have largely ebbed away, leaving frustration and apathy behind. Social standards have become harder, less sensitive, and more materialistic than before, more than ever devoted to the body's comfort and the mind's pleasure; they do not respect honorable poverty. The wide degradation of manners is an evil accompaniment of the downfall of ideals.

When the religious sanctions of morality become impotent, as they have so dramatically and so largely become in certain lands, there are grave results. When the inner life of religion has drained away, when faith and reverence are lost to older generations and meaningless to younger ones, it is inevitable that the outer life of society shall show chaos and crime and that men shall feel either disgust with their fellows or despair of them. When fortune is uncertain, when life is cheap, and social tempests prevail, men who do not see in this a warning to transcend all in spiritual self-seeking, are tempted to forget all in reckless pleasure-seeking. They are discontented with their personal situation and dissatisfied with the futility and senselessness of life. So they let themselves float on its surface, trying to forget, and repeat the lines of Ronsard, the sixteenth-century French poet,

> And since what comes tomorrow who can say?
> Live, pluck the roses of the world today.

The craving for physical excitement, the tendency to sordid intrigue and the unrestrained acceptance of animal impulses are fostered by much in our careless civilization and fostered to our danger. Personal or public catastrophe has driven the ill-balanced to find transient solace in cynicism and sensualism, which in the end are useless, when it might have driven them to fasting, prayer, and reflection, which may often be useful.

We have seen within a single lifetime changes of thought and view, of conduct and environment, so vast that hardly any farseeing prophet could have told about them and gained belief. Yet with all this, the hard fact remains that the moral character of wide groups of humanity is largely worse than before, the motivations more materialistic than ever. Many who were formerly indifferent to religion, still remain indifferent. Too many others consider spiritual study or mystical practice to be a useless luxury and declare that they have no time for it. A certain section of the intellectuals sneer at these things as escapism, never dreaming that it is they who are the real escapists. That the Unworldly could even be a part of the human being's proper business never enters their head. Their vision of life is definitely out of focus. The war did not drag them from their escapist attitude; the horror and shock, the blood and woe did not show its insufficiency. If a man talks believingly of spiritual things he must be, they think, either a naïve fool or a designing hypocrite.

Then anguish and despair of unfortunate victims of evil operations and evil oppressions have left many of them high and dry on the shores of doubt as to the existence of a higher power, and of skepticism as to its beneficence. The high tension, terror, and anguish of the times not only harmed some people but proved too much for other people. The First World War was the event that finally destroyed British novelist Thomas Hardy's faith in a beneficent God. The Second World War drove such a brilliant intellectual as that other British novelist, Virginia Woolf, to take refuge in suicide, and to leave behind the sad words: "I have the feeling that I shall go mad and cannot go on any longer in these terrible times." Life's agony proved too much for her feelings. The world's evil overcame her mind.

Many who once believed that there was a movement in the destiny of mankind leading upward to the Good now believe that it is leading downward to the Evil. Are they to be blamed if the dark fatalities of our times have wrought this unexpected change of faith? When goodness is mocked and good people thrown into despair; when the false, the cruel, and the diabolic are so powerful, it is not surprising that men's minds are stabbed with doubts. In the face of monstrous recurring and seemingly victorious forces showing so much malice and ignorance, bestiality and cunning, they may be pardoned if they think at times that all their best hopes are but delusions, all their religious and moral values mere shams. It is not possible to ascertain accurately whether the religiously faithless outnumber the religiously faithful, but all too many have become spiritually numbed by the tragedy and terror of what they have endured.

However, there are a great many others who hoped that after all this suffering, after all this horror, a new humility would come into the world, the humility which would acknowledge and reverence a higher power than Man's. When so many people in so many lands have lived to see fancied securities revealed as fictions; when so much has given way beneath them that they have to look beyond present distresses and around the corner of present afflictions, it was believed that this had taught those who were at all teachable the need of believing in God. There have been historical precedents for the notion that the destructive agonies of war and the chaotic miseries of peace might well bring many to a weary pessimism which would seek in otherworldliness what it could not find here.

The closeness or remoteness of the realization of such a hope is disputable, but one thing about it is not: the crisis taught above all, and continues to teach, that those who do not face the spiritual problem of their existence on earth decisively and finally will not escape mental insecurity and anxiety. It has not only brought up such questions but forced people to start searching for the answers. If they have been able to pass through the experiences of this war and this crisis without stopping to ask themselves at times what is the meaning of human life, they are doomed to go on suffering senselessly. Amid the crash of possessions, the shattering of faith, and the catastrophe of events, only those who have begun to find abiding values which will survive these disasters can really abate their mental suffering, relax their tensions, and reduce their fears. In the others, the awareness of an inner lack has become sharper, the feeling that an inner satisfaction is necessary but unfound has become stronger. Yet the idea of what is needed itself remains dim and vague or tragically wrong.

Cynics have said that man is still barbarian, that it is fantasy to hope for his spiritual betterment in the near future. But to say that it is folly to expect a quick and general spiritual revival is not to say that some spiritual deposit has not been left in the mind of a section of humanity by the war. The postbag of every effective writer on spiritual subjects offers evidence that a number of people are interesting themselves in these subjects for the first time and for reasons arising out of the world crisis. Their arousal from spiritual lethargy has begun to come, although it has come at a terrible cost. History shows that it is especially at such times of widespread distress, social upheaval, and shattered values, of religious crisis and moral challenge, that larger and loftier conceptions of life are sought and new spiritual movements are born.

If the war brought profound misery to mankind it also brought with it a profound opportunity to be humbled by sufferings, taught by reflections, and shamed by errors. Out of its wide suffering—this bath in human blood—all had the chance to arise, chastened, purified, and wiser. Hesitantly and confusedly, some did learn its lessons correctly under the dire pressure of events, purifying themselves of foolish beliefs and materialistic concepts. Its drastic shock and miserable aftermath led to the loss of some of their external supports; and this in turn to the loss of some of their internal supports. Swept by waves of pessimism, they sought for religious consolation or comforting prophetic messages or mystical experience. (The word "mystical" has possibly become too vague and too wide in meaning really to be useful. The word "spiritual" is hardly better. Yet there is no adequate equivalent in the English language to the idea intended. Sanskrit is better served. However, these words must be used for brevity's sake but they will be used here only when avoidance is too troublesome.)

After the First World War it was in the fashion to be cynical and lighthearted and superficial; it was out of the fashion to be intensely serious about the nature and destiny of the human soul. But after the Second World War, with its wider tragedy and deeper suffering, there is comparatively more earnest thinking about such a topic. Looking straight in the face at their experience, some have begun to think with truer concepts, and yearn to lift their activities to a higher level. Such an outlook has not been attained by most of mankind, but it has certainly been attained by certain individuals.

How many have been compelled by what they perceive of the condition of things on this planet to start a conscious search for the meaning of life? How much momentum have these movements actually gained? Are the marks of increased holiness, purer conduct, and decreased worldliness visible in this postwar era? It is true that more people seek spiritual truth now than did before the war. But their number is still so small and its increase so slow that the movement is very far from gaining decisive influence. Only a comparatively small number of persons has been aroused by the world crisis to seek the inner life. Those who care for personal idealism, who aspire for self-improvement, and who reach out after the divine, are still all too few. The regeneration which could have been the outcome of a war of this unusual character, needs to show more signs of beginning, if the expectation of a general spiritual awakening is not to fade. The great darkness which enveloped prewar humanity still envelops too large a part of postwar humanity. It is the cause of an avoidable mass of suffering and misery, of avertible sin and despair, which exist in the world and which can find no better solvent than such an awakening.

CHAPTER II

NO BETTER WORLD WITHOUT BETTER MEN!

IT WOULD BE easy for a generation which has seen unparalleled conflict and unprecedented evil to lose its faith in divine power or divine wisdom. This is what is happening to many people in this time; they are so preoccupied with the external circumstances of their life that they neglect its higher purpose. Their analyses of historic events and of human evolution are either not deep enough or quite misleading. What other result can be expected from men who lack the knowledge of the spiritual laws governing the causation of those events and controlling that evolution?

The times so vividly if briefly mentioned in various passages of the *New Testament* are upon us. Mark how they speak of one identifying sign being the appearance of false prophets. St. Luke warns us in burning words: "Take heed that ye be not deceived . . . go ye not therefore after them." The mistake commonly made in understanding these pages is to limit the reference only to religious and mystical prophets. But the teachers and leaders of destructive movements, whose dogmas have been received with emotional fervor and propagated with intellectual fanaticism, must not only be included in the reference but even given first place. They have diverted to themselves exactly the same kind of faith or devotion as that which is given to religious leaders like Mohammed.

A million people will eagerly follow a glib leader who raises contentious clamor and leads them to ultimate destruction, when only a few people will follow an inspired spiritual leader who leads them to true blessedness. This shows the faulty sense of values which prevails among people who are entirely ignorant of the fact that if their inner attitude toward life is wrong, their outer personal, political, and economic affairs will go wrong. It shows that the reason why the mass of mankind cannot make a success of their civilization is because they cannot make a success of themselves. Not having enough faith in, or leading by, higher forces, they put their faith in destructive ones.

When we hear the wonderful story of man's long rise we know that he holds within himself the power to conquer difficulty. He can make mighty changes, and move his world forward, but he can do this in a peaceful constructive manner only if he disciplines the violence of his animal nature. Society and surroundings are the consequences of history. The past experience of the human race and the traditional knowledge it has accumulated, cannot be dispensed with. It is for us to profit by it.

Those whose metaphysical foundation is dialectical materialism, exclude from their consideration of man the great truth that he is here ultimately for spiritual development.

They regard him solely as a fleshly body whose primary interests are material ones. But the fact that they turn away from this truth does not remove them from the sphere of its operation. So long as they hold such an incorrect conception of human nature as the materialist one, so long will the illusions of extreme egoism and the evils of bitter hatred flourish among them. Under the influence of such wrong thinking and limited understanding, the naïve men who engage in it are walking dangerously near the edge of a precipice. They live in a darkness to which they have become so accustomed that they believe it to be light. This puts them in a precarious situation.

The real struggle today is a confused and hidden one; it is not only the outward and obvious struggle which every newspaper records. It is between the great lie of a materialist concept of life and the great truth of a spiritual one. We call the first a lie because it asserts that we are here on earth solely to satisfy the appetites of the body and the desires of the ego. Throughout man's long history, his wisest seers and most illumined prophets have put forth their thoroughly tested discovery—not opinion—that the forces of Nature, God, brought us here to discipline those appetites and elevate those desires as a preliminary requisite to the higher purpose of life —the discovery of the Overself and the conscious union with it.

Millions have been deceived by the appearance of things into believing that their existence is physical and nothing more. Today they are eating the sour fruit of this false belief. Correct self-understanding would have shown them that they are not only creatures compounded of body, feelings, and thoughts but also of spiritual intuitions. That is why the firmest possible foundation upon which to build any social structure is the essential ethics of all spiritual teaching. Those ethics ultimately sprout from a mystically revealed knowledge of certain moral and spiritual laws which govern the universe. The new understanding of these old laws, which go far deeper than politico-economic doctrine, would necessarily bring about a new and better integration of society, which would then reflect ethical thought.

The impartial observer may seem pessimistic but he knows that world conferences will fail so long as statesmen go to them only to protect their present interests, to make patchwork solutions, and to avoid uncomfortable concessions. They will fail so long as rulers and peoples prefer a shallow to a deeper view. They will prove, as was predicted several years ago in an earlier book, mere delusions so long as a loftier ethical ideal and superior metaphysical knowledge do not animate them. When a materialistic civilization becomes outwardly impressive but remains inwardly impoverished, when political relations become an elaborate façade for hiding the spiritually empty rooms behind them, menacing problems are sure to appear on every side. The real contemporary problem behind all the other ones is the problem of mental and moral regeneration.

Those who know the hidden powers of thought in the life and fate of man, know that external peace cannot be successfully secured while internal war rages in the heart. Until men tame their angers, discipline their desires, leash their greeds, modify their materialism, and curb the cruelty and slaughter they practice on animals, the root causes of war will still remain. All they can do in the present stage of human evolution is to create an international institution which shall act as an international policeman. Just as the creation of city police forces has not stopped all crime but has nevertheless prevented much crime, so the creation of such an institution could not stop all wars but may prevent many wars. Every such proposal has its own special accompanying dangers. Yet, some proposal must be accepted and realized, whatever its dangers, because in no other way can the prospect of a more peaceful life open up more quickly for humanity. If coming history

should show a tragic failure to realize the contemporary proposal, that would be only because the deeper lessons of vanishing history, echoed here, have been insufficiently learned or
wholly ignored. But just as the grim necessities of war forced
overdue changes on us only when they were no longer
avoidable, so the grim necessities of peace will force upon us
those personal and national changes which many are still too
unevolved to make on their own. A new and better world
will come in the end, and after all. But to the extent that we
let it come out of compulsion, not out of volition, we have
to suffer greatly during its labor pains. In the end the Word
will replace the Sword.

It is questionable whether absolute harmony will ever prevail amongst men, unless and until they first fulfill the spiritual goal which God ever holds before them. Social life creates
its own problems, its own conflicts of group and personal
interests. National life leads to angry quarrels with other nations or aggressive invasions of them. In the world of manifested forms, each of which is different from all others in
some points, there will necessarily be friction at those points
at some times. A kingdom of perfect harmony on earth is
apparently not possible. The world's nature and human nature seem to forbid it. *But what we cannot find outside ourselves, does exist and may be found deep within ourselves.*
When Jesus once announced the good news to his hearers and
told them in plain words that "the kingdom of heaven" was
within them, he meant, if he meant anything at all, that the
most important and most desirable thing in life was not to be
found in any external place, thing, person, or position; it was
to be found only in the hidden strata of the thought and
feeling of man. The bellowing doctrinaire, who thinks otherwise, who persuades people to see only the surface of their
problems, may say what he likes but a physical utopia has
never existed and may never be found. It is like a mirage which
draws men on only to delude them. It is either an ever-

receding horizon or else a dream from which its deluded seekers must wake up. The dream's creator may paint pleasant pictures of an ideal society or even religious-ascetic community where all will be well and everyone will be happy, but the reality will never be like that, for it would still have to be built with the material of fallible and imperfect men.

If the ashrams, spiritual retreats of the Orient, and religious monasteries of the Occident, with so lofty and unworldly a doctrine as many of them possess, have been unable to develop perfectly harmonious and morally untainted communities among themselves, but on the contrary suffer from the petty weaknesses of pitiful human nature, what hope is there for realizing this dream outside their walls, where aspiration is less urgent and less deep? Where is the human material for such a superhuman society? Can it be found sufficiently anywhere today? Earthly millenniums are always postponed, never realized. So it has been in the past, so it shall be in the future. Any idealistic society or colony can be only relatively good at best, good only at and for a certain time and a certain place. It can never escape from the relativity, imperfection, and transiency which permeate this world. Human nature would cease to be its present ignorant self if it were to perform the vicarious sacrifices which the social or humanitarian or religious idealist's rosy but fallacious optimism expect of it. The paradise men want to attain is a condition they must *inwardly* create by slow degrees for themselves. As soon as men make themselves spiritually worthy of a finer world, they will have some approach toward it. A wiser practicality would not seek to establish a kingdom of heaven on earth, in the sense of a physical utopia, for its own sake. It would be too strongly imbued with the realization of transiency in all things and too profoundly perceptive of the inherent imperfection in all things to be deceived by such a materialistic aim. Rather would it seek to establish a better earthly home for mankind for the sake of using it as a springboard whence to aspire for the true kingdom of heaven, which is and always will be an inner one. It is not a spatial one. Jesus, the skillful angler of men, warned against looking for it, "Lo here! or Lo there! for, behold, the kingdom of God is within you." Yet not a few of his followers have fallen into the belief that this kingdom can be externalized. They believe that some kind of a sacerdotally controlled utopia can be created, just as a section of the materialists believe that only a sacerdotally free economic utopia can be created. The mystical dreamers believe that some kind of perfectionist community can be created. But a collection of imperfect human beings can never lead to such a result.

The truth here is that the external problems which torment man are really projections of the internal problems which he has failed to solve aright within his heart and mind. There is no adequate answer to the principal questions of politics and economics without first finding an adequate answer to the larger questions of life itself, which necessarily include the questions: "What is man?" "What are the real objects for which an organized society exists?" "What are the final ends to be worked out through its means?" Unless we lay hold of their correct answers, we shall only be working in the dark and wasting energies quite uselessly, or worse, gravely harm the human stuff out of which society is made. Ignorance of these answers is the primary cause of our present sad lot. The distress of today grips us like a horrible quagmire into which we sink deeper with every step forward, simply because we do not know and cannot see the proper destination toward which we ought to move. On the other hand, if we secure a clear conception of these objects and ends, we shall be able to work more efficiently, act more effectively, and live more happily. But how can we do so successfully unless we know the larger direction which the evolutionary forces of life itself are inexorably compelling it to take? Without a knowledge of the divine will, we may only stumble in the dark and perhaps hurt ourselves grievously, as we have already hurt ourselves during this tragic century. Hitherto, we have fulfilled our destiny blindly and unconsciously, which means painfully and stupidly. But the policy of spiritual drift will no longer pay. We might get away with it in easier times but we cannot get away with it in these sternly critical times.

The problems which press down on humanity may be mostly political and economic and therefore should be dealt with by economic and political measures. But their background remains moral and metaphysical. No solution can be a fundamental one which ignores these two elements. No way in which humanity can save itself from the danger which confronts it will prove satisfactory if it leaves out the spiritual way; every other way if taken alone will yield only failure as its result in the end. Only when the politician and economist, the statesman and the soldier will have the sense to perceive this and the courage to admit it; only when they will have the humility to declare themselves semibankrupt and with insufficient assets can the miracle happen and the aid of a higher power come to our rescue and do for us what we cannot do for ourselves.

What is best for the individual is in the long run also best for society. Whoever surveys the unrolled picture of his own existence or that of human existence as a whole and without prejudice will find this truth irrefutable. And if the individual can attain true happiness only by following a better way of living, society also can attain it likewise. If easier ways are followed, then lesser results must be expected. From this standpoint political, economic, and social reforms cannot by themselves lead to the true happiness of man. This is not to say that they are not needed, for they may lead to his partial or transient happiness. They are useful palliatives which may relieve his pain, not radical remedies which can cure his sickness.

An industrial economy which does not in practice recognize man as a spiritual being or the universe as outworking divine laws, breeds psychic perils for its people. Even if its planners provide a more satisfactory place in which the general mass of people can live, they cannot provide the ideals for which those people will have to live if they are to fulfill their incarnation's higher purpose, ideals which will in the end determine the fate of that place. "Man proposes, God disposes," may sound trite but is still quite operative. Those realists and rationalists who would dismiss the application of worthy ideals as being nothing more than dreamers' catchwords and impracticable slogans delude themselves.

Our failure to build a worth-while society is primarily a moral failure. But before there can be moral reform, there must be spiritual reform. This is the root of all the others.

We ought not in our judgment of materialistic doctrine preaching otherwise and the misguided men who symbolize it in the world today, misjudge the masses who have been befogged into it. We must not forget their ultimate quality, which links them with God. We must remember that in their blind unconscious way they, too, are seeking the truth; they, too, will one day stand hushed in the presence of the Spirit. They, too, will eventually accept the saving ideal of good will as against the destructive ideal of hate. They, too, will learn to know that the divine love is back of all events and that so soon as men turn to look for it, they will find it moving also toward them. Our Father is still in Heaven and our job is to recognize our sonship. This single truth is at the core of all spiritual teaching.

CHAPTER III

THE MACHINE AGE

TODAY'S WORSHIP of speed in living, doing, and making has produced nervous tensions which in turn have driven men to seek relief through artificial stimulants and narcotic drugs. The weaker-willed ones among them have done so to excess and maimed themselves in moral character in the end.

A different consequence of this worship seems trivial but is actually not at all what it seems. There has developed a contempt for lands where the tempo of change is slower, where the passage from an old-time way to a mechanized existence lags markedly. Behind this contempt lies a failure to understand why the people in those lands want to be left alone and undisturbed, why they prefer to work out their development at their own pace and not lose whatever inner contentment they possess. The two nations on this planet who have made speed a high ideal of living—have thereby become incapable of sympathizing with the wishes of backward peoples who prefer to preserve and continue their dilatory rhythm of living. The latter are satisfied to take only a little part in the race for power and possessions. They regard the environment of the Western nations as unattractive, the mental condition as a kind of madness, and the rush and turmoil as not worth the price involved. More curiously, they consider the machine as a kind of toy.

Nevertheless, despite their views, it is true that modern

industrial methods, because of their tremendous productive capacity, gained by mass techniques based on machines, have come to stay. But have they come to stay in their present shape? They give the worker his bread and butter but they also deprive him of inner satisfactions and individual functional value. They turn him to some extent into a machine part and bereave him of his manhood. Insofar as the machine robs him of his individuality and makes him perform the same few mechanical movements every day throughout his working life, it is liable to stunt him. The assembly lines in huge factories which pour out masses of goods do not make any demands on the creative skills of the workers but merely keep them engaged on repetition jobs. The physical arrangements and mental atmosphere of such factories are often harmful to the human nervous system.

We must have mechanized industry but we need not have it at such a heavy price. Those among the industrialists and economists who treat man, including themselves, only as a statistical cipher, or as a mere factory "hand" to be mass regimented as a mere instrument of production like the lathe, and not also as a sensitive, feeling, and thinking human being, atrophy his talents and spoil his feeling for creativity. They deal with human robots and are unconcerned with higher values. In their worship of the mechanized view of life, they lose their balance just as those other worshipers of the machine who denounce them politically in the name of enforced collectivism also lose their balance. Both are hypnotized by the modern form of materialism. Both believe the machine will so lighten labor and increase prosperity that everyone will henceforth be happy. Inventive technology can do and is doing wonderful things in this epoch, but it can never make anyone really happy. It has despoiled man of drudgery, but can it, for instance, despoil him of mental distress? How many of the millions of factory workers have developed mentally beyond the machines they tend? And how many celebrated executives of the business world have become anything more than mere automatons of the business world?

The panorama of our great cities presents a spectacle. For it is to these fast-growing many-peopled dwelling places of the Western world that the pioneers of today have been drawn. Great builders, great engineers, astute financiers, clever scientists, enterprising merchants, the millions who toil at their bidding, together with artists, writers, and other men of dreams, are all there. In the cities, forces of every kind fight for predominance; ambitions high and low strive for prizes in tempting dress. The field of business becomes at times almost a battlefield. Giants of intellect and cunning wage war therein. Like a huge mill, each town grinds out of its inhabitants what they possess of ability, energy, and courage.

City life develops human mentality. Its competition sharpens human faculty. This is good when balanced by the finer feelings, but bad when not. Life in the larger towns stimulates intelligence, fosters ambition, and develops personality, whereas life on the farms toughens the body, increases self-reliance but flattens personality. The men and women who live in overgrown cities have largely lost that direct contact with Nature which their farming forebears possessed. The values and virtues which city life develops in mankind turn into demerits and vices when it is carried to excess. When a metropolitan area is not restricted at a certain point, it creates trouble, danger, and evil. It becomes a contributory cause to the soulless materialism of its inhabitants. The size of this mammoth human hive which is a modern metropolis, is now idiotically inconvenient. The very difficulties of internal transport must in time force a reduction or rearrangement.

The quick growth of huge commercial and industrial centers has led to artificial, unnatural living. This has produced unbalance in mind and unhealth in body. The life of a family which knows only hard stone pavements, confining brick walls, and low plaster ceilings, which regards trees, grass, and flowers with awed amazement as unfamiliar things, which is incessantly subjected to the nerve-pounding noises of urban existence, is a life in some danger of spiritual hurt. Those who live in ugly alleys or in the rabbit-warren of tight-packed, treeless streets do not see the same bright mental horizons as those who live in leafy avenues. With the widespread use of motor vehicles and the consequent conversion of streets into nerve-racking centers of noise and hurry and incessant activity, each giant city becomes mentally poisonous to the human race, breeding psychological tensions and spiritual dissociations. The strident noises harm the nerves and disrupt mental health. A society which accepts them so unhesitatingly must tend to become a more materialistic one. It seems that nothing less than business depression, economic disaster, or even the threat of atomic bombing brings back out of the cities a people who have strayed too far into urban materialism, who have lost their touch with Nature and their intuition of spirit.

These large cities are our karma that express what we are. As we ourselves improve we improve them. In these environments into which we incarnate, we find the lessons that we have to learn, or we get the fruits of what we have done in the past or we find conditions which provoke us to change and improve them, and in so doing we develop ourselves.

The current belief that the existing industrial economy is the most efficient one possible, may be correct from a technical point of view but too often ignores its destructive effects on the human nervous organism, creative talents and moral character. A proper appraisal of its efficiency would take them into reckoning. To the degree that the actual appraisal disregards them, it does so because its fundamental view of man is one-sided and materialistic.

Today, when science has made life complicated and intellect has made man restless, a poised serene attitude seems be-

yond the horizon. Yet its need is an imperative one. Only a
philosophical mysticism can show how a man caught up amid
the complex maze ·of urban activities and struggling ·against
the speed and pressure of city life, jarred by its raucous and
flurried note, and perhaps, burdened also by the struggle for
economic necessities, may abolish his inner conflict and keep
his mind in sublime calm. But the multitudes are unready inwardly for such a philosophical approach, so whatever can
be done by outward means to keep their psyche better balanced, should be done.

The craving for the countryside's green beauty and healing
peace which expresses itself in week-end runs out of town,
or in little gardens surrounding a house, is at bottom a spiritual one. The severance from all contact with Nature for
long periods starves the city dweller of vital nourishment for
his inner being. Sadhu Sundhar Singh, the Indian Christian
mystic, once said that he always felt the spirit of evil to be
powerful in large towns. "To go into big towns is always
against my desire, and I have to constrain myself to do so. I
know why hermits prefer to live in caves and mountains. I
much prefer it myself. But I was told once in an ecstasy to
help others in this world," he added. He also thought that
materialism is more prevalent in towns than villages.

When a sensitive man walks in the city streets, after his
feelings have been healed by the solitary groves of Nature,
he feels remote from these houses that so often are not homes
but barricades for sorrow. On the other hand, it is rare to
meet a farm laborer who has a mind beyond the stolid drudgery of his toil in the fields. The romantic idealization of peasant life breaks down as soon as we think of the illiterate,
half-starved peasants of India and China. It is as foolish in this
twentieth century as the romantic idealization of the towns-
man's life.

The philosophic thinker does not attack the uprise of
industrialism, which was inevitable and necessary, yet he de-

fends the contemporary movement toward decentralization, because that is the environmental need today. He notes phenomena which any thoughtful observer can witness—the phenomena of the psychological and physical results of both urban and rural life. He counsels the need of a properly balanced economy, a way of social existence which will be developed all-round and not be lopsided or extremist. He may rightly deplore the repulsive evils which excessive one-sided unbalanced industrialism has brought in its wake, but he must justly admit that the standard of physical prosperity and comfort is, in every country, proportionate to the use made of machines. Critics should protest not against machine processes, which indeed are so useful and profitable, but against the way in which a blind industrialism has led the men and women employed to operate them, into unnatural living and loss of higher values, whenever it has failed to differentiate them as spiritually cored human beings from the mere machines themselves.

We of today cannot easily return to primitive or medieval conditions. The machine may be used against men and women, as in war, or for them, as in peace. The ascetic notion, popularized by such men as Tolstoy and Gandhi, that it is necessarily harmful and mostly evil, has a basis of partial truth but, taken alone and unbalanced, is unphilosophical. The machine is here and we must accept it. But this is not to say that we must allow it to master us, to enslave us. With a spiritually awakened artistically creative race, the machine civilization would no longer retard true growth but would be kept in its place and utilized as a useful help to promote this growth and elevate society.

Science and invention, organization and technique will open up great possibilities for the future physical comfort of mankind. The advance of invention saves the human race from monotonous and repetitive jobs and thus liberates the human mind for higher ones. If men choose to use this libera-

tion for degrading purposes, that is the risk accompanying
every racial advance. But if the risk becomes too great, if
human life is harnessed solely to materialistic aims, then inventions only hinder and do not help its true progress. Until
the world puts its mechanical inventions, as well as its reforms,
on a philosophical basis, as it will eventually have to do, every
new good gained carries a new evil with it. Speed is a help to
the quicker tempo of modern civilization, but we need not
therefore speed away with that which is needed to cultivate
our deepest nature, the true soul. A civilization whose merely
mechanical and external efficiency still leaves man an insensitive and soulless creature, is in the end a half-failure.

All this does not mean, however, that practical attempts to
create increasingly better environments should not be made.
The improvement of external environments is all to the good;
it may of itself help to create an atmosphere in which higher
ideals can be more welcome; but in the end it is no substitute
for, and can never displace, the improvement of the human
entity which has to dwell in that environment. Yet to offer,
as mystical but unphilosophic idealists so often offer, the pan-
acea for humanity's social troubles as being solely an individual change of heart, to do nothing more than sit down and
wait for this remote change to happen and to dismiss all
practical proposals, is to confess intellectual bankruptcy. It is
mere lack of balance and obvious narrowness of perspective
which make these idealists assert that a change in human nature is the *only* reform required. Their mistake is not in assert-
ing that a change of heart will yield a change of environment.
This is quite true. It is in rejecting the second while waiting
for the first. For there are bad things in human environment
which either prevent such a change happening or, if they cannot prevent it, hinder it from sustaining itself.

This historic panorama, which is a tragic reality to the millions who suffer in it but a mere shadow dance to the mystics

who meditate apart from it, is correctly evaluated by the philosopher alone.

Philosophy, because its ideal reasonably balances self-centeredness and altruism, definitely requires outer change to be made but at the same time still holds that man's largest hope, lies in so improving the individual character that the improvement inevitably affects all social relations with other men and spreads from within outward. It insists that although the forces which shape the external fate of men and nations are much more internal, psychological, ethical, and mental, nevertheless effectual contributions also come from the external, social, political, and economic ones. It agrees that the way of moral and mental evolution provides the real basis for worth-while change but it also asserts that such evolution can be helped and quickened by providing better physical conditions. It deplores the sad situation which shows our best thinkers beginning to forsake nineteenth-century scientific materialism and rediscover twentieth-century spiritual truth, while the toiling masses ignorantly lag some distance behind them.

Nowadays the way to the spiritual domain lies to some extent through the social one. The environmental ills must be ameliorated to some extent before people—the rich as well as the poor—can become aware of their inner ills and thence bestow their attention on a higher good. The man who is driven to an enforced and continuous preoccupation with the problem of earning a livelihood or supporting his family would be foolish indeed if he did not give this problem the front-rank importance which is its reasonable due. Even the man who is more fortunate is doing nothing wrong but everything right in providing himself with material comforts and modern conveniences, with a good home, decent clothes, and adequate food. The wrong begins only when both men set up these things as idols and worship them as ends in life, forgetting the higher ends; when their hearts are surfeited with attachments to them but remain starved of ideals beyond them and, most especially, when they secure them at the cost of spiritual values or in violation of moral integrity.

When men are actuated by altruistic motives but possess only a limited view of things, they seek to remove poverty of material possession in individual cases alone. If they lack wisdom they may do as much harm as good by their endeavors. When the same men arrive at a deeper view of things, they seek to remove poverty of material possession in society as a whole by going to its true personal and social causes. But when they are not only actuated by altruistic motives, but possess also the deepest insight into life, they seek to remove poverty of thought, poverty of outlook, and poverty of soul, alongside of the degrading physical conditions.

The need of tomorrow is for a social organism of a type higher than any now provided, an organism which will rest on conscious obedience to higher laws, which will make provision for the fact that man is also a spiritual being as well as a physical one. Our immediate hope for a better world does not lie wholly in a change from within, for that would be too great a demand, nor yet wholly in a change from without, for that would be too little a demand. It lies in a properly proportioned synthesis of the two. While the mass of people are principally preoccupied with wresting a livelihood, they can hardly be blamed for being indifferent to a higher spiritual and artistic culture. To them such a culture must often seem either quite remote or quite imaginary. Apart from their inferior training in intellect—not to be confused with intelligence—the essential factor in this situation is that they cannot give sufficient attention to such a search for truth or aspire after its personal realization until they are themselves less hindered by the inevitable dependence on economic conditions.

The four elemental, insistent, and stable needs of sufficient food, clothing, shelter, and fuel have always had to be satisfied before the cultural, religious, mystical, or metaphysical needs. It is true that the need of earning a livelihood has always been the most important need in most men's existence. The continuous drudgery merely to keep body alive, the constant enslavement to mechanical toil, the grinding effort of the everyday struggle for a livelihood leave many little time for higher thought and hamper the birth of nobler ideas. The physical despairs of the unemployed and the insecurity fears of the employed often bring out baser elements of the human character. They cause the mind to become negatively obsessed by its worldly problems, to struggle combatively against others for self-existence, to accept aggressive violent solutions of economic difficulties, and to stifle spiritual intuitions through envy or bitterness. Those who have to endure them cannot scent much of the divine atmosphere amid murky scenes of squalor. In earlier eras to a large extent but in recent eras or in certain countries to a markedly lesser extent, the thoughts of the masses, condemned to long hours of drudgery for a livelihood as they were, have inevitably occupied themselves mostly with what related to the physical body and its animal necessities. As civilized society changes its present materialistic form, they will be freed from the oppressions of overwork, unemployment, and excessive poverty, and take sufficient time for higher culture, aesthetic appreciation, creative unfoldment and nonvocational mental development.

It is not within the purview of these pages to discuss the arguments of those who would uphold the personal profit motive and those who would abandon it altogether. Both are actuated by an egoism which brings, and must always bring, friction along with it, but which has been inevitable in the course of human development. No one will work without motive, be it the building up of a collectivist state or the building up of a private fortune. The sage or the saint who serves selflessly, because he serves at the bidding of a higher power, alone escapes this necessity but such a man belongs to a breed apart. It is certain, however, that much industrial conflict could be resolved if the mental attitude of co-operation which involves some denial of the personal ego, were brought to bear upon it by both sides.

We are not concerned here with the extreme ascetic who consciously and deliberately sets out to try to live with as little as possible. His self-imposed renunciation has a certain nobility about it, whereas that which is involuntarily borne by the poor usually degrades them. He has taken to an exceptional path for a special purpose and when this is achieved, Nature may or may not eventually bid him return, as she bade Buddha himself return, to the middle way. But those who can find their happiness only in an environment of poverty, their spirituality only in an economy of scarcity, belong to primitive or medieval epochs and are no better than backward-lookers. Higher standards of living and the multiplication of wants are not at all evil in themselves, although if left unaccompanied by spiritual disciplines they may easily become evil, as they have in some Western countries. It is regrettable that the corrupting power of a prosperous state of society is historic, regrettable because in a well-balanced, spiritually alert character prosperity shows the good it can do rather than the evil. But for most societies—and certainly for the West—a time comes when a simpler life is the only way to a healthier one and when the refusal to accept it leads to sickness, decay, and self-destruction.

It is, however, the mental attitude we hold toward the multiplication of possessions which makes them good or evil. Good homes, adequate diet, and cultural participation need prevent no one from claiming and attaining their spiritual birthright.

Although it is not possible, with the faulty human material at our disposal, to make an earthly millennium, a terrestrial utopia; although political-economic perfectionism is a mere dream for emotionalist doctrinaires, it is possible to make a more co-operative beautiful world than the one which exists. This would need all the uncommon sense, all the clear concrete thinking, all the moral good will, all the wise artistic and spiritual leadership, all the imaginative enterprise which our best men can muster. If we cannot succeed in bringing an impossible dream utopia down to earth, that is no reason why we should not try to bring a little fragment of it down.

It is quite inevitable that we should move toward a higher form of civilization. The war gave the individual and the state an opportunity—often unwelcome—to indicate where they stood in life's struggle and to demonstrate what goals they really pursued. All, including those who emerged badly shaken and badly battered, are being driven by widespread chaos either to develop themselves in new directions and readjust themselves to new evolutionary currents, or through selfishness, blindness, cowardice, and inertia to disasters ending in destruction.

We can understand these happenings aright if we understand them in terms of a far wider universal change embracing the whole of human existence itself. The war marked one stage of a titanic turning point in the mental and moral history of mankind. It was actually an outward sign of an inner conflict between the forces of light and darkness, which still continues. Behind the visible crisis, as expressed in tremendous historical events, there is secreted an invisible crisis, which is indeed its activating cause. The conflict today is outwardly between political groups and economic systems. But inwardly—and therefore essentially—it is between opposed views of man, of his life and purpose on this earth. It is a conflict between utter materialism, conjoined to harsh idealism on the one side, and partial materialism, conjoined to partial religious faith on the other. We are witnessing the final convulsions, the last desperate activities of the murderous nature left in man by his former animal reincarnations.

It goes against the grain of human egoism to accept the pithy point of the centuries-old Spanish saying: "Truth, although severe, is a real friend." And even the few who can receive it will doubt whether the claims of philosophic principles can be equated with the claims of mundane practicality. In ordinary times, they would have solid basis for their doubt. But we live in extraordinary times. Life today is a challenge which cannot be evaded.

CHAPTER IV

THE CRISIS OF SCIENCE AND INTELLECT

Scientific Advance Leading to Self-Destruction. Man's personal necessity spurs his mental ingenuity. Inventions follow in the track of each conscious need. Nature is yielding her amazing wonders to the human exploitation of them. No living man today can escape the beneficial as well as the bad results of scientific activity. Most are helped in some way, many are hurt in some other way, by these consequences of its rapid and spectacular advances. Someone listens to a man's talk although he is two hundred miles away, with nothing but a slender wire or an unseen wave between them; this aid comes from the thought of scientists and the working of engineers. A man falls dead at our feet, struck to the ground by a carelessly speeding automobile; his death is ultimately due to their thought and working, too.

The reasoning intellect in its high perfection as we see it exemplified among the great scientists of our age is something which deserves and demands our high respect. Their

scrupulously exact methods of research and carefully method-
ical observations are to be admired; their cautious attitude is
extremely valuable and quite necessary in its proper place.
We are not of those who despise the cultural and scientific
achievements of the intellect in order to praise the mystical
achievements of the intuition. We have no desire to detract
from the wonders of modern science in order to point out the
wonders of ancient mysticism. We cannot accept the dogma
that conscientious reasonable thinking is wrong for the spiritual
aspirant but right for the worldly materialist. Too long has the
mystic been unfriendly to the intellectual processes and uneasy
with the practical ones.

The scientific and industrial age was inevitable if man was
to go forward in the development of *all* his faculties, and
not merely of some of them. The work of science and intellect had to begin and extend itself. It was a necessary phase of
human evolution. Only those who have traveled widely in
primitive countries know how great a jungle of absurd superstition and parasitic custom suffocates the inner and outer
lives of their inhabitants. This is the heavy price they have
paid for complete but blind faith in traditional ways. The
good done by their faith is undone by the harm done by
their superstition. Philosophy indeed bids man develop his
reasoning powers. Equally with science, it bids him be on his
guard against the superficial view, the incorrect statement, the
exaggerated emphasis, the unsound premise, the unreported
fact, the fallacious reasoning, and the distorted picture. It
respects, and sympathizes with, André Gide, the French intellectual, when he cries out for integrity between his reason
and his religion, in these words: "I want to honor God with
every part of me." If it warns him against the dangers into
which most intellectuals fall—the dangers of pride, arrogance, narrowness, and intolerance—this is only because man
ought not, as his thinking power and critical judgment grow,
become less humble, reverent, and prayerful, but more so.

He ought to strengthen and not weaken his higher instincts. The loss of a belief in a higher power than his own or Nature's, the doctrine that physical environment alone molds character, the materialism that becomes both an interpretation of the universe and a code of conduct—these are a few symptoms of changes that have been promoted by excessive worship of the intellect. What has actually happened to its modern devotees is the exact reverse of what has happened to the primitive peoples, and therefore just as baneful in its own way. As those peoples pay a heavy price for their blind faith, so they pay a different but equally heavy price for their blind skepticism. The good achieved by intellectual progress is now amply offset by the harm which accompanies it. There is no other way, for both the primitives and the moderns, out of this situation than to readjust their attitudes in such a way as to restore their balance.

No one will understand the complex world problem aright if he does not see that these deep changes in the human problem are partly responsible for it. Modern progress has given the human character width without depth, fluency without wisdom. Science has led the thinking portion of humanity in two divergent directions. It has destroyed the spiritual faith of a large group but reinforced the faith of a smaller group. This paradoxical result need not be as puzzling as it seems. For both groups have interpreted their facts and observations according to their innate personal inclinations, tendencies, and feelings. Men differ so widely in their dispositions that such a result was inevitable. But this is not to say that both results are equal in value. They are not. The first one misses some of the profoundest lessons which all experience affords and which scientific data do not really contradict.

The activity of our external and surface progress blinds men's eyes to the truth that no civilization which fails to achieve balance between the materialistic and spiritual forces can endure. Its own heavy materialism eventually causes it to wobble. This is one apocalyptic meaning of contemporary world-shaking events. Modern civilization has been worked out to its logical end and has been gathering the harvest of its own sowing.

Many justly accused Hitler of imperiling civilization but never saw that their own so-called civilization was itself steadily growing, through lopsidedness, into a great peril to mankind. Exponents of popular science became ecstatic when picturing the paradise into which applied science was leading us all. They did not care that it was a paradise for the head which left the heart to stay outside, or that it was at best a paradise for the body and left the spiritually and intuitive and morally sensitive parts of man untouched! They did not realize that his ethical character, his actuating motives, his attitude toward his fellow men, and above all his understanding of life's ultimate ends are still the real power which drives the machinery provided by science. Modern history has shown what they forgot, that whenever man improved the external face of life but did not retain his mental balance, he paid dearly for every such improvement. He wandered further away from the original center of his being with each step. For every new facility which his inventive brain thought out, he paid by the loss of spiritual power. Those self-styled practical realists who formerly saw the postwar world as being miraculously changed into a paradise by machines, inventions, new materials, and economic readjustments but did not see any necessity of a parallel inner change in humanity, have been proved self-deceived dreamers by events themselves.

It is not long since these people quite pardonably thought science's progress and industry's advance would solve all the problems of living. Yet the more they burned incense at the altars of progress, the more the fates mocked them by dealing gigantic blows at the civilization which was to have experienced this progress. The more their perception into the cyclic character of history was dulled by prosperous moments and scientific discovery, the more they resembled men walking toward the edge of a precipice. The more they identified their highest good with physical and intellectual development alone, the more did primitive and barbaric forces arise to shatter that development. They failed to see that although reason, when rising to its purest metaphysical stretch, becomes impersonal, and ennobles man, when it descends into its murkiest materialistic depth, it becomes mere selfish cunning and turns his best into his worst.

The naïve belief that science could so improve the state of man that utopian happiness would eventually be his, is falling rapidly by the wayside. Everyone can see now that it still leaves his moral nature untouched, his animal nature ungoverned, his weakness for false paths undisturbed. Everyone can see that his house may be packed with machines but his heart may still remain empty of satisfaction. The notion of interminable progress was one with which science first flattered its devotees and now frightens its victims. It was attractive enough when the nineteenth century watched the passage from steam to electricity but dreadful when the twentieth century watched the progress of hand grenades into rocket bombs. The smug satisfaction that everything is getting better and better is going. The unhappy realization that progress can be too one-sided a thing is taking its place. To see so much strife and disorder in the world, so much bestiality and irrationality may well cause many to wonder what kind of progress this is. These times must be seen in proper historical and psychological perspective if they are to be seen aright. Then it will be seen that the technical progress made has not compensated for the spiritual regress which has accompanied it. The glaring disparity between them arrests attention.

The era that is passing cannot be described as wholly unspiritual, but the tendencies which came uppermost between the two world wars may fairly be described as such. That phase harbored a civilization which sang poems in honor of its own romantic industrial, mechanical and inventive advance. This advance, in its place, was proper and necessary. But when it was bought at the price of broken moral laws, enthronement of intellect above intuition, greed, selfishness, violence, and the loss of faith in, and reverence for, any higher power, such paeans of praise betrayed a grotesque superficiality, for the movement became advance toward a precipice. Who can see any end to this degenerative process which is at work among us? Each decade of the last hundred years has seen more of pride but less of reverence, more of information but less of wisdom, and more of frankness but less of goodness than the preceding one. The loss of these qualities is to be mourned. We pay a great price for supplanting God-worship by Thing-worship.

Because we have the automobile, the airplane, and the atom bomb, we think that we know more than our own ancients and the exotic Asiatics. We do, but we only know more about things. Actually we know less about ourselves, about the hidden purposes of life, about the world of inner reality. We do so little that really matters, so much that is comparatively trivial. The range of knowledge among the ancient philosophers was limited but the depth of thought was not. Thus it was possible for the more mystical among them to achieve this miracle, that with fewer facts at their disposal they reached truer *ultimate* conclusions about the universe than we moderns have done, as well as a truer knowledge of the essential being of man. This need not surprise us if we remember that the same science which tells us that we must base our search for truth only on the facts adduced by the senses also tells us that the senses themselves are limited, unreliable, and imperfect. The mystic, so often criticized by the scientist, might well be ironical about such a situation!

Science has gone out and investigated the universe in every direction except one—the scientist himself! Such is the pressure and tension of our so-called civilized life that it is less and less possible for men to find time to look at their own selves, still less to look into their own selves. That is why those who take the materialistic view of themselves have been able to form such a large conclusion from such little evidence. They would have done better to withhold their verdict than to pass an unfair one. This lack of religious feeling, this indifference toward mystical experience, this paralysis of veneration for higher things and moral laws, which began a couple of centuries ago, could not show its bad consequences in all their terrible fullness and visible shape until sufficient time had passed. That has since happened. Violence and war, greed and hate—these are the bitter fruits of the loss of faith in a higher power and loss of belief in those who can commune with it. If they have opened the door to hopelessness for the greater number of mankind, the blame must rest upon this negation to which they can ultimately be traced. The intellect, unwarmed by feeling, unillumined by intuition, betrays man into the illusion of truth. And such a state is far worse than the ignorance of truth. This is why the cold scientist has unwittingly contributed more to human evil today than the illiterate peasant. It is merely man's intellectual vanity that causes him to believe that he can eventually make his earthly life exactly as he wants it to be by the powers of scientific knowledge. There will always be a number of incalculable circumstances to control or even to prevent that.

The appearance of science and the growth of intellect were not evil phenomena in themselves. They were indispensable and necessary to the full evolution of the human entity. In their *ultimate* origin they were not less spiritual than the religionist's faith and the mystic's intuition. But the misuse of them was evil, as the extreme unbalance into which they have pushed that entity was also evil.

The hour has come to wake to what we have done to ourselves, to what a one-sided science and an icy intellectualism have done to us, and to seek a balance which will rest on them, yes, but also on faith and intuition. And since we have so much to support one side of this balance, yet so little for the other side, there is demanded of us a concentration of aspiring effort, an urgency of awareness in the matter of spiritual development. Modern man needs a spiritual counterpart to the phenomenal external advance of the past couple of hundred years because all the stately and impressive achievements of applied science cannot hide the inner emptiness of his life. He needs airplanes and auto cars, yes, but he also needs higher satisfactions and a change of mental orientation even more. He needs to make new valuations, find uncommon ideas, create new thoughts, express generous attitudes, make expansive experiments, and, above all, he needs a new spiritual dynamism. His civilization should balance the just claims of heaven and earth. This is not an unessential theoretic need but, in these stresses of world crisis, an urgent and practical one. Never before was it so vitally important to man that he should nourish his mind and heart from divine sources. Otherwise the tower of Babel which science, civilization, economics, and politics have been building together is in danger of crashing to the ground and crushing its worshipers.

It is often asked why the existing religions have been unable to hinder the spread of materialism. This is partly because they are so old, and consequently to some extent devitalized and uninspired. If the tragic apprehensions of our age are to be negated, it can be only by the birth of a new spiritual impulse. Whether that happens inside or outside the old religions and the new cults, or both inside and outside them, is not at all so important as their followers are led to believe. No religion, no cult, no group has yet succeeded in securing a monoply on God's inspirations and revelations, the Overself's grace and salvation. What is important is that this impulse shall be born *in the hearts of men*. For what they feel deeply secretly and privately within themselves, is what will govern in the end. Humanity was given a respite of twenty years between the first two world wars to amend its ways and improve its goals, to turn away from past mistakes. The failure to exploit that opportunity was a costly one. The second peace brings the same chance and the same respite. The smug satisfaction with a life exempt from the knowledge of, and reckoning with, life's higher purpose cannot go on indefinitely. It has to culminate. The hour is not too far when mankind must either wake to this purpose and become aware of the first beginnings of spiritual truth or rue the neglect. Those who stop their ears to life's contemporary challenge, because it disturbs the settled current of their life, escape nothing. It is well for all who lead men or direct thought if they can read the signs of events aright. Tremendous new developments are lying like seeds embedded in the earth of this century. These belong indeed to its very nature. Their appearance is assured.

Man—Animal, Intellectual, and Spiritual. The violent movements, bellowing with passion rather than promoting constructive thought, which have been such a world-stirring phenomenon and which masquerade as new religions for the young, rise partly because the old religions will not bravely meet and face present-day tendencies and partly because the old systems will not cope with the new needs. These faiths have accepted the scientific conception of man as a reasoning animal, and history has shown how dangerous this is when accepted as the highest possible conception. If the body's existence is all we have to tend now and look forward to later until it crumbles to dust, then the stupid folly and violent crime of mankind may well be excused.

The animal develops the use of its five senses. Man in his animal body has this same use. But he is raised above it by several important differences: his faculty of speech, his erect physical posture, and the dramatic fact that in the sphere of mental operations he is able to achieve what no animal can achieve. Whoever examines for the first time a corpse in the dissecting room will find that the human animal's brain is structurally more complicated than all the others. This is not all. If he examines the quality of the brain he will observe its marked superiority. Why? Because one grand difference between man and beast is a difference of *mind*. No animal can comprehend what a man may comprehend or has, like man, the capacity to feel intellectual hunger.

The eyesight of an eagle and the swiftness of a deer are far superior to those of a man. Yet the reasoning intelligence and creative imagination of a man are far superior to, and far more valuable than, the instinctive intelligence of any animal. For his intelligence enables him to invent an ingenious telescope which permits him to see what even the eagle cannot see, and his imagination enables him to re-create the physical world in his own way and thus to construct an amazing airplane in which he can outfly the fastest bird. His power to reason out, and his capacity to premeditate a course of action, imagining its probable consequences, also segregate him.

Animals, birds, fish, and insects can all enjoy gross physical pleasures but cannot enjoy aesthetic pleasures such as those of painting and music. That is the exclusive human privilege. His potentialities still further enable man to surpass the animal in a totally different way for they lead him into an altogether higher world of being. In him, life, for the first time, begins to reflect upon its own significance, and thus attains metaphysical thought. There is no animal other than the human which can reason abstractly, and feel the need to understand truth and turn away from error, to judge appearances and appreciate reality. This is because it is a species on an altogether different level from all the others. It has progressed nearer to the capacity of recognizing its own metaphysical entity and such reasoning is one of the signs of this progression. It is not only the power to become conscious of himself as an intellectual being that elevates him over the animal; it is still more the power to become conscious of himself as a spiritual being. If the possession of abstract thought distinguishes man and makes him a higher being, linking him with a brain which can compass the universe and pierce some of the mysteries of physical life, the possession of intuition enables him to unfold the sacred soul. If the animals cannot follow him into the realms beyond physical sensation, into the realms of creative art and abstract thought, how could they ever follow him into the realms beyond even those two—into sublime mystical experience and reverential spiritual feeling?

If man were really nothing more than an animal, as our materialists say, he would be quite content with his mental finitude and his physical appetites. The squirrel which sits and gazes at me from its perch on yonder tree is so content. But man is not. Why? Because something within him prompts him to seek the Beyond, urges him to rise to the More. And that "something" is nothing less than the undiscovered presence of his own divine soul. It is not enough to be practical only. The beaver is also a practical creature, but the higher life, of which no beaver can form a concept, truly distinguishes man from it.

The scientist who regards religion as another word for superstition, and who thinks of himself as nothing more than the body, is in a sorry state. He has lost four valuable characteristics which elevate and, among others, distinguish the human from the animal creatures: faith in an unseen higher power, humility and reverence at the thought of it, and the capacity for prayer to it. Freud, for example, denounced religious belief as an illusion to be got rid of in a more evolved society, yet himself harbored the illusion that science alone could provide all the guidance in life which a man needed. How many men who once thought the same as Freud, continue to think so now, after the dread experience of scientific war has revealed their inner poverty and brought them to their knees in utter helplessness or agonized prayer?

In this feeling of religious veneration, intimate worship, and personal aspiration directed toward an unseen Power and Mind beyond himself, man has climbed upward to heights where no animal can follow him. No other creature on earth than the human creature is able to create, receive, or contemplate the mysterious concept of a God, much less the idea of its own spiritual being. Even more, he alone may pass from intuitive feeling to the full bloom of mystical experience of his Overself, which men call the soul within. It is this that links him to, and is a ray of, the ultimate existence, the World-Mind, which men call God. A man or a woman can develop into its awareness, but a peacock or a leopard cannot. The dim distant echo, the muffled intimation of the soul's existence deep in his heart, is an uncrossable difference from the animal. It manifests itself in a twofold way. First, there is moral conscience, a sense of right and wrong, a desire for and an ability to choose the good or decline the evil. Second, there is the capacity to take compassionate thought for other creatures, to feel unselfishly for and with them. Where is the animal which practices loving and genuinely unselfish compassion toward other animals? It exists but only as an extreme rarity.

Lest these thoughts leave us with too large a superiority complex let them be countered by remembering that there are several points wherein the animal shows up more favorably than the human. Two will suffice here. The placidity of a cow has been a subject of scornful mention by several writers yet the tensely nervous and half neurotic modern city dweller might profitably exchange his tension for this relaxed attribute of the cow. The failure of human beings to act according to their knowledge or their beliefs, whether due to weakness of the will, conventional hypocrisy, or unconscious motivations, is unknown in the animal world, where self-expression is spontaneous and perfect.

Domesticated creatures like the dog in the West and the cow in the Orient learn from their association with man to follow quite intelligently a few of his questions, some of his words, and many of his commands. This is merely incidental, but illustrative of the law of development.

However, the animal kingdom represents a stage which is evolutionary for the life-waves coming up from the plant kingdom but retrogressive for those already in the human kingdom. The utterly selfish struggle for survival of the fittest, the use of violent murderous force against other creatures merely to support and nourish existence, is natural and proper in a beast but immoral and improper in a man. Such supposedly human attributes as anger, greed, hate, and the desire for revenge are really animal ones. In war they find their worst and fullest expression. As he evolves into the realization of his truly human possibilities, so will man drop these unhuman ones from his heart and banish war itself from his activities. As peace is felt within himself, so will it fall upon the earth accordingly.

The atheistic faiths, following a false lead of discarded scientific theories, and entangled in the cobwebs of their own thought, have also misconceived the thinking nature which they conjoin with man's animality. Theirs is a kind of mentality which calls itself scientific, but is really pseudoscientific. It all too precipitately dismisses the mystical as superstitious, the metaphysical as meaningless, and discredits both immediately on hearing of them. It is too impatient with their supposed insubstantiality even to discuss them, let alone investigate their facts, which a true science ought to do. Its twin is the kind of mysticism which refuses to free itself from the superstitions which have so long half-strangled its own tradition. Truth can deform beauty or deny intuition only at the cost of no longer being truth. The materialist or the scientist who fails to grasp this, fails in life. But nor does the mystic, who ignores fact and misplaces faith in order to secure intuition, secure it. He secures only its pretense.

The arrogant pride which comes from a well-developed intellect, is a powerful impediment upon the path to philosophic truth. It gives the ego a conceit about its own importance which prevents it from making that humble obeisance before the Overself which is an indispensable prerequisite of the latter's self-revelation. If the strange mystery which hides within life and men has baffled the keenest minds, this is because they tried to impose their own conditions upon its solution, instead of accepting those which inexorably inhere within it. The methods used and faculties needed are basically so different in kind that science regards the exploration of mysticism as unprofitable. It is true that the exacting character of scientific criterions is beyond the religionist's and the mystic's total fulfillment; but this is not necessarily through opposition to them. It is through the total difference of conditions governing the spiritual experiences.

Whoever listens impartially to the intellectual bickerings of our time will soon come to know that intellect alone does not yield certitude. The intellect can present a plausible case for the belief that all things in life and the universe are being guided by an Infinite Mind to good ends, or it can present an equally plausible case for the contrary belief. Only the intuition can tell quite definitely that the belief is true. Only the prophets and mystics—if they be fully developed—can rise to certitude and *know it* to be true. A mechanized godless view of the universe did not bring our moderns nearer to certitude. On the contrary, it brought them in the end nearer to doubt and confusion. There is no other road confronting science than the road leading from physical fact to metaphysical truth, from observation made by the senses to illumination found by the mind. Science must rise from concrete results to the abstract meaning of those results, that is, from materialistic physics to mentalistic metaphysics. In this way alone can it complete itself.

There is a mystery in man's own mere existence, let alone in the world's existence. No one who really feels or deeply thinks can fail to recognize its presence. The materialist evades it. The mystic explores it. The philosopher explains it. When a man's thinking first stirs vigorously it may embrace the materialist conception of himself and of life. But when it enters the stage of maturity, it must perforce abandon such a superficial conception.

Whoever asks of an unillumined reason what it is neither competent nor qualified to give merely falls into self-delusion. For it is thinking itself, when working at its highest pitch, which tells him that the soul's nature or the world's reality cannot be known by thinking! The Spiritual Self can reveal its own nature to him only by means of intuition, not by thought, although thought may be used as a springboard whence to attain intuition. Therefore the first step is to set up a difference, not in kind but in quality, between those thoughts which are discursive and those which are intuitive. The first are common and everyday, the second uncommon and infrequent.

Thinking confuses itself while experience contradicts itself. All the confusion which comes from holding a mass of contradictory ideas and all the tension which comes from seeking to achieve by self-effort what the personal self can never achieve unaided, lead one day to mental and emotional exhaustion. This in turn forces the self to let go, and provides favorable ground for the birth of intuition. When thinking realizes its own imperfections, it will realize the need of silencing itself at the point of its farthest reach. Here it will have to call in the help of a technique like Eastern yoga or Western meditation. This is *a part only* of the price and the prelude of a man's initiation into the quest that leads straight to the serene center within his flickering mind.

Thought and reflection must walk very delicately here. No mental system, no intellectually constructed edifice can do this. Nevertheless the intellect in its thinking about what is beyond itself, if it is scrupulously honest and unfalteringly humble, may eventually succeed in annihilating its own tyrannical power. Reasoned thinking completes its loftiest mission when it enforces upon itself the recognition of its own limitations, when it perceives that its most liberating ideas cannot liberate itself, and when it thenceforth places its services at the disposal of mystical contemplation of the Un-thinkable. It can tell us that although the Overself is beyond our thinkable comprehension, it is not beyond our possible experience. We have to find the truth not only in our thinking but, also and more, beneath our thinking. For the silence out of which the function itself rises is divine. The course which will always have to be taken by our rational intelligence when it seeks to understand life, must be a course that starts with the World, proceeds to Man, and ends with God.

That it is possible by a process of abstract thinking to attain knowledge of what is beyond thinking itself, may seem paradoxical. But this is not really the claim. Thinking can lead us to its own source, but there it must halt. It points to what is beyond itself but it does not yield the realization of that which transcends it, except indirectly. And this it achieves by merging itself into the place of its origin when its own task has been fulfilled; but it will do so only if introverted, concentrated and sustained.

The Intuition Beyond Thinking. "Why should I believe in God? Why should I so live as not to injure others' welfare?" Intellect, unhelped by revelation or unguided by intuition, can never be equal to the task of adequately answering these questions nor of perceiving "the why, the whence, and the whither" of human and cosmic existence. Alone it is powerless to judge these matters accurately, it must call help in—the help first of intuitive feeling, then of mystical states, and lastly of philosophic insight. All it can do is limited to answering another and grosser kind of question.

This attitude toward the use and value of reasoning seems to puzzle some students. They detect contradiction in our alternate approval and condemnation of its use, in our alternate esteem and deprecation of its worth. This apparent instability on our part needs a little explanation for their benefit. Where logical thought separates itself from the realities of experience, we condemn it. Where it builds on a foundation of scrutinized fact, we uphold it. Where thinking of any kind cannot possibly penetrate, we bid it be still. Where thinking of a special metaphysical kind leads to the threshold of true intuition, we bid it be active. Thus there is no real inconsistency between our statements.

The creative values got by intellectual research are kept and preserved in the transcendental higher knowledge instead of being discarded as worthless or dispensed with as hindrances, as one-sided or half-developed mystics often discard them, but they are not permitted to set up a barrier to human possibility. Although true insight cannot be a mere product of intellectual exercise alone but must emerge from something which transcends the intellect itself, nevertheless such exercise has its place and value. It helps to dispel illusions, check superstition, evaluate and discipline emotions, and map out untrodden territory for exploration by the way of intuitive feeling and mystic experience. Reason can analyze and intellectually interpret what intuition already knows. Thus it gives deliverance and rational satisfaction to intuition. It occupies a particular position and performs a particular function, but does not exhaust the possibilities of man. When he understands that reason and intuition must work with and for each other; when he comprehends that they are not irreconcilables; and when he ceases to regard their alliance as incongruous, he becomes the gainer in every way. Just as reason is essential as a disciplinary check for intuitive feeling, so intuitive feeling is most essential as a disciplinary check for reason. Otherwise the thinker will be only adding to his stock of intellectual constructions.

But although reason must check feeling, it must not be allowed to replace feeling. That would be an error. For the finest flower in man's garden is intuition, which is nothing else than feeling purified of its egoism and enlightened by the Overself. Excellent ideas may be spoiled in the public mind through historic association with words which have been misused intentionally. Hitler has cast a shadow, for instance, on the word "intuition."

Materialism is an intellectual illusion. The cleverer its adherent thinks himself to be, by reason of his adherence, the more he deceives himself. As he sinks deeper into it, his intuition is proportionately paralyzed. Intellect without intuition is a blessing to man only up to a certain degree, beyond that degree it turns into a veritable curse upon him. If through enslavement to past habits or domination by logical intellect, a man refuses to heed and obey the intuitive feelings that float up from the nonego self, they will become fainter and fainter until they leave him altogether. When intuition speaks in its silent and subtle way but is not recognized for what it is, there will be a vague uneasiness for a time, some misgivings, perhaps some conflict even. But if it is not obeyed by a certain time, its voice will be no longer heard and the ego's victim will have to eat the fruits of such disobedience. When he obeys the dictate of his inmost intuition rather than the suggestion of others, he walks aright. But when he yields to them and does what they expect, wish, or advise in contradiction of intuition, the latter is weakened and begins to desert him. If he will only heed, trust, and obey his intuition it will direct him to his best and protect him from his worst.

The sturdy struggle of reason against passion, intuition against suggestion, truth against self-interest, individuality against the mass, and contemplation against convention is an unending one. But it is also an honorable one. We must not, we dare not, surrender either the right to think or the power to intuit for ourselves. It is both a blunder and a sin to take the easier path. We have witnessed in our time its terrible consequences in the case of whole nations.

Civilization has supplied us with the means of communicating thought in ways that would have astonished our forefathers, but it has given little attention to supplying us with ways of cultivating intuitive thought. Machines may be developed to give us the first, but only man can do the second. We may telephone from New York to Bombay but the value of what we say is the real test of our progress. And we shall really begin to say something worth while when we learn to be docile and receptive to the feeblest of intuitions, maintaining our loyalty to it against the exaggerated cautions and excessive prudence of a frightened intellect.

CHAPTER V

THE EGO IN EVOLUTION

WE WHO LIVE on the outer crust of a planet rotating its way through endless space, belong to the most tragical and critical of all its eras. That is why we must begin to search for its meaning for us. To discover what that is and to reorient our lives accordingly could make the impending era the most blessed of all, but not to do so could easily make it the worst.

That the universe has a meaning, and that human life is not a mere wandering from nothingness to nothingness, is the unhesitating affirmation of philosophy. Although in its fullness it offers a wisdom too subtle, a morality too lofty, a mystique too strange for the mass of humanity to care for, much less to comprehend and live up to, this is not to say that it is useless to them or has no message for them in the gravest crisis of their lives. Without asking everyone to become a mellow-minded philosopher, without asking anyone to study light-bringing philosophy, it yet asks for a hearing for its message on humanity's present situation.

This word "philosopher" too often means today only a mental speculator, one who has attended a college course in such speculation or who has read a number of treatises on it. It has broadened out, like so many other ancient terms, into an umbrella word to cover widely different things. Can some way be found tersely to differentiate the name "philosophy" from the academic weavings that pass under its label? We refuse to renounce the use of a word whose high and honorable derivation is revealed by its Greek roots: "the love of wisdom." That men and time have degraded its use is regrettably true but that is all the more reason why it should be rescued and its original meaning restored. Here it is reserved, as the Orientals still reserve it, for the inner core of man's loftiest culture, which has come down, more quietly and less known than the outer forms, through the ages among the few who cared for it on every continent in religious, metaphysical, and mystical intuitions and experiences.

There is, there can be only a single universal and external truth. Because the Real exists always and can never vanish, the Truth exists always and can never vanish. No prophet ever reveals it for the first time, no seer discovers it. All only rediscover it. It never changes or evolves; only its form of presentation does that. But before it can manifest in our world, it must find human minds sufficiently prepared to be able to receive it and sufficiently developed to be able to comprehend and teach it. Such exquisitely sensitive men are the inspired prophets, the authentic seers, the true philosophers of history.

This wisdom is really so ancient that it sounds as if it were quite new. How ironical that the first principles of human culture should have become the latest principles! Its teachings are given a new importance, a fresh dignity by our own generation's tremendous need. The philosopher who follows with his special knowledge and farther sight the world drama which is being enacted in our times, knows that more than human forces are determining its ultimate course and sees that higher laws are shaping its end. He may make no claim of omniscience but he may claim to know something about matters which, although most important to human life, are often most neglected by human beings.

The crisis which now faces the world is something it has never had to face before on so wide a scale. Most men feel helpless before these catastrophic events that have succeeded each other so swiftly during the past few years. The human mind is too discomposed to gather their significance at all adequately. We have to ask ourselves the question why it is that such unheard-of historic happenings, such revolutionary inventions, such evil machinations, and such tremendous mental ferment should agitate humanity precisely at this point and on so wide a scale in its age-long career. Why did they not manifest themselves before? It is a mistake to look for historical analogies to the present situations. It will shortly be shown that the crisis today is not only unique in its tremendous area but also in a very special way. We are not only at the end of a historic cycle in human life but also at the end of a cosmic cycle. The first has happened before and will happen again, but the second is a situation which has not been paralleled in so large a measure during post-Atlantean times. This is why human history has reached its period of gravest importance, human destiny its period of gravest decision in recorded annals.

The twentieth century has witnessed more reversals of human thought, conduct, and government than any other epoch. It has witnessed the placid egoism of the formal, the orthodox, and the conventional being shaken up with more rapidity than ever before. In no other period than this midcentury of ours could such a tremendous combination of forces have developed. In no other period could such a dramatic and universal contest between the powers of good and the forces of evil so openly have happened. Yet in no other period was it so possible for the ordinary man to learn the true laws governing life, and in so rational a way.

The entire population of this globe is collectively passing through an all-round transition between one kind of life and another which has yet to replace it. Whether we take a materialist standpoint, or a mystical one, whether we call it the play of visible environmental forces or the outworking of the World-Mind's invisible designs, the result is the same: all must agree that an old order is dissolving, a new one being born. Everything has its place in the divine World-Idea. The great and grim happenings of our generation must also have some meaning in that thought, but this does not mean that they are arbitrarily sent to us. We have in large proportion brought them upon us ourselves, under the eternal law of compensation and the universal law of evolution, which constitute the essence of that Idea. The knowledge of these laws forces us to look from a different point of view at the suffering engendered and consequently with different results.

The cosmic laws exist, for if they did not everything would be in confusion. If the sun rose today it might not rise tomorrow. If there were no such laws the use of human free-will would be without meaning. Human life receives its full significance only when such will can be exercised. These laws express the will of God, and to the extent that we make our individual life conform to them, we are doing the will of God. Therefore it is good for man to ask in prayer what this will is and to seek to know through intelligence what those laws are.

A whole era is being brought to a close, hence the disintegration of values and institutions. Its own grave defects, its own moral backwardness, and its own ugly materialism have eaten like corrosive acids into its body. We are witnessing an immense planet-wide liquidation of outworn forms, false ideas, hypocritical institutions, selfish attitudes, and spiritual stagnations, even though the channels and forces of this liquidation are themselves so evil that they introduce for a time a worse state of affairs than the earlier one. For the good is being disintegrated along with the bad, the true is being cleared away along with the rubbish, and the beautiful is being destroyed too. In this transitional age when the evolutionary forces press and act upon humanity, both from within and from without, the predominant moral characteristics are everywhere being relentlessly forced to show themselves as they really are, and without disguise. And everywhere men are reaping with dramatic inevitability the consequences to which those characteristics lead. In the end it is what they deserve. It is the business of the law of recompense in this century relentlessly to adjust the accounts of all those groups and interests which have been dominated by the animalistic ego. History has become dramatically apocalyptic. This is indeed the "day" (that is, the period) of judgment spoken of in the Bible, the time when the scales of justice are in full operation for all races, all classes, all nations, and all religions. These are the scales in which the structure built up by humanity, and humanity itself, are being weighed, measured, and appraised.

But the operation of this law is only one of the factors in our complex situation. For not only is a process of world accounting responsible for so much contemporary upheaval but also a process of world development is responsible for so many present-day changes. The impersonal forces of the first produce shock, of the second, surprise. The phenomenal material progress of this modern era is partly due to the speeding up of tempo which always accompanies the last phase of an evolutionary trend, and partly to the outward-going character of the impetus behind this particular trend having reached its final and consequently largest expansion. The seething ferment of our times continues. It is a period of constant turmoil and incessant change. Why? Because the evolutionary pressure of hidden forces at work on this planet is now impatient to turn us from an outmoded past to a creatively new future.

Ordinarily, human nature has changed in the past with the utmost gradualness and the utmost slowness, but the pressures of life today show the need for a quicker adjustment. All the forces which underlie this transition are not easily perceptible, except to intuitive minds and clairvoyant perceptions. The consequences of their activity will not be felt until this fact is more clearly and sharply formed, but they will be even more momentous than are the ones already showing themselves. The stimulus for the present historical period of human development is coming both from within and without, from the unseen world and from the physical world. This inner pressure is making itself felt everywhere. The world gropes blindly with its problems; it is unable to grapple successfully with them because it dislikes to perceive that an old historical epoch is dissolving rapidly, that disturbing and disintegrating events are clearing the way for a new one which will later strive to take birth, and that it must adapt itself accordingly. The war and the peace are but the gateway to a new era, even though that era itself is still at the end of a long avenue.

The transition prior to a new cycle is slowly beginning its work. Its pressure is compelling men to pursue new avenues of inquiry, to thirst for wider awareness of life, even though their immaturity leads them often to mistake evil for good, the malign lie for the beneficent truth. Else why have the multitudes in Asia ended their long lethargy and begun to feed avidly on their new opportunities to learn reading and writing and thus become more knowledgeable citizens of the world? Why have the laboring masses on most continents been so insistent in demand and so restless in behavior? Why have lands which were asleep in medieval backwardness been aroused by war and crisis and forced to open themselves to new and worse as well as new and better ideas? It is because universal ferment is stirring up both the evil and the good long latent in men's minds. Those alone can read the riddle of our time who possess its key, which is that the old order of materialistic thinking, the old ways of looking at life, are being brought quickly to the surface in their most extreme forms, only eventually to be inexorably shattered by the shock of surprising events.

Men are merely puppets in this tremendous process, and they can neither control nor stop it. That the course of events is bigger than men, that the trend of world destiny is beyond the control of individuals, is illustrated by the history of our own times. Not even Hitler, with all the strongly dynamic energy he evoked in himself and inspired in others, could change this inevitableness. It is an illusion bred by historians whose only guide is logical intellect and external observation, that any particular person is so important and so powerful that he is able to alter the character and fate of his times, or even the mind and fortune of his nation. It is true that the rise of every movement coincides with the career of some remarkable man. But all that he does, all that he can do, is to provide in himself the conditions whereby karmic forces and evolutionary trends may achieve their aims for his age or people. It is inevitable that if he is used as such an instrument, his own personal aims will coincide with them at the time. It is his genius to perceive and provide for them.

The karmic forces and evolutionary processes now active

are hidden imponderables beyond any individual's control. If we see a particular man seeming to shape contemporary destiny, this is merely an appearance. Such a man is but an instrument for powers higher than himself, whether supernal and holy or infernal and devilish. Therefore, when men capable of great leadership appear on the scene, sooner or later they come to possess an influence commensurate with their greatness. It is only seemingly true that men are anterior to movements, that the outstanding epochs of history were inaugurated by outstanding persons, but it is really true that they are the focal points expressive of such movements and epochs. Every great movement, whether creative or destructive, has always seemed to be the achievement of one man—the child of one leader—but that which gave it the burning impulse of birth, and fed it with strength that it might live on and do its work, came from outside the man. It is not that a single individual at the helm of affairs remolds the life of a people but that the hidden forces of evolution and the historic forces of destiny find a fit outlet for their work in such an individual. For it is not alone his personal ambitions and desires, capacities and defects, which dictate the course of his people's history but also the inexorable operations of these two powerful mainsprings—self-incurred destiny and the evolutionary World-Idea.

In short, all heroes and all dictators, despite their illusion of self-creation of a movement or revolution, are really channels for impersonal forces as they enact their spectacular parts in the world drama. Destiny plays the last card, the winning trump, as usual. History can be understood properly only on a twofold basis—the personal and impersonal. The first points to the purposes, minds, and talents of the men who figure most in it, the second points to the great universal forces which use them. In the tremendous events which have unfolded themselves all over the world for several years past, there is plenty of evidence that new forces are entering men's minds and rousing men's unconscious approval or opposition. But behind all secondary issues and unworthier ramifications, behind the colossal struggle between the relatively good forces that are lifting them upward and those relatively evil ones that are dragging them downward, the will of the World-Idea is imposing itself.

Nothing could be more abnormal than the age of new, quickly changing conditions in which we are living. We find it hard to let the past impose itself too strongly upon us when it is so inadequate to the new problems. Our eyes are forced to concentrate themselves more upon the present and future, to look forward rather than backward. As in everything else, a double reckoning is needed here. There is a credit and a debit side of history's account. We need courage and initiative to separate ourselves from the bad and outworn things; we need wisdom and calmness to retain the good and useful ones.

People have made almost a religion out of their civilization. To point out its shortcomings as well as to predict the consequences if not remedied in time, is to commit sacrilege and blaspheme before their god. Yet this same civilization shows enough symptoms to indicate that they have approached the extreme limits of materialism with terrifying consequences for themselves. There is no real way out other than a reaction against this extreme position, no real relief except to turn automatically and spontaneously away in the opposite direction, that is toward their spiritual nature. The insufficiency of the unillumined intellect in practical living has become more and more revealed to them, so they have to turn away from it to the intuitive within themselves simply because there is no other direction in which they can turn.

The path of human evolution is not a straight line, but a zig-zag spiral which jerks from side to side, as well as up and down. This cycle of alternating human development is a historic one, and can be found throughout man's past. Thus certain tendencies or movements, such as materialism, appear as recurring phenomena in history. The evolution of the living being is marked by a spiral movement which brings it back again and again to corresponding but not identical conditions. Not all portions of humanity are at the same place in this movement. This spiral-like character of the circle explains why some nations or races seem to be rising but others falling, why some are weak and helpless when formerly they were strong and dominant, why some are inert and backward while others are active and purposeful. The world has passed through and is now on the last lap of the downward arc of the phase of excessive materialism. The reaction from it has already begun in our time, under the twofold pressure of external events and internal directives from the Higher Power, or rather man's own Overself, exemplifying the will of God for this time. These spiritual influences are working upon mankind everywhere but working more through the individual hearts than through official organizations. They exist in countries where the ruling powers are openly materialistic and irreligious as much as in countries where the ruling powers are not. If human evolution were left to man alone, or to chance alone, this might not have happened, but it is compelled to obey universal laws.

For twenty years after the first World War civilization was given a long opportunity by karma in which to set its house in order. It failed to do so. The vital period for mankind, a period which may roughly be called the crucial period, lasted for about twelve months before and eighteen months after the next war's end. If chaos occurred then in some quarters of the postwar world, crisis prevailed in others. Hope in many lands and ruin in others marked those opening years of the peace, necessarily full of confused suggestion and experimental movement, of swift change and articulate discontent—all following in rapid succession. Like an old tree, the old era was being torn up by its roots. But all were conscious that somewhere ahead either a tremendous transformation or a tremendous collapse awaited them. The time was short. Decisions had to be made hurriedly. The spiritual trend of this generation, and consequently its physical destiny, was largely decided within those two and a half years. It was then that the future pattern of the world's present and coming destiny was largely shaped.

This second postwar period is, in its way, just as important as the first period was. For on the wisdom or foolishness of the personal decisions which have been and are now being made, on the spiritual courage or cowardice shown by leaders and led alike, depends the happiness or misery of millions of people. The first step to cure present miseries is to change our personal and national thinking, to stop thinking in terms of materialism and start thinking in terms of spirituality, to cease cut-throat selfishness and begin mutual co-operation, to lighten emphasis on physical needs and increase the emphasis on spiritual ones. Humanity has reached the turning point in her young life. She must prepare to take up the responsibility of maturity. She must give a nobler direction to all this tremendous dynamic activity, a deeper significance to all this rushing energy. The change that the evolutionary forces of Nature are asking from us is a drastic one, yet if accepted and made, it would be our best guarantee of victory over the destructive forces.

A calm perception of mankind's moral limitations and a philosophical acceptance of them need not lead to a dismal and paralyzing pessimism. For a colossal evolutionary movement is always in progress which Nature has guided and activated with infinite patience to its present point. We may understand that mankind is on the upward move, however slowly and through however many dismal lapses and retrogressions. Some change more quickly than others but no man is what he was ten years ago. If the inevitability of change must be granted, then inability to go back and be what he once was must likewise be granted.

Simply because he cannot, man will not remain a static creature. He must go forward—or degenerate. But his forward movement is an enduring one whereas his backward movement is only a temporary one. For that which ever impels and enables him to evolve is a force which ever exists within himself. It is none other than the force of his higher self, his divine soul. This is the secret energy which is lifting him upward and activating his development. If his evolution depended only upon the whim of his personal self, then it would be an uncertain and often hopeless process. That the mysterious power which belongs to his Overself is the real driving power of his evolution is the best assurance of his ultimate achievement.

Consider that the numerous living cells which compose the tissues of our bodies will themselves one day evolve into individual human beings! The spiral-like wave of evolution is infinite, carrying the minutely small onward to the unimaginably great.

In these terrible times the quest of this Overself has an enhanced value. Quite apart from its personal results, the knowledge that higher laws still rule the world and that the forces of evil are doomed to self-destruction in the end saves its possessors from despair and gives them hope.

The Ego Crisis. It was pointed out in an earlier work that tremendously accelerated change is a dominant note of the present period. However much we may dislike interruption in thought and behavior, we cannot escape the changes—both good and bad—which are being pressed upon us. We must recognize this insistent and unseen pressure as a challenge and adapt ourselves to the good in it as well as reject the bad in it.

Millions of people had their whole life uprooted during the war. They were cruelly dragged from their familiar surroundings, ruthlessly parted for years from their old homes, and separated from their communities of which they felt an integral part. How many lost or were robbed of nearly all they possessed—life, health, land, houses, money, business, furniture, even most of their better clothes! They were not only mercilessly stripped of things, but in many cases were forcibly separated from wives, parents, or children. Statistics revealed that in England alone more than half the civilians moved to new residences during the war. Memories of the once-comfortable past became tortures of regret while pleasant hopes for the future were turned to unpleasant anticipations. The easier fate often belonged to those who had to make a change because of their work than to those whose connections were with the armed forces, but often not.

Why should this law of change dominate the world of physical forms as well as human affairs? Why cannot a permanent social form, a stable individual existence be created and maintained forever? For answer let us go into the secret structure of every atom. What do we see? Ceaseless vibration. Let us go next into every human mind. There we will see the perpetual birth of a progeny of ideas. This is its very nature. But these facts remain half-truths unless we couple them with the major fact that behind the atom is the everlasting Stillness of God; behind the mind is the witnessing Silence of the Overself.

However often history may have repeated itself in the past, it has not repeated itself today. For the situation now is unique. It is a *world* crisis, and not merely a continental or national one. It touches *all* humanity, and not merely a section of it. This is the first time a situation like it has ever risen. *Such an external event is in line with the extraordinary internal event which marks a turning point in the spiritual evolution of the human ego.* The outer conflict which materially affects mankind has been matched by the inner conflict which troubles its subconscious self. It is more necessary than ever amid the turmoils and dangers of today to understand something of the divine Idea inherent in the universe, and cooperate intelligently and willingly with it. These studies have therefore an importance which is not realized by most people.

The World-Mind does not work quite like a human architect, for it is not separate from its materials or activities. Therefore, when the phrase "divine Idea" is used in these writings, it should be understood to mean not an architectural plan or pictorial drawing but the inherent necessity whereby manifestation follows a certain way and not a different one. Everything in the cosmos is passing through various stages of unfoldment. And because it originates in the divine substance, all the possibilities of such unfoldment from the lowest to highest are inherent in it. They do not have to be planned for. They are already there as part of its innermost nature.

Every man who looks back on his own life may discover that it has moved onward in certain noticeable periods, each of which was the expression of a particular physical or mental trend. Every nation which does likewise may make the same discovery about its collective history. And because it is the inner life which, after all, manifests itself in the outer one, because it is the underlying Idea which molds the character and form of every epoch, it will be highly profitable to make clear to our own consciousness what is the special Idea which is coming into birth during this present time when an entire epoch is so obviously disintegrating before our very eyes. We must look at, and judge, contemporary history by its secret connection with a special evolutionary crisis which intellect only obscures and insight alone reveals.

It does not need much examination of the facts to show that human evolution works through three successive phases: the physical, the intellectual, and the spiritual. If the human entity is to develop its capacities at all, it has to develop them through a self-centered individuality combining the first two. This is a natural and necessary phase of its history. The divine Idea for human evolution has a place for the personality's self-centeredness, for out of this development of egocentricity, this intensification of separative consciousness, the human entity differentiates itself from all the others. It is necessary for man's progress that he include the extraverted and egocentric attitude. For a time it serves a useful purpose in his development. The various capacities of the physical body and potentialities of the mental-emotional psyche are brought out by it.

Out of the unknown life of man's unremembered past, there comes down to him the legacy of being able to know and do so much more than any animal can. The selfish and possessive instincts, the materialistic and extraverted attachments in human nature are not there by any degeneration on its part but rather by its own development. They are natural results of bringing out its latent capacities and faculties, of expanding its consciousness from more primitive stages through a quest for individualized life. They are a part of the rhythmic evolution which is such a feature of the divine World-Idea.

How else could Nature form man's ego unless its informing life and consciousness had been given a wide enough experience, unless they had been allowed to journey through the bodies of the adder, the tiger, the cow, and the horse for example, and gain the attributes and consciousness that such bodies could manifest? They were not merely useful but quite necessary in the making of the ego, the "I am."

When this finite center of consciousness finished the preparation in other kingdoms of nature and began its life as a human ego, the development of its selfish nature was necessary and useful to its ultimate goal. This provided it, through desire, with valuable motives for activity and, during the earlier and intermediate stages of that life, was its strength and glory. The ego had to enlarge its field of power and experience and expand its sphere of acquisition in the course of its progress. The multiplication of desires and the struggle of egocentricity, with the consequent intensification of personality, as well as the growth and extraversion of mental faculties, were necessary phases of its unfoldment.

Man could gain his fully individualized awareness of himself, of others, and of his environment in no other way. During the long course of his history, it was through this very selfish extraversion that man gradually manifested the potentialities with which nature endowed him and thus both expressed and developed himself. It was a natural and essential process, which brought him the requisite experience and the resulting knowledge of his own individuality and powers. It was an indispensable phase of his development that his ego should grow in strength and expand in consciousness.

The yearning of young egos, impelled by desire and in need of experience, was for activity. The yearning of old ones, disappointed in desire or satiated with experience or inwardly urged toward truth-seeking, is for rest. How many series of earthly existences, how many a wave of successive enfleshments, separate the first group from the second! The only reason why the great mass of humanity failed spiritually to grow up more quickly was not one for which it can be blamed. It had not had enough time, and the richer experience which comes with time. Dozens of more rebirths were and are needed to gain the deeper consciousness, the finer perceptions which distinguish mature persons.

Up to the present point in his development it was the proper and useful business of man to acquire capacities and possessions, to differentiate himself through selfishness. But in doing this he lost more and more his spiritual kinship with Nature and his intuitive guidance. This middle point of his evolution is when intellect awakens and develops, which is why it is the most dangerous one. For here the ego is most strongly individualistic, most stubbornly materialistic, most filled with selfishness, most wedded to the use of cunning for its own gain and consequently most harmful to others. Many of the egos which have incarnated in contemporary bodies have reached this extreme limit of individualization but have been the most unwilling of all to make the about-turn for which evolution now asks. They refuse to join the next trend, which is toward harmony, peace, and co-operation with others, toward mutual help and service, toward a more spiritual and less sensuous world-view.

The spiritual evolution of the human race is partly a struggle to overcome the strong obstacles of its own self-regarding animalistic and extraverting tendencies; partly a discipline of the intuition-crushing intellect. There is nothing wrong in these tendencies by themselves and in their place. But when they entirely dominate consciousness, they give rise to extreme selfishness and cynical materialism. It is an inevitable result of past and present phases that excessive attachment to the animal-physical side of life should rise within it and that selfishness and wrong-doing should rise in the relations between the egos, that evil should become as active as good and even, at certain periods, more active than good. An evil creature is simply an insufficiently evolved creature. Such a stiff thickening of egotism, such an extraverted attachment to the physical personality is unavoidable in the human entity's development. It cannot be prevented. But in doing this it naturally strengthens its own selfishness, and its own antisocial attitudes. This eventually brings about clashes with other egos. It begins to sin and consequently to suffer. The evils which follow in the train of such selfishness, such as the competitive attitude which later grows into the combative one, and the acquisitiveness which grows into aggressiveness, cannot be escaped. Yet carried too far, such attitudes defeat the very object of all this evolution. Real evil appears only in the human kingdom, where the union of human intellect and animal desire produces creatures capable of wickedness such as no animal is capable of. A stage has now been reached when it must be halted and when the ultimate goal must be recalled to view—the goal of elevating the ego's consciousness to the

Overself's. This need not be done in all its fullness; only the simplest, most elementary recall, such as popular religion suggests, is enough.

Man has now fully appeared on Nature's scene and the necessary mental instruments for effecting his spiritualization have already been developed but they are being misused for what are often antispiritual purposes. The higher opportunities provided by physical birth are either frittered away in vanities or abused in sins or neglected in other preoccupations. The ego is like a child that wants to remain in the stage of childhood forever. But life will not permit it to do so. The time for its crossing over the threshold of adult spiritual responsibility has come. It must face the serious issues of existence, the why and whither of its presence on earth.

When we speak here of the human ego, it should be obvious that the reference is to its evolutionary stage as found in the largest number of human beings upon this planet. That is, the reference is not to the small minority now in incarnation who have passed beyond this stage. It is this majority which stands mostly at the mid-point of evolution.

It can go farther along the present road only to self-destruction. Its progression on this planet has reached its final climax of individualization. If it is to evolve it must be henceforth by adding the controls, checks, and compensatory balances of another goal. It must dispense with the excessive personal selfishness and intellectual materiality which lifted it to its present capacity, but which when unbalanced blinded it also to its best interests and truest knowledge. Their growth was only a particular phase essential only for a particular period. That period is now drawing to an abrupt close.

Today the individual entity's needs are inevitably different. In order to become man it had to develop egotism. In order to surpass man, it will have to submerge egotism. Then only can the ruthless struggle and cruel history of human relations surely be ameliorated. In the balanced practice of self-help and accommodation to others, in the cultivation of spiritual faith and intuition, the next phase of its progress lies. It has moved far from the protozoa and has now reached a point in the evolutionary scale where a considerable change-over to another direction has become imperative. It must take the great step forward to a higher understanding of its own existence. Every day that it delays doing so, invites further suffering. The evil misdirection of its own physical and intellectual forces has come too dangerously near to being a total one. The species Man approaches the most critical hairpin bend in inward and outward life. With the twentieth century at its meridian, this self-worship, this materialistic intellectuality, and this excessive outward-turning begin to lose their evolutionary value.

The aggressive animal forces in the ego are especially making a desperate stand to keep their ancient rule. What we see all around us is partly a visible manifestation of the invisible convulsions through which it is passing. Its own fierce resistence is reflected in the international situation. If both leaders and led persist in ignoring the new orientation, their convulsions might well become dying ones and the civilizations they have built up may disintegrate with them. In this state of extreme extraversion and aggressive egoism, millions of people have become quite blind to the higher purpose of human life. They consider Man merely a thinking animal, the moral struggle between right and wrong merely a matter of expediency and convenience, the aspiration for goodness merely a morbid pathological condition. Too many other human beings have fallen even farther than this. They have said, "evil be thou my good."

Because humanity in the past has been living in a vicious circle of ego domination and consequent suffering, this circle must now be broken. The unfoldment of selfhood through a series of lives on this earth has reached its culmination. It has led inevitably to a situation where the strength and violence of the "I" must be checked if it is not constantly to injure itself and others by excessive blindness, grasping, and possessiveness. Although every living creature possesses egoism in the form of self-preservation, only man has brought it to such socially dangerous extremes because he alone has brought intellectual cunning to its service. It has reached a point where it must either submit itself henceforth to the checks and controls of the higher self, or it will provoke the gravest danger of destruction for humanity.

The human entity's inordinate clinging to its combative animality and selfish personality is being challenged and attacked by world forces and turned into a cause of its own psychic suffering. The tremendous tension which has risen in its consciousness because of its inner resistance to this evolutionary pressure working both from within by spiritual influences and from without by historical events, has been too much for many people. It has unbalanced their psyches and caused much semi-insanity. The critical point has been reached, the farthest point of their straying; beyond this they will be in danger of losing whatever spiritual qualities still remain. In developing and inflating this egotism, they have gone farther and farther away from the divine source of their being. It is now being carried to the extreme resulting in such widespread atheism, aggressive selfishness, and open immorality, that the danger of utter self-destruction has risen. The aggression of the animal ego and the perfection of the lower intellect have gone as far as they should for the present cycle; their attenuation must begin. If too few individuals and no nations are voluntarily willing to start the process, the forces of destiny will co-operate with the other factors to arrest the present trend still more drastically. The shock of such events to the nervous system would then induce different moods and even different views of life from those previously prevailing. Thus the evolutionary compulsion is being laid upon the extraverted and inflated personal ego to abandon its present position and take the path of return.

We know that this is physically the most exciting time in history. Do we know that it is also spiritually the most critical time? Humanity has been led to the crossroads of its incarnated life. It needs to pause and reflect. The hour has struck in the ego's cosmic journey when it must choose whether or not it will turn round to face and then begin to obey its own divine soul. It has come to the end of its severest evolutionary cycle. Deeper into darkness it will not be allowed to go. Higher into light it does not want to go. Forces both inside and outside itself wage a titanic war for its right and wrong guidance. It has arrived at the climacteric period of its long history. Its approach to this evolutionary crossroads is indeed one of the most powerful influences contributing to the present world crisis. Events so constantly shape themselves that the situation must be faced; momentous decisions are so constantly required that they cannot be put off nor their demands ignored. It may respond to those moral ideals and nonmaterialistic beliefs which the spiritual teachers have always set before it as essential to right conduct and thought, or it may reject them.

All this is the result of the tremendous evolutionary twist in conscience and reorientation in consciousness which the unwilling ego is being asked to manifest. The result is clash and conflict within itself and, because the pressure is also synchronized with the operations of karmic destiny, clash and conflict in its external life. The wars and crises, revolutions and famines are both outward symbols and natural consequences of its desperate resistance. Among the first effects of this inner evolutionary change, along with the noble, the good, and the self-sacrificial, all the evil in humanity's character has been thrown up to the surface, all the ugliest passions have found release. Horror and violence, lust and greed, fear and hate, envy and spite have been openly glorified. But this is the night before the dawn, the desperate struggles of the trapped beast in man.

Our own sins and sloths, errors and materialism, sent us a Destroyer. God has yet to send us a Deliverer. Hitler appeared as a gigantic figure holding the center of the world stage and armed with a whip which slashed right and left, among his own countrymen equally as among all Europe. It would be a large error to believe that the world was punished for Hitler's sin alone. Not one man's but the accumulated results of millions of men's selfish thinking and negative feeling, animalistic passion and unethical doing went into the catastrophe which overwhelmed more than a whole continent. The long insufferable agony of wartime horrors and atrocities, bitterness and distress, deserves special thought here. In its size and cause, its strangeness and technique, the war was the outstanding event in the external history of the nations. Yet it was simply a part of the general world crisis, albeit the most vivid, violent, and dramatic part. Its grim pressures began the process of forcing co-operative attitudes and social fusions upon the individuals and classes within most countries, but the relaxed tension of peace's onset reversed the process and saw fresh returns of the egoistic attitudes.

In the delusions of the ego and in its ignorance of the true nature behind that which expresses itself in the personal and vertical pronoun "I" are th esource both of the evil it does and the ignorance it shows. In its unchecked selfishness is mankind's worst adviser. So long as it considers its personal good as the all-important consideration, so long as it does not see that the interests of others are to be thought of along with its own, so long as, wherever the two collide, it always sacrifices the second to the first instead of wisely balancing them, so long will events and experiences befall which, through pain and disappointment, will try to tutor it out of this error. If, in its long past career it was quite proper for it to seek its own, to expand its rule and strengthen its position, the new evolutionary bidding is to place itself under the rule of the higher self and to balance its own interests with the common interest. The inordinate attachment to its own interest, values, and views into which it has fallen marks the extreme limit of a long phase of development.

The inflated personal ego is everywhere—in politics and religion, in art and business—attempting to resist the internal and external forces that would reduce its tyranny and undo its selfishness. It is stubborn, unwilling to budge from its position. This is one reason why philosophy reiterates that neither economics nor politics will ever adequately solve humanity's problems, not even its material problems, because they are at bottom spiritual problems. No matter what sphere of human activity we look at, there the personal ego may be found perversely defending itself and aggressively clashing with other egos. Its desires and possessions, its ambitions and prejudices are the real goals which it aims to obtain or retain behind the façade of tall talk which it often puts up. This is as true of the political and economic spheres as of the social and religious spheres. Hence, philosophy leaves to others the securing of external reforms and devotes itself to exposing and eliminating the ego's tyranny. It teaches men that what seems the longest way—improving themselves—is in the end the shortest way to the goal of improving their environment. Thus it gets at real causes; the reformers get at mere effects. Those who do not come to the truth about life (that is, philosophy), out of its own inner attraction, will one day have to come to it out of the need of self-defense in the struggles of living. Such a day has arrived in our own times. Those who still fail to recognize this—and they are many—are mere escapists, hiding from reality but likely to be dragged out of their corners by Destiny's rough hand.

Whoever has eyes to see may recognize that the war should have been a period of tremendous awakening, to compensate for its terrible devastation. If that awakening has so far taken a political and economic turn, this was inevitable. But a religious and intellectual one has yet to follow. Humanity should not have tried to go back to the old prewar way of materialistic life. It had the chance to go on to a new and worse way or a new and better one. Few have escaped being caught in the whirlpool of contemporary events and therefore being influenced for better or worse by it. Of those who lived through terrible experiences, what they suffered themselves or saw others suffer has been too drastic not to leave an ineffaceable impression upon their character. The experiences of the past decade should have led them to a different standpoint, whether higher or lower, from that which was theirs before it began. The world crisis should have carried such men's thoughts to a position which even to a single generation earlier would have seemed so idealistically advanced or so degeneratively alien as to be unthinkable and unimaginable during this century.

In a transitional era of such quick-moving events as ours, and of such titanic events as those which have happened in our own lifetime, it is foolish to consider problems only by the light of what was. Prewar appraisals do not hold good for postwar times. If a man or a nation finds out that he or it has taken the wrong road, the sensible thing to do is to turn around and get back to the right one. A new direction should then be taken. Yet this is rarely done—such is the impetus of the past and the pressure of habit. One of the strongest supports of the ego is habit, the automatic memory of the mind and feeling-nature. It sustains and preserves the selfish past or the wrong past by bringing it into the present. It arms and equips the intellect in its domination over, or resistance against, the intuition. Behind the evil and grief of war and crisis is this good—that they bereave us of habits that imprison us in thinking that is evolutionarily outworn, in attitudes that are too personal and in conventional lies that are absorbed from society, civilization, or tradition. Giving them up is part of what the Mystic of Galilee meant when he asked us to give up the self. Such a curious idea as that we must give up our self in order to find it must seem like an irritating paradox to the intelligentsia, and must necessarily be dressed in homely parable for the simple. But we ought not to run away from a paradox; it is really a cloak which covers the deepest and therefore the most valuable kind of thought.

The human ego must make the first faint beginning to renounce its sovereignty in favor of the divine Overself, or be driven by implacable fate in the same direction. The necessity of a change in thought and feeling as a preface to a change in humanity's tragic fortunes is an absolute condition. The repentance must be an active one, the change of heart must be shown in a change of life. Negative emotions are to be checked, evil deeds stopped, the animal nature disciplined, and spiritual exercises started to overcome spiritual sloth. The path of humanity must now begin to lead homeward again toward awareness—however slight—of the higher self. Willingly or unwillingly it must round this crucial point and change the direction of its inner life. Such a change necessarily involves and expresses itself in penitence. Consequently the supreme spiritual message today is a call to repent. Those who sincerely respond to it will be "saved," but those who refuse to heed it, whose egos rebel against the higher view of life, condemn themselves to further and worse suffering.

Certain types of fanatical leaders represent an easily recognizable section of the latter group. Their blinded followers are indeed unlucky; there is no room for permanently maintaining such a position in the dawning era. They are trying to hold a doomed fort, the end of their era is nearing, whether by self-surrender or external catastrophe, for the evolutionary forces are inexorable.

Such is the process of reorientation which will, when a certain point in history not far off is reached, develop increasingly in the human psyche, such the passage from an outmoded materialistic egoism to an incoming spiritual awareness. As this evolutionary development goes on, the ego will be less and less victimized by its senses and animality, hence less and less materialistic in its thinking. The new tendencies will affect not only its quality of consciousness but also its moral attitudes.

Always in times of social crisis and more especially in a time of immense cyclical transition like our own, when an evolutionary change-over of the ego is secretly impending, men do not evolve slow step by slow step into high spiritual truth, but reach it suddenly and dramatically. They experience it with all the force of an unheralded revelation. Although there has already begun a period of marked intellectual and social awakening, a longer time is necessary before the culminating point in spiritual awakening is reached. The mind has still to travel some distance before it will even admit that such a change is possible, and still farther before it will readily discern the first signs of its happening. It would be a misunderstanding to believe that this change could be so abrupt as to be most evident in sudden improvement to everyone. What will happen is that the prompting toward such sudden improvement will manifest itself, because of the tremendous pressure of certain situations that will later be created by the world crisis. There will and can, however, be no compulsion upon anyone to accept this prompting and act upon it. The human ego must choose to follow the divine guidance of its own accord before the external benefits of such a course become evident.

The Inner Challenge of the Crisis. If we consider for a moment how obsolete today are the ideas of nineteenth-century physicists about the structure of the atom and hence about the nature of the physical universe, we may see what a large advance has been made away from the falsity of nineteenth-century scientific materialism. Yet, although the scientific basis of materialism has largely disappeared, the industrialistic basis of it has not. This explains in part why the general mass of people in "advanced" countries still think and act as if it were true. The religious camouflage under which it is often hidden does not alter its real nature. It is not only out-of-date, but it has all the errors which out-of-date scientific knowledge often has. If the full implications of what had been developed in psychology, in psychobiology, and in nuclear physics could be thoroughly comprehended by the atheists, they would be compelled to abandon their negative belief. The subatomic investigations of a great scientist like the late Lord Rutherford proved metaphysically favorable to nonmaterialistic doctrines. But Rutherford himself, because he underrated the value of metaphysical thinking, did not perceive that they showed forth how matter hid the energies of a nonphysical reality, or, as a highly illumined Oriental seer once said to us when we mentioned atomic research to him, "the energies of that infinite and eternal being—the World-Mind, God."

In France, England, and America, not a few influential intellectuals, who once led thought into skepticism, cynicism, and nihilism, have themselves been led by a further process of their own reasoning, based upon the further data now available, to deny the very materialism to which this same reasoning first led them and to renounce the antispirituality which was its original fruit. It is more than ironic, it is tragic that science which first destroyed religious belief in existence of a reality beyond the material one, should now begin to provide the evidence needed to support that belief. For the help has come so very late. Modern civilization is in danger of destroying a large segment of itself, partly because of the military weapons which science has put into its hands and partly because of the mental materialism which science created in its earlier ignorance. The history of many past civilizations is written today in sand and water; two hands are ever at work in writing that tragic tale, the first being the one all see—man's own; the second is one which few see—the irresistible hand of a higher power.

For too long most people thought that the search for a higher purpose in life was not so important as the several lower purposes; it did not even matter. They needed to be shocked into awareness that nothing else can take its place. The wars and world crisis provide these shocks. The sudden appearance of the atomic bomb on the world scene is a symbol of the abruptness with which the challenge has come upon us. It offers humanity the choice to survive or be destroyed. But to survive it has to change its old thinking. This final discovery was needed to startle and alarm humanity as never before, to arouse and compel it to face the fact that the old ways of dealing with certain problems are useless now. It is a reminder of the futility of clinging lazily to ideas stamped with the materialism that must pass away. Through the atomic bomb the human intellect is entering the psycho-electric world behind the atom, but it is doing so prematurely, before it is ready or worthy to do so. The World-Power is not only creative but also destructive, as the staggering changes in starry bodies and our planet Earth, changes which have happened in the past and will happen again in the future, exemplify. To meddle with it before being morally prepared and spiritually knowledgeable to do so, becomes as dangerous to man, when devoid of any knowledge of the spiritual laws which govern life, as when informed by that same knowledge it becomes helpful to him. Physical and intellectual advance have gone far enough and should be halted for a while until a spiritual and moral advance restores the lost equilibrium. The crisis is closing in upon us. At a certain point its results will not only stop our further blind advance into scientific and technical power uncontrolled by an ethical attitude toward that power, but also show that we are not strong enough to live without spiritual resources.

Our definition of war is too limited, too exclusively physi-

cal. For the visible war is only an effect, an expression of
what already exists on the mental level, the true cause being
the invisible war of thoughts and feelings. While one group
of men are filled with hatred or glower with anger at another group, while they spit forth hysterical recrimination
and denunciation, they create the mental conditions which,
if sustained long enough, developed intensely enough, and
returned by those they oppose, can one day be reflected in
open strife or even physical war. This could happen by a law
of inevitability, even if war itself is feared and undesired.
Such forces express animality and have been struggling for
power before our own eyes and seeking to control humanity's very life. Yet this outer conflict is only a universal expression of what is going on in the individual man. That is
why it cannot be resolved on the plane of political rearrangement alone, or on that of military war alone. Each person
who refuses to try to resolve it within himself, which can
be done only by disciplining his lower nature and turning
toward his higher self in faith and love, is in a small way responsible for the world's discouraging condition. Two roads
open out before every individual in today's as in every great
crisis of his life. One will lead him farther on the way to his
Overself, the other farther away from it. The demands which
this epoch makes on him are tremendous when compared
with those of former ones. He cannot adapt it to himself but
must adapt himself to the epoch. Such a time of transition is
no time for intellectual or emotional stiffness.

   The problems of the world crisis cannot be evaded but
have to be met somehow. The problem of learning how to
live has to be approached afresh, not merely dallied with as
in normal times. This problem is always with man but only
when it is thrust so insistently and so overwhelmingly upon
him does he realize that he may drift on from hastily impro-
vised and therefore insufficient solutions to one new crisis
after another, or else seek entirely new solutions. When ex-

cessive immersion in the means of existence, that is, the body with its passions and appetites, the ego with its emotions and intellect, becomes so extreme that man forgets its end, that is, integration with his true being, then the forces of destiny and evolution put pressure upon him to bring about a search for some freedom from this immersion (which is one form of materialism). The form taken by such pressure is usually suffering. Humanity could never have been brought down to the depths of misery and suffering to which it has been brought, and made to endure so much that seems unendurable in retrospect, if there had not been grave weaknesses in its character and defects in its judgment.

The idiot fury of two world wars punished civilization for its errors. Their effects taught some people some wisdom and virtue but they have taught more people much materialism and evil. There is naturally a time lag before the meaning of an experience catches up in consciousness with the experience itself. But even allowing for that, what has been learned by too many is not enough or not correct. If they had learned from their sufferings to remove the causes which originally brought them into being; if they had shed their errors and righted their outlook, then history would have taken a better course. The emptiness of a life activity devoted to materialistic aims alone and the futility of a life view limited to what satisfies the ego and the senses alone, become their own retribution in the end. The need of finding a meaning to life exists more today than ever before. It is pressed upon them from outside by these alternating crisis. They must face the inescapable issue: either to live in a more reasonable and reverent world and find true peace or to fall back into the old prewar chaos and find fresh strife. The urgent need, the insistent demand made by the evolutionary forces is a courageous break with wrong habits and false beliefs on all levels—spiritual, intellectual, and worldly. This alone can save them from the disastrous consequences of committing further follies.

We stand at a moral crossroads. The grave moment of choice is here. It is true that the world has often been sick and required healing. Today its sickness has become critical. As the crisis in which we live today has tormentingly lengthened so has it progressively worsened. The more we delay drinking the medicine of truth the more sick we become. That medicine would compel us increasingly to view our situation with complete impartiality. For the causes of human misery look into the human heart and see its moral selfishness; look into the human mind and behold its spiritual ignorance. Every kind of frustration, every condition of failure, every sort of disappointment has come to teach us that our way of life is faulty.

Life today is more than ever a challenge by the events we are responsible for, by the destiny forced upon us and by the pattern of the World-Idea, to become aware of our spiritual ignorance and to give up our self-admiration. The man who has not found out his spiritual origin and higher destiny may be excused, but the man who has not tried to find it out is blameworthy.

Man's Need of a Higher Power. Everywhere today we see that the human being has misunderstood itself and misconceived the World-Mind's will for it in this era. And because there is a price to be paid for all mistakes, everywhere we also see human distress and human suffering. The way out of these afflictions is being desperately sought but seldom found . . . for it is being sought in the wrong direction. There is only one proper way out, and that is to correct the misunderstanding and to remove the misconception. This needs a dramatic change of moral attitude, a large renunciation of materialistic outlook, and a quick reversal of spiritual indifference. A change in thinking is the first way to ensure a change in the world's condition. In changing himself, man takes the first step toward changing his environment and in changing his environment he takes the second step toward changing himself. For the first step of self-change must be a mental, not a physical one. He has lived a materialistic life which is but a half-life. Therefore he will profit best in these difficult days by subduing pride and being perfectly frank with himself, even to the point of putting on mental sackcloth and emotional ashes. His mental attitude must effect an about-face. He must heed that inspired bidding, *"Repent—and be saved."* This has been the divine message for all such times but it is especially applicable to the present time. The only cure for the newest chaos in which the whole world has fallen is also the oldest one. Those who wait for the announcement of miracle-working prescriptions wait in vain. The truth that is around the corner is as old as mankind, only the face it shows is fresh and the clothes it wears are styled to the century itself. Some thousands of years ago India's sacred writing, "Bhagavad-Gita," proclaimed that there is peace and prosperity on the earth for those who will learn and follow the laws of the inner life.

To say that the higher powers have created a crisis of human destiny in order to compel human beings to face the inner challenge is true. To say that human history and conduct have themselves created it is also true. These two halves must be put together to get the whole truth about the dark events which have overtaken humanity. Every attempt to save itself that is only an external attempt and not also an internal one, is foredoomed to failure. This needs to be remembered by all peoples because all peoples have been caught in the world's challenging situation, even though their particular responsibility is less in some cases, more in others. It is not the Europeans and Americans who are alone being challenged today by their creations, but also the Indians and the Chinese, inheritors of the oldest civilizations on the planet. We are not of those who eulogize the Orient as the sole abode of spirituality, and titter at the Occident as the polluted

abode of materiality. Each hemisphere has its own special
faults to set right, each has strayed from the path ordained
by God for it and consequently both are being involved in
the crisis. All peoples, all races, have reached a point where
the road traveled can no longer be traveled, where going forward and retreating backward are both impossible. What then
are they to do? The obvious and only correct answer is to
get off the wrong road and get on to a new one.

The ultimate destiny of the world—as apart from its immediate destiny—is to become more spiritualized and not
less. Every man who believes this will understand that society
is as good or as bad as the individuals who compose it, that
there is no magic which can make a good civilization out of
bad individuals, a golden new order out of the leaden old
characters. He will consequently believe in the need of fine
character to guide a people, rather than in cheap slogans. He
will look for guidance from men who believe it too, not
from those who believe in the materialism which darkly shadows everything. This is why philosophy points to the need of
human reformation for any durable reformation of society.
This is why there is no nobler task today than diffusing that
knowledge about man himself, which he least possesses and
most needs. This is an even more valuable service than reforming the society in which he lives, although that is perfectly proper and absolutely necessary in its place. The task
is not only to reaffirm that under the law of compensation we
get back the results of our own good or evil doing, not only
to advertise to an ignorant blinded world that the Overself
exists and is the supreme value; not only to show that it is an
experienceable reality and not an imagined fancy or a specu-
lative concept, but also to advocate to an indifferent complacent world that the Overself's life must be brought into its
own practical everyday life.

In the end, humanity will be driven to have recourse to its
pure spiritual teachers, after all other guides have led it into

material ruin and mutual destruction. No other refuge is left for stricken humanity than this one. The notion that their teaching is of no use to men of the world, versed in the facts of life, and aware of the compromises involved in business and political affairs, is a delusion which dates the origin of man's unnecessary and avoidable sufferings. It is indeed the greatest of errors to regard such guides as impractical visionaries. Their vision of what is happening around them is never circumscribed by personal considerations. Having rid themselves of narrow views and parochial prejudices, having learned to think of human affairs in large terms and through long vistas of time, having transcended the limitations of a merely intellectual approach and entered into an intuitive one, they are in a good position to understand the course of past history and to discern meaning behind the veils of present events. They can satisfy the deep-rooted need of the human mind to discover some worthier significance in life today. Hence their philosophy is not irrelevant to the purposeful activities and practical interests of men. They know the true causes of humanity's distress and the true remedies.

The declaration of eternal laws and revelation of universal patterns must be made anew. The sooner we discover that there are spiritual laws which cannot be outwitted, the better for us. Never before did the function which the philosophic sage, the religious prophet, and the mystical seer could perform in society be so needed yet remain so neglected. We have no worship for their wisdom, revelation, or guidance, only for the engineer's mechanical skill, the tradesman's fortune-making capacity, the entertainer's escape-providing talent. The old spiritual teachers with their intuitive or clairvoyant penetration into the inner side of things, and their certainty about truth only because it was their experience and not their opinion, gave merely moral injunctions against all the ugly emotions and passions, especially hate. Today the scientific laws of the power of thought must be given out to explain these injunctions, and to warn us that negative mental-emotional states reflect themselves in physical war, strife, trouble, sickness, and even misfortune. When, for instance, a man so easily loses his balance as to fall into a wrathful state at the smallest provocation, he is exposed to many dangers—such as fights, sickness, accidents, and loss of friends.

The war was a warning to begin afresh and a reminder that the Day of Judgment is at hand. Yet out of its definite evil there arose a certain good. In such hours of tragic need which the universal conflict so often brought, a number of those who had lived empty, frivolous, or materialistic lives were driven by hitherto suppressed instincts to seek outside help or transhuman support. Today, humanity is reaching a dead end where, on its own admission, its problems have expanded to almost insoluble proportions. Its wiser leaders begin to confess that it needs help from sources beyond itself, that human power unaided by spiritual wisdom and strength is not sufficient to deal with such wide and explosive problems. It has come to witness in its own time how a rapidly developing civilization unillumined by spiritual content must end in tragedy. The painful contradictions which were always inherent in materialism came glaringly to the surface during the wartime climax of world crisis. They forced many to look beyond their own resources for guidance and strength. Where else could they look except to religion, mysticism, or philosophy? Events opened a passage into their hearts through which a spiritual impulse could enter less obstructed by the obstacles which formerly blocked the way. A world in crisis has found that without higher guidance there is only perplexity. These are critical and momentous times. Spiritual values alone stand out as the really worth-while and enduring things today. There is no other hope for present-day humanity than this earnest repentant effort to lift itself. We have to find a more spiritual way of looking at life, or pay the penalty for failure to do so. There can be no standing still.

The world has fought long enough against the truth, but in the end it will find no other way out of its troubles than by accepting it.

The divinity within us, the Overself, is always there even when we disbelieve in it and its presence is the secret why sooner or later there must be a reaction in human life toward spiritual values. Only after we realize vividly our human insufficiency and our human inadequacy are we likely to turn toward it for help, sustenance, and strength. When we feel deeply how imperfect is our knowledge, how uncertain and limited our happiness, how weak and sinful our character, we may become sufficiently humbled to turn our faces imploringly and devotedly toward our higher selves for relief. It is thus that we are really able to progress. The need to progress from an inferior to a superior kind of life was never more urgent than today. We must take the lesson of the prodigal son deeply into our mind and come, like penitent sinners, to prayer before the higher power.

When contemporary man looks outward on the contemporary scene he is distressed by its violence. When he looks inward for the soul's comfort, he is bewildered by its silence. To the objector who says: "We know nothing about a higher power and we have lost the capacity for simple faith in it," the answer is that there is a way whereby he may discover by his own inner experience the truth about its existence. But he must follow this way and practice its methods. "Knock and it shall be opened unto you," does not mean that a single act is enough. Rather does it involve a whole series of acts. Nor does it mean that knocking in the wrong way or at the wrong door will bring about the desired opening. This single sentence of Jesus, put plainly out of his deep insight into universal laws, embodies a whole course of instructions.

Faith which humbly acknowledges the existence of a higher power is a true instinct planted in the heart of humanity. It is supported by the proper use of reason although it may be throttled by the unbalanced use of intellect. Let no one be ashamed to kneel in prayer, or irked to sit in meditation. Because a man professes such a faith or practices communion with his soul, it does not mean he thereby discloses feeble intelligence. Why should the modern man leave religious faith and mystical practice to women? Have not an innumerable galaxy of historical stars in the past been men who drew the power for great deeds from these deeper sources? Rightly understood such faith and practice do not enfeeble men or narcotize their minds; it is only superstitious religion and false mysticism that do so. Rather do they exalt the mind and calm the heart. The reverent worship of, or inward communion with, a higher power is indispensable to the fuller human life.

A great and holy mystery lies enshrined in the world's blatant failure and heavy crisis. When humanity finds itself with its back to an impassable wall, when it seems to reach the utmost limit of disasters, when the agony of utter helplessness crushes it down, it stands close, very close, to the Gate. If in such moments it will reorient its thoughts in sincerest self-surrender to the Divine and in fullest humility of the ego; if, too, it will calmly accept the disvaluation of all earthly things which truthful reflection upon its situation should yield—then the climax of its outer suffering and inner defeat will be reached. If, with patience, repentance, reform, and acceptance of life's higher purpose accompanying its prayers, it will stretch forth its arms into the darkness and plead that Peace may come forth again, it will not plead in vain. The higher Self will take a hand in the game, taking possession of the conscious mind at the same time for some memorable moments at least. Relief will mysteriously appear and rescuing hands will move toward it. Courage will rise and the strength to support what is unchangeable will be given, thus promising a tranquil heart even in the midst of a troubled life.

CHAPTER VI

MAN IN SORROW AND HAPPINESS

THERE ARE at least six things whose quick attainment and uninterrupted continuance all of us unconsciously desire but which none of us ever find in their completeness. We want: a happiness unmixed with sorrow, a life unbroken by death, a health unsaddened by sickness, a freedom unhindered by restraints, a knowledge untormented by questions, and a harmony with all other people.

The tragic riddle with which life confronts us and which has to be solved, if we are ever to know peace, is that the instinctive nature of man bids him seek happiness but his inner life shows sorrow and sin, his thinking mind shows conflict and doubt, his outer environment pretends at times to give him happiness but never does. It gives him, instead, occasional pleasures but soon brings misery and pain treading at their heels or appearing as their background. How can anyone be happy today, it will be asked, when most of his existence is like that? What, then, is his highest happiness and where is he to seek it?

Moreover, intelligence tortured by such terrible events as our war-wounded and crisis-stricken generation has seen, demands that they should at least be redressed by a higher purpose. And it demands an answer to the further question: "What is the function of suffering in human life?" All these are questions no longer for those alone who are interested in religion and theology. They are for all mankind, whose existence and future have become so uncertain and so imperiled.

Everything which happens to us may be considered in two different ways. There is no painful event in a man's life and no sorrowful contact with another person which cannot be regarded from two different points of view. Each result may be correct but, by itself, it cannot be complete. On the one hand, there is the practical, personal, obvious, and immediate approach. On the other, there is the metaphysical, impersonal, profound, and ultimate approach.

All talk notwithstanding, the fact remains that very few people are really in a position to contemplate their own lives and fortunes with the genuine detachment demanded by the metaphysical approach. For our natural and human view of them is based upon our finite reactions, our limited senses, our short-range perceptions. In the midst of personal anguish, it is easy to lose perspective. Three instances will show this clearly enough. First, we rarely stop to weigh our own distresses against other men's. Second, when we are inclined to murmur against hard fate, we rarely balance our troubles against our advantages or our physical difficulties against our spiritual possessions. Third, when our personal situation works to our advantage we are often satisfied with things as they are, but when it does not, we become discontented with the world as it is. The insufficiency of our ordinary attitude toward experiences and events is that our perspectives are too short; we divorce them from their relationship to the larger problem of the universe itself. We fail to see present distresses from a long-range metaphysical standpoint. The truths uttered by philosophy, however sympathetically, may seem cold and drear—at the time—to one who keenly feels a personal anguish or is brokenhearted over a family bereavement. They may offer no comfort to the suffering man. Yet they cannot be denied by the wisdom of the mind even when the limitation of the heart refuses to receive them.

It all depends on where we stand. If life is a constant burden to some, it is luminous inspiration to others. Is it not a curious fact that the same trouble which weakens one man adds strength to another; the same disappointment which renders one more selfish renders another more sympathetic; the same difficulty which dulls one mentality rouses the intelligence of another; the same environment which helps to degrade one person stimulates another to overcome it and thus to evolve. A reverse or disappointment which hardens and embitters one man against his fellows may soften and mellow another man. The same experience which multiplies the mistakes of fools, corrects those of the wise. "A fool is he who soon forgets Depression's lesson when 'tis passed," wrote Ratnasekharasuri, a wise old Indian master of the Jain faith, five hundred years ago. The hard reality and harsh truth of these lines is still needed today.

We naturally resent the painful character of certain experiences and question the wisdom which brings them to us, even though we may admit in calmer moments that they have really helped to shape our character or sharpen our intelligence. A just philosophic attitude demands, however, that we balance these resentful feelings against the joyful appreciation with which we greet pleasant experiences. In the midst of grim relentless torment we cannot see its use or justice, but in the calm long-range perspective of time we may see it as part of the divine leading toward our true goal. If a certain kind of unpleasant experience is necessary to the growth of our character, and if life eventually gives it to us, it is then not only to be met with resentment and depression, if we must indulge in such negative superfluous luxuries, but also with constructive analyses and the will to make it serviceable in some way. If prosperity has created an arrogant pride in us which will ultimately lead to our downfall, poverty may create the humility which can save us. Loss of fortune, loss of health, or loss of friends are extremely unpleasant but they are sometimes competent tutors in disguise. Whenever this is so, it would be an error to call them evils of life; more correctly, they are ills of life.

When we can gaze down impartially and indifferently upon our own person, the troubles and burdens which travel with it will assume a changed garb. We, with our limited viewpoints, want only what we call pleasurable situations to exist but the Infinite Intelligence, with its infinite viewpoint, is wiser. A continuous personal happiness is not always the best life even if it were obtainable, which it is not. Unpopular though these views may be and unpalatable though their first taste is, unless personal wishes rather than observed fact are to rule our thinking, we have no other alternative in the end than to accept the findings yielded by the higher standpoint, even though we accept them reluctantly and sadly.

Many sufferers see no chastening lesson to be learned from their loss or trouble; rather, they feel it to be senselessly damaging to their material and moral life. Quite often there is apparent justification of their attitude but it is only a superficial justification. Under the precise operation of cosmic law, life would not have brought it to them had it really been unearned or else unnecessary. To understand what is happening to us individually as well as to mankind collectively, we need to use not only the ordinary social, political, economic, and other concepts which the historian uses, but also two special concepts which a true philosophy uses. They are: the factuality of the law of recompense (karma) and the ultimate irresistibility of spiritual evolution (the path ordained by the World-Mind for man). They have been explained in earlier books, but in their use and application here their meaning will gradually become clear.

Both men and nations are disciplined either by the sad consequences of their own actions or by the necessities of their inward growth. The destiny which foreordains so many of our sorrows is self-earned, partly during the present and partly during anterior lives, or else wholly during the one or the other. We are not punished by a God who sits remote from our struggle and indifferent to our misery. We are punished by our own sins, deficiencies, misjudgments, incapacities, or disequilibriums. What we have wrought in the lives of others will ultimately be wrought in our own, when the natural nemesis of the law comes into effect. We shall start removing our miseries as soon as we start removing our ignorance of the laws and their governance of life—not before.

Suffering seems useless when it forces concentration solely and entirely upon its own pain, when it arouses resentment, and when it creates despair. How, then, could it help our spiritual progress? This criticism is only a surface view. Something of instructive or redemptive value is always being achieved through it. The divine laws are impelling everything and everyone onward and upward. We are moving little by little in spite of ourselves. But we are moving through the pain and suffering generated by blindness, incapacity, and selfishness. The mistakes in action which we make lead to results that in turn lead to doubts about ourselves, about others, about our beliefs and attitudes. Thus life tends to correct our world-view, for our deeds are unconsciously based upon this view.

How often has seeming trouble masked approaching better fortune? How often have exterior frustration and disappointment led to interior consolation and development? How often has a crucial test of character been masked as good or evil fortune and an excellent opportunity been hidden in an apparently unpromising or trivial affair? There are tragic and terrible events which seem utterly evil at the time they happen but which seem disguised boons later. When suffering, like a surgeon's knife, is applied to a rotten part of character, the operation may be as durably beneficial as it may be temporarily painful. The experience of outward loss may turn a man to inward gain. It is an unpleasant happening but also a thought-provoking stimulus. If the suffering that follows wrong action dramatically discourages any tendency thereto and picturesquely deters its repetition, we must cease to look upon pleasure as the only good and pain as the only evil. The cosmic force, which deludes undeveloped minds into taking the sense reports of things as their real nature, reflects itself in the cruder force which deludes developed minds into taking evil situations as good ones and good situations as evil ones. We are spiritually shortsighted. We do not always know what is good for us, do not always see a friendly hand in disappointments that turn us from a foolish, harmful wrong or unsuitable course. No dictionary has yet taught us the true meaning of pain, pleasure, happiness, and sorrow. There is no situation so evil that the philosopher cannot see some good in it, nor any situation so good that he cannot see some evil in it. Only, what he may mean by these terms will be based on a long-range view, too long indeed for the mass of conventional people to appreciate.

It is true that life at times brings even good people anguish and disappointment. For them to watch a dear friend or near relative fall into wrong courses that yield sorrow or disappointment in the end, and to feel that there is nothing they can do about it, is a particularly sad experience. But it is also true that it brings, if only they will accept them, the compensation of sounder judgment and the consolation of higher values. Or perhaps some horrible experiences have brought home to them the fact that their attitude was inadequate to explain and meet all circumstances. In that case, to suffer and suffer blindly until reason calls out in rebellion and emotion questions loudly in despair, is not without evolutionary meaning, for it forces either a needed revision of this attitude, a needed development of new capacities, or else a needed deepening of the understanding.

Not all sufferings are earned, however; not all descend

on us in punishment or retribution. Some come only under evolutionary law out of the infinite will and wisdom of the Overself, to help us, either as single persons or as entire peoples, develop better character, evolve new qualities, and foster more intelligence.

Quite often we do not see the benefits of our sufferings until they are long past. Sometimes, in a chastened mood, we can fill in the pattern which was woven between a past act and a present circumstance. But sometimes we cannot. In that event we may be able to do so many years later, when more of the pattern of our whole life has unfolded itself. Alas! the education which comes through mistakes and failures sometimes seems to come too late to be of use in this lifetime, when it is not till middle or old age that we comprehend its lessons at all. But the reality is that we shall carry them over to the next birth.

Are those who repeat old errors and blunder again and again into old sins incurable of them by life's painful lessons? This is not really so. It is unfortunate that they do not usually know at the time that they are making these mistakes in judgment, displaying these faults of character, or committing these sins in conduct. Indeed, it is often not until some years later that they may make this startling discovery. It is equally unfortunate that others learn their lessons at a high cost and often learn the wrong lessons in the earlier and more limited stages of their experience.

The extent to which they learn from suffering may be very small. Hence, time and plenty of it is needful. That is, they need to come to earth again and again. This educative result cannot be achieved with a single experience. It is necessarily a cumulative result, achieved through innumerable experiences extending through many lives. What men gain in spiritual growth under ordinary circumstances and in a single life is often so infinitesimal that we might well believe the incarnation a wasted one if we looked at it alone. But we need to look at a whole lengthy string of incarnations before we can see clearly that it really must have contributed to the appreciable gain there shown. We may not see what nature has evoked in them by the processes of experience through which she makes them pass when it is so slight but nevertheless it is still there.

Every ego passes through numerous births from which it gradually but inevitably learns the art of living. These experiences are intended to release latent virtue, unfold latent wisdom, develop latent power, and expand both intellectual and intuitive consciousness. But they do not do this all at once. Hence, it is confused and bewildered by their apparent aimlessness, their seeming cruelty. They will certainly do so ultimately, however. Time has a mysterious value and will transmute the deepest woes into a benign wisdom. Eternal lessons lie hidden behind day by day experiences. In the moment of illumination when the necessity of sorrow, frustration, or adversity is at last perceived, in that moment the mind overcomes its bitterness and mitigates its pain. It perceives, then, that the divine Idea is here to befriend it, not affright it.

For the man who is striving to become spiritually conscious, distresses provide either stimulus or opposition. Generously to forget an old grudge lifts him to a loftier plane. If he can discipline his emotional feelings sufficiently to keep the ego out of them for a while and then look back at his miseries and heartbreaks, his difficulties and defeats, he will see a meaning in them and a purpose to them. From that serene disengaged insight he will deduce the existence of meaning, order, and intelligence in the whole world. He will understand then that all this dismaying experience has not been in vain and that its roots have lain largely within the needs of his own development or within the defects of his own character. These distresses are in every man's path, he who nears attainment no less than he who ignores the very thought of it. They must be regarded impersonally, studied, and understood, if they are to be overcome through wisdom rather than repeated through ignorance. They are tutors, albeit expensive ones. They are, if used rightly, ways of learning nasty but needed lessons and improving low or inferior values. They teach some particular aspect of truth, and thus stimulate progress.

Humanity swims forward on a stream formed from its own tears. The real purpose of the shifts of experience, with changes of fortune from joyous to miserable happenings, is the ideas they suggest, the attitudes they elicit, the characteristics they draw out from it, and the revaluations to which they direct it.

We must learn to discipline the senses, re-educate character, and develop intelligence. If reflection has not already led us to do so, the painful experience will inevitably lead us to consider its necessity. After all, if such an experience makes us perceive clearly and forces us to note consciously that we are seriously deficient in certain essential qualities and thus starts us on the way to amendment, it contributes to our progress. How, then, can it be evil? Is it not better to pass through it as through a training school, even if it involves a purge of our inefficiencies and our errors? It is necessary so long as certain lessons remain unlearned, and so long as it teaches where argument fails. If it brings home the consequences of having chosen wrongly, it justifies a place for itself in the universal scheme of things.

The hour is here for us to associate ourselves *consciously* with the two laws of compensation and evolution. We may base our general policy of living on selfish interest, on upsurges of emotion, on calculating cunning, or on idle drifting with the tide of circumstances. In consequence, we may find momentary benefits but we shall not find permanent ones. Or we may base it on philosophy. If we do so, we desert the old game of trial, error, and suffering and begin to live by *under-*

standing. In that case, it is not the unexpected but the expected which will happen to us.

If a man can look impersonally at his own present life and analytically at his own past history, comprehension will begin to be born and later, out of that, mastery. He to whom the pursuit of moral excellence and practical wisdom is something more than a phrase will find both in the fortunes and misfortunes of existence helps to achieve his aims. He will see the mistakes he has made, what psychological causes led up to them, and what external consequences they themselves led to; and seeing, he will suffer. If this suffering engraves a new and higher attitude upon his mind, it will not be regarded as something to be avoided but rather as something to be accepted. If, perceiving this, he co-operates consciously and deliberately in the gestation process, he will triumph over it. Out of the suffering, thus properly regarded, he will draw a heightened power to control his lower self and a heightened capacity to understand it. Every fresh experience will then become like oil to the flame of his growing understanding.

This result is arrived at only because he changes his attitude to that of an eager learner and rejects the egotist interpretation of life for the impersonal one. To others, suffering merely brings dulled consciousness but to such a man it brings a cycle of new growth. Whatever severe anguish enters his life for the first time or the fourth time, be it the unheralded turn of fortune for the worse or the unanticipated anxiety of surprising events, be it the wrongdoing of a human being or the tragic news of a written letter, be it a painful illness or a tremendous failure, he instinctively asks himself such questions as: "Why has this come to me?" or "Why has this person entered my life?" and then reflects impartially, coolly, and slowly, until he can discover its physical or inward significance. For life would not have brought it into his experience if it were not his due, which means if he had not earned it or needed it. Such philosophical analysis often shows him that causes within himself are responsible for many external happenings. Awakened by suffering to remove defects or to cultivate needed qualities and thus improve himself, he transmutes it into an asset. Every defect in character or deficiency in judgment is seen to lead in the end to a deficit in happiness. The problem of making right choices or wise decisions is no easy one.

Men can help change the course of their destiny by changing the shape of their character, intelligence, and talent, or the form, energy, health, and condition of their body. If they inertly accept themselves as they are, they must also accept the fulfillment of their destiny. When the law of recompense lays out this destiny with hard living conditions or unwanted misfortune, they are dissatisfied with its harshness. If, instead, while trying to relieve the conditions or remove the misfortunes they gracefully accepted the law as a just one, they would demonstrate wisdom and shorten the period of suffering.

Where a sufferer finds that he cannot mend a bad environment or cannot undo a tangle of bad karma, then he should mend the way in which he views them. Where he cannot quickly adjust his outer circumstances, he can and must adjust his inner self. When he cannot extricate himself from a disharmonious environment by the integral use of intense endeavor and inspired imagination, he must learn to look on it with new eyes. It is the use that he makes of his sufferings that determines their values for him. With the recognition that his faults punish him and his weaknesses betray him, with a wise and impersonal attitude toward his troubles—whatever his personal feelings may be—he can turn them into assets. But if he lets those feelings sweep him away into bitterness, hatred, resentment, malice, fear, or selfishness, they will remain as debits. It is not only unscrupulous conduct and injury of others that brings eventual retribution. Bitter thoughts and resentful feelings, negative ideas and unbalanced emotions will affect not only the quality of a man's character but, if strong and prolonged enough, also the quality of his fortunes. Troubles may come to him which would not otherwise have come. Enmities may be created or kept alive which would not have touched him or, touching, would have died down. If his experience of life has soured him, he may be sure that his thinking about life has something to do with the unhappy result.

When the mind's negatives reach a certain degree of strength, a certain depth of intensity, or when their repetition extends over a sufficient period of time, a physical manifestation may eventually follow. A man's actions are largely predetermined and his fortunes largely predestined by no other power or creature than himself. Both arise out of his own nature. He may take a misfortune as a final defeat and sink by the wayside of despair. Or he may take it as a first challenge and rise to the summit of determination. In the end, it is his *thought* about it that matters. His attitude toward these happenings is not less important than the happenings themselves. The creative thought comes first; its visible results will come later. The finer the quality of the one, the better will be his satisfaction with the other. This is no mere dream but solid actuality. Experience advances this thought and history affirms this truth. Mussolini kept a loaded revolver in a drawer of his desk for several years, ready for immediate use against his own life if events went too badly for him. How much did this sustained concentration on death by shooting have any relation to the fact that he did ultimately die in that way?

There is no man who cannot achieve some degree of improvement in his character and his conditions, often in his health too. There are always creative uplifting forces lying latent within him waiting to be drawn on and used for his progress and his service. It was a favorite practice with the young Disraeli, even so early as from the age of fifteen, to utilize his creative imagination and picture himself as England's Prime Minister, which height he did, of course, attain.

Where a man—even a whole people—finds himself in terrible affliction and desperate straits, with everything done that he could have done and yet no way out, it may be worth his while to consider a method of seeking relief that was universally used among the ancients who are long dead and is still used to some extent among the Orientals who are now alive. Let him become an ascetic for a time, "put on sackcloth and ashes," in the picturesque Biblical phrase, and by this enfeeblement of the ego's habitual pride and humiliation of its self-sufficiency, he may succeed in prayerfully invoking the aid of higher forces. Such an expression of his own helplessness will become more effective if accompanied by penitent prayer, by fasting, and the restraint of passion, or through a restricted diet and other disciplines. This philosophic procedure is an heroic one and few may feel able to follow it, but the results are nearly always good and even sometimes miraculous.

With all its blunders and all its sins, humanity may profit by its sufferings, its blood, and its tears, and reach forth to grasp the truth that a divine process of compensation and justice does rule the world. The failure to understand such cosmic law and the neglect to obey it are responsible for more of its miseries than any other single cause. The terrible fact is, so many people fail to make this link in comprehension between their sins and their sorrows that their painful experience is apparently wasted. This failure is the result of their letting themselves be deceived by the blind ego and misled by the lower emotions. It is a truth, although often obscured at times by a cloud of bitter feelings, that the disappointment of personal expectations and the frustration of worldly desires are often one way in which life seeks to educate the ego and discipline its character. The inability to perceive this does not really waste the experience, for the subconscious mind has absorbed and memorized it. At some time, in some way, it will be digested into significance, however slight.

In his strivings for what he believes desirable, man does wrong or commits mistakes. Later, the results are reflected back to him in sorrow and trouble. It is neither strange nor accidental that the same painful combinations of circumstances seem to repeat themselves in so many different people's lives. Man is ordinarily neither amenable to reason's voice nor obedient to intuition's promptings. If he is to acquire elevation, he must first acquire experience. His long evolution operates by providing from without an increasing area of experience and from within an increasing refinement of consciousness. Out of the conflict of human emotions, he is working nearer to divine intuition; out of the struggle of human ideas, to divine intelligence. He will come to see in the end that there is no other way to overcome suffering than by conquering evil, removing ignorance, or developing capacity. Good is the only real power and evil a shifting phenomenon like the cloud. In yielding to evil or being content with ignorance, he draws to himself suffering and the eventful result of suffering is to force him to turn his face back again toward the good, the true, and the real. He cannot forever travel along with a makeshift happiness and a substitute salvation. The experiences of life have meaning, purpose, and instruction for him. Each earthly incarnation provides him with them and thus with the means of self-development. If this purpose is achieved, then the suffering which intermittently accompanies those experiences can be called evil only from a narrow and limited view of things. He gets knowledge at the cost of such so-called evil, experience at the price of such suffering. Out of these recurring lives on earth, he accumulates diverse experiences and passes from error to truth. All of them, both good and evil alike, are in the end a means to develop character, nurture intelligence, and unfold intuition. Out of their fruits, he accumulates the tendencies, knowledge, instincts, and attitudes which make him what he is. More than that, his consciousness eventually opens up on a higher level.

Nature directs her operations to this end. Life is not so monotonously futile as it seems. Each entity's suffering becomes a medium through which in the end it evolves a higher form of its own life. If it can look upon every experience as an opportunity to learn wisdom and thus draw nearer to final enlightenment, nothing that happens to it will be unfruitful and everything can lead to a mental or moral enlargement. And what is not less valuable is that such an entity will also draw nearer to true happiness, whose quest is consciously or unconsciously the most magnetic of all its motivations. But if we are skeptics and do not believe that a moral law governs our existence or that a spiritual purpose has been set for our fulfillment, we shall then deceive ourselves utterly about our experiences. We shall rejoice over events which will later bring us suffering or moan over events which now bring us to a halt in evil, and therefore dangerous, courses.

It is sensible to bemoan past experiences if at the same time we try to learn the lessons they teach, but if we do not make this effort, then it is silly. In the first case, we convert stumbling blocks into stepping stones. In the second, we whip ourselves quite needlessly. We may use our agonies of such experiences to burn out the ego's dross or we may permit them to increase it. The choice is our own.

Most people think only of improving their fortunes, few of improving themselves. Not that philosophy would balance the one against the other, for it recognizes that their spheres are different, but that it would stress the foolishness of ignoring higher values. All men create certain values for themselves but evolution forces others upon them. So long as they are too obsessed with their own immediate aims to care for the ultimate ones of human life itself, so long will they suffer the inevitable consequences of their obsession. All other blunders follow inexorably from this, the primary one. If you want to wish another man well, the best you can wish him is not increase of fortune but increase of wisdom, not more good health but more intuitive awareness of his Overself. For with these two—wisdom and awareness—he will also be in a better position to secure the others—fortune and health.

The School of Sorrowful Experience. So many people ask why God permits such a vast world crisis to oppress mankind and the horrible menace of a Third World War to engulf mankind. They point out that both crisis and war are filled with evils and sufferings, and so stippled with dark wicked forces and callous inhuman sins, that the general effect seems only to brutalize and degrade mankind. The worse that world conditions become the more some think in their despair either that God does not care for humanity or even that there is no God at all. Where, they ask, are the signs of spiritual evolution in such happenings? There can be no correct answer to these questions unless we clear our minds of the confusion involved, which is itself the result of a one-sided egocentered outlook—whether it be the outlook of the gross materialist or of the unenlightened religionist.

Too many have been stirred by their compassion for suffering creatures to disbelief in, or even hatred of, the God who permits such sufferings to exist. But let them not deprive God too hastily of his much-praised goodness. Let them not believe also, in their limited finite and dim understanding, that the Infinite Intelligence is capable of making any mistakes. Do not the earlier reflections suggest that some part at least of life's sorrow and pain is neither meaningless nor purposeless in the divine Idea? Does it ever occur to the doubters that the normal attitude toward suffering, as toward death, is not the attitude which that Intelligence takes toward them? That whether a painful experience is really evil (or good) is largely relative to the character or situation of the person undergoing it? That when they ask in prayer for its relief *as an evil*, they ascribe human characteristics to the Supreme Spirit and thus unconsciously claim knowledge of it? If they could form any conception of the Infinite Power with their limited minds, it could not at best be more than the merest illusion of the Power, since the latter is utterly inconceivable to human thought.

It is a fact which is everywhere admitted that the nerve strains to which people have been subjected by this crisis generate fear, hopelessness, and even despair. It is also a fact that it is natural for some human beings to seek a way of escape by sinking deeper into a sensual and frivolous life, and for others to find it in religious or mystical devotions. The first group take the way which is easy on the ego, but the escape which they find is illusive and superficial while the second group take the way which is hard upon the ego but more helpful in the end. Those who take neither of these ways, nor the third way of immersion in politico-economic hopes which are also illusive and superficial, although in a different manner, fall into stolid dulled apathy.

If one purpose of human life upon this earth is to unfold spiritually and if a section of humanity is driven by the pressures of crisis and the sufferings of war to seek such unfoldment, why should not the World-Mind permit these drastic happenings? The same Nature which gives us mild balmy summers also gives us arctic winters. The same universal laws which bring the sunlight of noon also bring the midnight of darkness. The same Power which is bringing infant humanity through its first fumbling steps toward self-realization is also permitting it to fall and bruise itself because only so will humanity ever learn to walk. Who can deny that at least one section of humanity needs the whip of suffering to act as a lesson in its moral education or as punishment for its blind sins or as stimulant to wake it from stagnation into evolutionary movement? Those who will take the trouble to look deep beneath appearances for realities may even see in these very same world happenings the vindication of the World-Mind's care for humanity and a demonstration of Its presence in the world.

To seek any way of escape from devastating happenings which seem to creep closer and closer, without including the way of trying sincerely to fulfill the spiritual purpose of life on earth, is to live in a fool's paradise. The indifference of man to the silent pleading of Truth and his displacement from the spiritual center of his being, cannot last forever. It took the dangerous stresses of an unexampled war to offer the second chance of a great initiation to the world. That could and should have been a purifying process for those who had become too attached to earthly things and who did not trouble to bother about why they were here at all. Since pain and suffering are never welcome and seldom understood, the voice of woe rose in a long lament and echoed over the whole planet. All were being given another chance for self-regeneration, yet few knew it in their surface consciousness! Not only may intense suffering help to arouse a lethargic nation or an inert individual to neglected duties, but if not too prolonged it may also tend to wake latent will power.

It would be absurd to declare that all affliction serves destiny's ends. After we have made all allowance for those calamities which are born out of our own errors and sins; and also for those with which the Overself forces our individual or collective development; and after we have further allowed for those which are the natural consequences of the interdependence of mankind, affecting us through the frailty and imperfections of other people, it must nevertheless be admitted that there remains a proportion which are not of our own making at all. Whence do they come then? Although the suffering of human beings is often indicative that they have strayed from the right path, a part of it is always coincidental with human existence itself. The affliction to which they are exposed may not necessarily be the consequence of personal karma. It may be the consequence of being human. Whoever understands this statement, understands already a quarter of the Buddha's teaching. When he pointed out on how precarious a balance all human happiness rests, he pointed out a salutary fact. The truth of his teaching about the essentially sorrowful character of life is usually disguised by the pleasures and relaxations of life. It becomes apparent to the generality of people only when it is thrust prominently into their consciousness by horrors and tragedies such as those of war. Our generation has had the tragic character of existence thrown into sharp relief. It has glimpsed dimly by its own painful experience what philosophy always knows clearly by its tranquil reflection. Among many other things the war and crisis have been bold and unforgettable demonstrations of the fact that suffering is inseparably allied to life in this world. It is in fact forever with us, albeit on an unimpressive and unimposing scale. It is so familiar that we tend to remain untouched by its normal existence. Only the extremely thoughtful who love truth or seek peace take note of its ever-presence and seek also for some deeper solution of its meaning or durable escape from its burden. Where is the joy which is not sooner or later mingled with sorrow? A happiness which is not mixed at some point or at some time with misery, can nowhere be found on earth.

The tides of fortune and wealth, pleasure and pain, ebb and flow for all men, for would-be philosophers no less than others. Nobody can alter this natural law, as nobody dare ignore it. It is this tantalizing alternation that constitutes the general human experience. But whereas the philosophers try to keep a stable mind through all such changes, the others do not or cannot. This is because men whose happiness can exist only in company with external things, have not found happiness at all. For it will flee with the first flight of those things. If pleasure is eventually turned into pain, if joy becomes later a source of misery, then the happiness they get from such emotions is sadly limited and pathetically deceptive.

We younger peoples of the West must begin to learn what the older peoples of the East have long been taught by their religions and philosophies. We are being led to dissatisfaction with much of earthly life in itself and irrespective of its circumstances, to a perception of the impossibility of finding peace and happiness among earthly things alone. We have been too greatly in love with activity for its own sake, too infatuated with physical things and possessions, too deeply bound by our lower desires to care for an outlook which had the slightest tinge of such Oriental pessimism or ascetic detachment. We have failed to see that no scientific improvement in the outward circumstances of living and no practical advancement in the outward arrangements of living, could be enough by themselves to bring us any lasting satisfaction. If other men do not interfere with our contentment, if Nature herself does not interfere, then Destiny, with her uncertainties and changes, may interfere with it. We have to learn that at some point within our heart we must pass over from sole dependence on outer things for true satisfaction to more dependence on inward things. We have to create within ourselves a state of mind which will of itself give us the peace and happiness that the world in the end so often fails to give us. But all this said, it is still needful to remember that telling sweltering men in the hot tropics that life is suffering, as Buddha told the Indians, may be to impart acceptable wisdom, whereas telling eager, ambitious, and comfort-loving Euro-Americans the same thing may be to talk unacceptable nonsense.

He who recognizes that the power behind life is a beneficent one and that even the evils of experience are turned to ultimate evolutionary good, easily becomes an optimistic dreamer. On the other hand, he who recognizes that this earth is not his true eternal home, that all human experience is stamped with transitoriness, imperfection, and change, easily becomes a pessimistic observer. A third type usually begins with the thought that worldly life is a source of joy, but often ends in old age with the thought that it is a source of sorrow.

The philosopher, however, does not let his belief in the ultimate goodness of life push him to an extreme optimism, nor his belief in the ultimate unsatisfactoriness of life push him to an extreme pessimism. Intellectually, he couples and balances the two points of view; spiritually, he attains the perception of life's sublime and sorrowless basis. This lifts him above both the shallowness of optimism and the cheerlessness of pessimism, and keeps him stayed in inner peace. Is it possible to get such a happiness, which is unlimited by chance and which will never abate under any change of circumstances? Philosophy answers that, if we pursue its fourfold path to a successful terminus, we shall surely get such happiness.

Either in reflective moods inspired by art, nature, and reading or in relaxed ones prompted by extreme gratification, some people feel vaguely that there must be some kind of grander and nobler being than this sadly limited earthly one, which is all that they know. But only when suffering or privation has emphasized the tremendous contrast between the two, is their feeling likely to stir the question whether they propose to do anything about it and thus start the aspiration whose fullest expression is the path to finding of the soul, or the quest of the Overself.

Death is the only thing in life that is absolutely certain. It is more than a thousand years since Shankara Acharya, the Indian sage, remarked that he is indeed a fool who wastes this precious chance of gaining salvation which birth as a human being gives him, and fails to profit by it. Yet during our passage from childhood to adolescence and thence to maturity and old age, engrossed as we are in the personal cares and physical pleasures of living, we rarely deem it necessary to undertake a search for this higher salvation, which comes from knowing and surrendering to the impersonal truth about our existence here. This is because earthly life binds us hand and foot and spiritual ignorance holds our eyelids down. But, in the end, we can no more escape from following its quest than we can escape from eating food. For it is an inexorable necessity of our inner being. Whether we like it or not, we are walking into the spiritually ruled life anyway, but, if we fail to do so willingly we will walk into it backwards—with all the disadvantages of such a movement!

There is on the one side, a hard and long way to truth and there is, on the other side, a hard and short one. The first is the way of being tutored by time, Nature's evolutionary pressure, and by the results of our thoughts and deeds. The second is the way of voluntarily going out in direct search for the true goal itself. The first slowly works out the meaning of those parts of its experience which are distressing. The second deliberately tries to get at their roots and cut off their further growth. We may flee from sorrow into various kinds of escape, including the one which hides in the refusal to believe it may one day touch us too; but, ghostlike, it again returns to haunt us. Or we may face it, study it, and understand it through philosophical perception, when it will be inwardly conquered forever and outwardly avoided wherever possible.

When, by virtue of loftier prenatal lives, a man is capable of following a purer, wiser, and more spiritual course but refuses to do so, then the Overself will show its hand in one or another way, and bring about his return. It may release a series of rapidly changing karmically derived events, which will show up vividly, abruptly, and forcibly the foolishness of his present course. Or it will offer him attractive opportunity after attractive opportunity but always terminate each experience with disappointment, disillusionment, or pain. Or it may cause him to lose everything in a catastrophe, and thus for the first time find himself. Such a revolutionary result is of course not only true for the individual destined to engage in the quest during the present incarnation; it is true for all mankind at all times. Or, sometimes at the height of his greatest successes, sometimes in the depths of his greatest pleasures, it will make this man who has once been privileged to glimpse the Real—however briefly—suddenly perceive the limitations of success or the unsatisfactoriness of pleasure. Such a thought will come to him as a continually recurring, mentally depressive, and action paralyzing intuition. It will indeed be a momentous message sent by his higher self, and one whose answer will save or shatter him for the rest of that incarnation.

All the varied experiences of our existence, the gratification as well as disappointments, turn to profit if they drive us to seek an answer to the question: "What is the higher purpose of life?" When we discover that, along with whatever joys they bring, these experiences in the external world harm our senses and hurt our feelings and that this alternation is their unavoidable constituent, we are then inwardly prepared for the idea of seeking the enduring happiness of the Overself.

How few can show themselves stronger than life's joys! Yet they are the ones who can also show themselves stronger than life's sorrows. So many seek passionately for the shadows of life and miss its mystical substance, while so few ever go into reflection upon their human journey at all. Such reflection would show that we search for happiness only because we do not have it, yet feel we ought to have it. This statement is as true of the most brutalized and most animalized man as it is of the most refined and most advanced one. The need is felt to be paramount. Why? Philosophy answers, "Because the real essence of personality is the divine soul. Because this soul continually exists in a state of unbroken happiness. Because even if we find all that we want physically and intellectually, we would still remain discontented, still go on with the search for happiness, for the single reason that we had not yet found the soul itself. Because we unconsciously and indirectly know this and therefore always hope on and hold on, clinging to life despite all the sufferings and struggles that it brings us. Because whenever we observe how innumerable are the creatures, whether human or animal, who cling desperately to life even under the most horrible conditions, we observe also evidence of a subconscious recognition that the earthly incarnation possesses a value, purpose, and meaning beyond its immediate ones."

How little, at this immature stage of seeking amid externals, do men know that the treasures of bliss, satisfaction, and possession are really all in themselves! The feeling of being incomplete, unfinished, and imperfect harasses them; much of their unrest rises from it. But although they may experiment with various means of assuaging it, although they may seek satisfaction on different paths, they cannot overcome it except by taking to the final quest. Although they think they are seeking happiness through the physical body, they are in fact seeking it through the spiritual mind. This is so and must be so because of the constitution of their own nature. This is why no sooner is one desire satisfied than another rises to replace it. Thus, every thirst of the inebriate for further drink is really a thirst, at a physical and lower level of development, for the Overself's bliss. All men are engaged in this search for the second self but most men are engaged in it quite unconsciously. They are seeking its stable satisfaction in different transient ways. How few comprehend that their need of the divine self is a permanent one! Most want to enjoy life in their way, which often is entirely dependent on external things or on other persons, not in the philosophic way, which, while including these things or persons, is yet inwardly independent of them. All troubling desires fall away and unchanging emotional rest is attained only when the goal of philosophy is attained.

The serene happiness of the soul can never be broken by the anguish and misery of its shadow, the person. No grief or passion, no fear or pain can get into it. That part of his being which always remains in heaven, is the Overself. That part which descends to suffer and struggle on earth, is the personality. The two are indissolubly linked, although ignorance sees only the person. This separation in consciousness from the Overself is the fundamental, if hidden cause of man's perennial search for happiness, now in one thing or through one person and then in or through another. But a happiness unhindered by some accompanying or subsequent sorrow, he never finds. How could he, if it does not exist in anything or anyone outside? His longing will never be satisfied until it is diverted to, and satisfied by, the transcendental Overself. All through his successive appearances in different bodies, he is seeking the wholeness, the benign happiness, and the blessed fulfillment of union with his higher nature. When he discovers and finally accepts that earthly things are transient and contradictory, that the pleasurable are tied to the painful, and thereupon makes this search a conscious one, he is said to have entered on the Quest.

All forms of life in this world, being finite and limited, involve suffering. But life in the heavenly world, which is not a distant place but an inner state, findable even before death, is gloriously free and therefore without suffering.

The six things mentioned on the opening page of this chapter, always desired but never found on earth, are so elusive precisely because they belong to heaven. But heaven is a state of mind. It is indeed mind in its own purest being. Therefore, man may yet attain them here and now so long as he searches for them in the region of thought and feeling and does not limit himself to the region of flesh and blood. "The cause of happiness or misery is no other than one's own self; it is an idea of the mind," teaches Krishna, the divine messenger, in another ancient Indian text, the *Srimad Bhagavata*.

CHAPTER VII

MAN'S WILL AND GOD'S WILL

RELIGIONISTS call God, "The Merciful," but it would be equally correct to use the opposite epithet, "The Merciless." For if they feel grateful to God for the pleasant things and fortunate events, they should logically be grateful also for the unpleasant things and unfortunate events. But they aren't. It would be wiser, therefore, to stop ascribing both to God and start ascribing them to the true source, which is mostly in themselves. People who ask for divine blessing, whether from God direct or from one of God's saints, usually ask for it in the form of material benefits and worldly advantages. Such people do not comprehend that the divine blessings may be sent through physical sorrows and worldly misfortunes, not less than through more agreeable ways. A little impersonal reflection upon the course of past events might enable them to discern good in apparent evil. Keats, with the intuition of a spiritual poet, felt this too. "Do you not see," he wrote in a letter, "how necessary a world of pain and trouble is to school an intelligence and make it a soul?"

The sufferers of today are the seekers of tomorrow. When it will not open of its own accord, then the heart may have to be broken to let God in. When a man's life has lost its bearings, then the ego may have to be mortified. For only when its own personal rule flickers out, will a diviner one flame up. The World-Mind's method of human attraction, and hence of human development, the mysterious therapy of its holy grace, involves the use of suffering as one of its features. If the hand of man is responsible for so much of his own or another's misery, the hand of God must be *ultimately* responsible for all of it. For the divine wisdom has ordained the laws which in turn ordain that man shall pass through the realm of affliction before peace rests on his face.

We may get the meaning of suffering only when we get a whole picture of it, of the bright and the dark parts, both. Some, like Mary Baker Eddy, rightly perceiving its irrelevance on the highest plane, wrongly deny it any proper place anywhere at all in the divine Idea. Others, like Charles Robert Darwin, persist in looking at the shaded part of the picture only and remember the earth for its savage beasts and biological struggles, not for the food it thoughtfully gives them or the flowers it generously provides them. Both see it in limited perspective. Still others, who persist in talking of Nature's cruelty to man, ought to ask themselves whether it has ever been equal to man's cruelty to man? If there is too much cruelty in Nature's arrangements for man to approve of them fully, let him consider that perhaps there was no other way to make them if Nature's goals were to be achieved. If his heart continues to protest, let his head nevertheless bow down, knowing that it is in the presence of a wisdom which is unutterably infinite. If the governing laws of this universe were not beneficent, there would be no hope for mankind. But, on the contrary, there is every ground for ultimate hope.

It needs remembering that the evils and pains of life have only a passing existence and are relative to the good and joys of life. Their own existence is in the end controlled by the divine laws and used for the divinely based universal outworking. Such complementaries and relativities follow by necessity as soon as this outworking itself begins afresh with every renewed cosmic period. How could any universe come into existence without *both* good and evil, light and darkness, joy and sorrow, coming with it? Such duality is the unescapable and tragic side of its manifestation. The existence of the one opposite is a necessary consequence of the existence of the other. Those who ask for a painless world do not comprehend that they are also asking for a joyless one. The ebb and flow between the opposites of joy and anguish, possession and loss, gives a man a sense of values which he could not gain to such a vivid degree in any other way. Experience of one kind provides a needed balance for the experience of its contrary. This helps him to form a just estimate of bodily and earthly values, a truer perception of its transiency, and thus brings him closer to the consciousness of spiritual life.

To refuse a place for suffering in the divine plan when we judge it solely by our finite human feelings, is to detract from our evaluation of the divine wisdom. We see the part only and lament the evil and pain that darken it. There is no place for these ugly shadows in the sublime Overself; they belong only to the world of appearances. Here they tragically exist; there they could not even exist. This is the paradoxical situation. They cannot be denied, as some dreamers deny them, but the reality behind them, the original Power behind the universe itself, is good in the highest sense. Could we but see the whole, we would discover that the Beneficent and the Beatific have never been dethroned. Unenlightened man hears the world's agony alone whereas philosophic man hears *both* the agony and the melody hidden behind it. Pain and sorrow do not represent the whole truth of life. The pain is an everlasting Bliss temporarily lost. The sorrow is an eternal Peace momentarily obscured. Love will one day soothe the human tumult; light will flood the world's darkness. There is an infinite wisdom inherent in the cosmic Idea which the tumult and darkness may momentarily hide from our perceptions but which they can never obliterate.

The World-Mind is the origin of Life. Ours is not a dead universe but a living one, because it is a mental one. All creative movement of this wonderful cosmos is a memorial to the hidden Mind whose presence called it forth. The expression of its genius is everywhere to be found. This Mind being a single one, not two or three, can manifest only a single kind of intelligence. It is not higher in some places and lower in others. Everywhere, in every part of its cosmos and behind the life of every one of its creatures, this supreme, infinite and all-knowing Mind is at work. And because it is infinite intelligence, it yields an infinitely intelligent World-Idea. There is indeed overwhelming evidence that this is so. If reason requires an orderly principle behind the operations of Nature, both the mystic's intuition and the philosopher's insight find it. A man cannot expand his knowledge of the inner working of Nature without expanding his reverence for the stupendous sagacity of Nature at the same time. Its existence back of things hushes the mind in amazement even when the first signs are detected, and much more when the full presence is discovered.

The world's evil and misery cannot possibly be exempted from its knowledge and sovereignty. When, even where he cannot understand the misery nor condone the frightfulness, a man can bring himself to accept the logic of its existence and with that accept the universe too, he will know a great peace. Is it so hard to develop this capacity of acceptance when reason shows him unerring wisdom in so much that he can understand, when intuition tells him that love resides in the inmost heart of God's ray—the soul—and when revelation informs him that all is ultimately for the best in what he cannot understand?

Many are those who object that much suffering misses its purpose because it does not carry its lesson with it on the surface, that a punishment which is not recognized and understood as such, loses its moral effect and defeats its beneficent purpose. This criticism is especially applied to the deferred consequences of acts done in earlier births, although it is a criticism which fails to remember that everyone who resents having to pay for the mistaken acts done in former lives which he knows nothing of and who therefore considers the payment unjust, will always accept without the slightest question the advantages and benefits which come from the right acts done in those same lives.

The first answer is that if suffering were the *only* method brought to bear upon the ego for its spiritual development, the divine Idea could justly be accused of being brutal rather than educative. But evolution of man's mentality and character develops in a twofold way. It works from the outside through his environment and from the inside through his heart. Hence, alongside the experience of suffering there is also gracious instruction to explain its meaning. This is given externally by human teachers through religions and philosophies, and internally by the soul itself through direct intuitions and valid reasonings. Since adversity and pain teach only a negative wisdom, the need for getting a creative understanding of life still remains. Therefore it is that some among those who have risen on the crest-wave of insight, are sent back into the world or come of their own accord, or are brought from higher planets to point out to others the more positive ways and truths. Suffering by itself does not instruct man nor lead to character reformation. Its work must be complemented and completed both by enlightenment from within and enlightenment from without. In the first case, the quality of the thought and the intuition he brings to the suffering, contributes toward its educative effects. In the second case, the quality of the spiritual teaching he receives and the spiritual reading he does, has the same result. His own reflection about it, or upon other men's teaching about it, brings out its lessons. Inspired prophets, teachers, sages, saints, philosophers and mystics have appeared among us in every century and one part of their mission is precisely to make those lessons clear. Men do not care to heed them simply because they do not connect the impersonal statement of those lessons

with their own personal lives. But it is their duty and responsibility, not the teacher's to make this connection. The fal-
lacies in their unconscious interpretation of life's meaning will
have to be pointed out to them by further painful events
where there is no disposition to have them pointed out by
human teachers.

This leads to the second answer, which is that the very
obscurity of any causal link existing between sin and suffering,
or between ignorance and suffering, or between incapacity
and suffering, is intentional and deliberate. For it compels
the sufferer to put himself the question: "Why has this come
to me?" In the search for a satisfying answer he slowly unfolds his intuition and develops his intelligence. The suffering
passes but these faculties remain. This whole situation thus
becomes a device to bring them out of latency and fulfills
an important part of his general evolution. Suffering remains
his teacher only until he is willing to accept tuition at the
hands of prophets, seers, or sages, as well as internally from
right reflection and intuition. If he will not listen to any of
these divine teachers, then he must listen to the disagreeable
consequence of his own wrong actions or personal deficiencies. If he will not correct in himself the faults productive of
intellectual mistakes and ethical misdeeds, if he refuses to
learn from history and religion, from those gifted with insight
or inspired with revelations, either the lesson that wrongdoing
does not pay or the need of developing what he lacks, and if
he is not capable of learning in any other way, then life has
no other recourse than to teach it to him through personal
anguish or ignominious humiliation.

It is deeply significant that the Cross, which is the emblem
of sorrow and pain, is likewise the emblem of salvation.
Every man is here on earth to become conscious of his super-
earthly self. Until he does accomplish this task, he will be led
through varied experiences in many births, experiences that
will be punctuated at time with pain, grief, and disappoint-

ment but tinged at intervals with joy, pleasure, and satisfaction to make life bearable. He will certainly accomplish it despite all lapses and all setbacks because the eternal law, the living principle of his own being, will force him to do so. He will be made to embark consciously on it in the end because he will discover it to be the only way to desirable happiness. The divine Overself does not pursue him in the sense that an ardent lover pursues the beloved one. But neither does it remain aloof and indifferent. It sits serenely in the heart waiting to welcome his return, knowing well that its power of magnetic attraction will draw him, as his own evolving spiritual values will lead him to seek it, and that instruction and suffering will finally make him aware of its presence. Such patience is immeasurable just because the love is immeasurable. The divine love is limited only by his openness to it and his receptivity of it. And because it is an incredibly patient love, it will not and does not *compel* him to turn away from his servitude to earthly attractions, which turning is the first form that such openness or receptivity must take. A salvation into which he was forced, in which his free will had no part to play, and with which it did not co-operate, would not be true salvation.

"The healer of all thy difficulties is remembrance of Me," said a Middle Eastern prophet. The only thing asked of every man is to turn about, change the direction of his outlook and face the Overself. Everyone is destined to come into its enlightenment. Once he has found this presence, felt this inspiration, surrendered to this power, it will carry him serenely through whatever troubles and crisis, buffetings and upheavals life may bring him. In this liberation of the self from its own desires, he will find fulfillment of the self, the true satisfaction which those very desires are unconsciously seeking. He will come, in time, to feel that this is the high purpose for which he himself came into this world and that all other purposes have unfairly consumed more time and energy than they deserved.

The human quest of happiness is too often frustrated by some hideous *physical* circumstance, condition, lack, or defect. The human entity is driven in the end toward the non-physical, that is, toward religion, mysticism, and philosophy. And thus we arrive at their immeasurable value for man (in ascending degree) and at the important consequences of his personal world-view. For we gain from suffering, as from travel, partly what we bring to it. Our faulty conduct of life is the natural outcome of our faulty concept of life. Without the guidance of spiritual teaching, we muddle our few opportunities, waste our precious years, and misdirect our limited energies. But when we begin to shape conduct by its principles, we begin to dissolve personal disharmonies. A spiritual understanding of life, which attains its best form in philosophy, assuages the pain and lightens the struggle of life. In hours of trouble or danger, in agony of emotions or flesh, we may derive a little or much relief by letting the mind take hold of its great truths and by musing earnestly on them. But at all times they may be dwelt upon with much benefit. Their study gives significant form to the flux of life's changes that would otherwise be meaningless and goalless.

Common Errors Concerning the Surrendered Life. Nothing in the view presented in the foregoing pages should leave any room for indifference or callousness in the practical result, should prevent anyone from extending the hand of sympathy and help to sufferers. Nor should he deduce from them that philosophy is in quest of self-suffering, self-deprivation, and self-martyrdom; if he does he makes a grave mistake. For it never ceases to remember that if there are sorrow and pain in the movement of life, there are also grace and mercy, pardon and love at the heart of life. Nothing so far written should lead anyone to the wrong conclusion that he should cease to cultivate sympathy for those who suffer, nor should it stop the hand that goes forth to relieve distress.

Those messengers from the Infinite Being like Jesus and Buddha could not have brought pity and taught goodness if that Being itself were really cruel. If they no longer suffered in themselves, they still suffered for others. The pain was a vicarious one. But this must be noted, that their thought was not so much for people's bodies as for people's minds and hearts: and that their compassion was principally directed not toward physical sufferings, but toward mental ignorance; toward overlooked causes rather than mere effects.

A true mystical philosophy does not joyfully hug the pains of life to its breast. It recognizes that although happiness is primarily an inner condition, it cannot be sundered altogether from outer conditions; that the materialism which makes light of human will and everything of human circumstances is as unbalanced as the idealism which does exactly the opposite; and that if the kind of response we make to the external world is important, what the external world does to us is not less important.

Nor has it much use for the attitude which insists on suffering miseries because it always accepts them as the inescapable decree of God, or for that other which waits helplessly for God to come and deliver it from its difficulties. Many Eastern and even some Western mystical leaders have rightly taught the virtue of letting God manage the universe by not attempting to interfere with his operations and the wisdom of believing that God knows better than we do how to conduct its affairs. As a direct consequence of this, they have adopted and preached to others a cult of complete social and personal indifferentism, with the wholesale resignation of all happenings as being expressions of God's will. They have taught their devotees to submit to, or acquiesce in, all events of whatever character, and to abstain from interfering with the course of events by some helpful service to mankind.

Such unrestricted and unqualified counsel to submit blindly to all circumstances, because they are God's will, is sometimes judicious but sometimes dangerous. The history of religion is quite alone eloquent on this point. How often has selfish priestcraft, serving the interests of a discredited group or despotic monarch, adjured suffering men and tormented women not to mend their present tribulations but to endure them unresistingly because divinely willed! How often have energies which could have been directed toward improving conditions remained unused in useless hopes of pleasing God! This weak attitude was long exploited in India to claim caste —originally a sensible and flexible arrangement—as a divinely ordained, rigidly unalterable institution; it was also taken advantage of in medieval Europe where each man was supposed to be born in the place and class proper to him, above which he was not given any chance to rise.

Philosophy freely admits that some circumstances, events, and happenings are certainly divine leadings for us, whether pleasurable or painful, and it will be wiser in the end not to resist them. But it also says that others are devilish in origin and should certainly be resisted. Otherwise, they may lead us into error and disaster, or encourage their originators to commit further crime. Again, some events are the sweet fruit of good destiny and therefore represent opportunity which ought to be seized. But others are the bitter fruit of bad karma and therefore represent traps, snares, pitfalls, or troubles which ought to be warily guarded against. The correct attitude is flexible; it is neither to assume rigidly at all times a fatalistic willingness to become the passive prey of events nor a bold determination to dominate them at all times.

It is plain that nobody can hold his life entirely in his own hands. Everybody is himself held in the hands of the Overself. But the advice so often given to aspirants by religionists and mystics to yield to all events as being the actualizations of God's will, to resign unresistingly to whatever happens and

whoever comes because it is ignorant egoism to do otherwise,
is not accepted by philosophy unmodified as it stands. It is
certainly true that there are situations when there is no other
recourse for anyone except humble submission to God's will
in the faith that God's wisdom is interlinked with it. It is also
true that in the end God turns all circumstances, all events,
toward the furtherance of the divine intention for the universe. But this does not justify everyone in blindly accepting
them always as being God's immediate will. They may not
be. They may be man's will. The error of those who would
have us submit universally to all sorrowful and evil events
because they represent the divine will is to forget that if we
submit unintelligently, uncritically, and uncomprehendingly,
if we do not study the meaning or lesson behind each experience, then God may send the same troubles again and again.
For that which really sends us so many experiences is God's
law of recompense.

Our tragedies and troubles do not happen to us by chance.
A divine law brings most of them as the reaction to our own
unworthy thoughts, as the correlation with our own improper
desires and foolish deeds or as the consequences of our own
personal imbalance. This law does not forge a cast-iron
fatalistic chain around us. What it does is to make a situation which, be it remembered, was created by our own previous thinking and doing, develop in a particular way *if we
do nothing thereafter to make it develop in an alternative way*.
Mere acceptance of the painful consequences of bad karma
is not enough. Passive resignation to the inflexible decree of
God's will is incomplete. We must add understanding to the
acceptance, comprehension to the resignation. Otherwise, we
suffer blindly and deprive ourselves of much of the profit
which hides behind our pain. The *inert* acceptance by would-
be religious devotees and mystics of such evil conditions as
always being God's will can be characterized only as a pathetic sign of their intellectual bankruptcy. The practical

result is that they regard sitting down and doing nothing, that is, idly waiting for things to drop into their laps, as the highest kind of human conduct. The dangers which beset such a passive attitude are serious. Not least is the danger of abandoning their life to mere chance and their will to mere circumstance.

The extremist advocates of nonresistance ignore the evolutionary need of cultivating both intelligence and will. The way in which we meet external situations and worldly events depends on these two factors as well as on our moral status. A total acceptance of, and passive resignation to, each situation or event because we believe that God's decree is expressed by it, deprives us of the chance to develop intelligence and exercise will. But such an activity is part of the divine evolutionary Idea for humanity. Blind acceptance of every event, apathetic submission in the face of every situation, and pious yielding to remediable evil really means failure to co-operate with this Idea—which is the very opposite of what their advocates intend! When the celebrated Sufi mystic, Al Hallaj, was visited by Ibrahim Khawwas, he asked his visitor: "O Ibrahim, during these forty years of your connection with mysticism, what have you gained from it?" Ibrahim answered, "I have made the doctrine of passively trusting God to provide for all my material needs specially my own." Al Hallaj retorted, "You have wasted your life."

A proper use of intelligence may save us from falling into grievous blunders. For a merely mechanical resignation to the will of God may, on occasions, cause self-deception, abet laziness, and excuse selfishness, whereas a wise resignation is always discriminating, reflective, and profound. If we have the right kind of resignation, a resignation which does not preclude intelligent self-effort, then these difficult situations will be squarely met and honestly faced. Each new experience of the human situation becomes, if intelligently analyzed and rightly met, an asset to human character, a sharpener of human intelligence. The resignation which philosophy does accept and emphatically teaches is perceptive and not blind. It does not regard God as a glorified despot and God's will as an arbitrary fiat. Accepting Plato's precept to Aristotle: "Be sure that all punishment which is inflicted upon men by God is not tyranny, but that it is correction and instruction," it uses its intelligence to discover what in its character needs such correction and what in its mentality needs such instruction. It refuses to drift fatalistically with events. It rejects the assertion that they are necessarily God's will and therefore unchangeable or not to be changed.

While on one hand it repudiates this mystical indifferentism, on the other hand philosophy repudiates the humanistic self-sufficiency exemplified in those who scorn the mystic's inward attainment. While it points out the intellectual, ethical, and practical errors of mysticism, it is much more emphatic in pointing out the errors of materialism bloated into dangerous self-conceit by dramatic scientific achievements. While it counsels understanding of what lies behind the event, it teaches drawing from within the will and strength to bear what cannot be remedied.

The world war and world crisis have dealt shattering blows to the once complacent beliefs that the human intellect, unaided by any higher power or diviner light, is wise enough to build a happy utopia on earth. The benumbing mystical idea of leaving everything to be done by God and the arrogant materialistic idea of doing everything by man are both unacceptable extremes. Philosophy teaches that only in their union and consequent mutual modification does a right attitude lie. It advocates the exercise of human will to the utmost, the continuous application of human knowledge, scientific and otherwise, to the improvement of life in every direction. But, at the same time, it seeks to understand what is the divine will for us in every situation and advocates the surrender of the results of all these efforts to this higher will.

It gives up all unprofitable anxiety about results and thus keeps its inner peace, but it does not give up the efforts which can make or modify those results. It points out that the problem of bringing into working harmony the teaching which bids us resign all to God and the intelligence which bids us shape life by will, can be solved only by keeping a flexible mentality. Its acceptance of the factuality of infinite intelligence permeating and ruling both cosmic events and human existence leads to a peace and contentment which may be easily misconceived to mean inertia or indifference, cowardice or enfeeblement, laziness or fatalism. These things are not part of the philosophic life. On the contrary, it calls for personal effort and inculcates personal responsibility; but it also says, "Do not put forth that effort in any direction that would be useless because doomed to disappointment, or that would be foolish because leading to dissatisfaction." It sets limits upon desire and teaches the unwisdom of excess.

The gnawing unrest of insatiable appetite destroys all peace of mind; philosophy says we must know when to put an end to it and we must practice the self-denial necessary to do so. It takes care to point out that the wisdom of letting go and renouncing is primarily an inner one, which may or may not have outward consequences. It admits that the final step is to limit our desires, to stop following the common unthinking trend of endlessly multiplying them, but at the same time points out that this admirable simplification does not mean that we need necessarily impose discomfort upon ourselves.

Such a negative attitude toward life as that proposed by extreme asceticism does not satisfy the modern man. Yet his spiritual needs are no less great, indeed are greater, than medieval man's. Is it not better that he seek something that is within his reasonable reach, something that will uplift and exalt him while he yet remains usefully at work in the world? He may be as comfortable and as modern as he likes, if only he will strike a balance between worldly needs and spiritual aims. Poverty is not the only gateway to purity. The better way calls for a selective synthesis of physical with spiritual, a prudent reconciliation of hitherto divergent trends. It recognizes that the real evil does not lie in the physical possessions. It understands the importance of thought, that "As a man thinketh in his heart, so is he."

Even the leisures and luxuries of the rich are not necessarily antispiritual. They could be and they most often are, but they need not be. The wise man must beware of the dangers of wealth, yes! but he need not therefore fail to appreciate its values. Not all authorities on Indian mysticism, which is supposed to support the contrary view, do so. The *Siva Samhita*, an ancient and respected palm-leaf text, says: "Let a householder also exert himself in yoga, his wealth and conditions of life are no obstacle; if free from attachment to them he will get the signs of success." The quest of physical comfort and the wish to accumulate possessions are natural needs and not bad in themselves. Only when they are permitted to dominate the heart of man and absorb his time to disproportionate excess do they become bad. In that event, after a certain time, a compulsory re-establishment of lost equilibrium will be brought about by karmic forces.

It is praiseworthy and not blameworthy for men to endeavor to improve their position in the world. The desire and search after more earthly possessions are perfectly valid. There is nothing evil in physical things themselves. Nobody should be asked to make himself unnecessarily miserable in the name of spiritual self-discipline nor to submit to intolerable degradations in the name of spiritual resignation. The philosophic idea of sane equilibrium would preclude it while its exhortation to self-improvement would oppose it. This ideal offers a fuller, better balanced view. It conquers desires but refuses to make a fetish of discomfort.

But it warns man that life holds finer, more vital, and more durable things. If he persists in making a monomania of possessions and in becoming obsessed by position, he will miss those finer things. Evil begins only when he permits them to stupefy his mind, when he lets them obstruct the inner spiritual purpose of his life on earth. Buddha may have gone to extremes when he taught that even all the pleasant material things of life were, if considered against their background and consequences, really unpleasant and hence to be shunned. Certainly we must simplify life at some point and surrender it if we are ever to have peace, and certainly, too, when the search after possessions becomes never ending, unbalanced, or unethically carried on, it is no longer valid.

It is much the same with the taste for healthy pleasure, the urge for amusing relaxation, and the desire for light entertainment. They are natural and right. It is not wrong to attend to these human needs. Philosophy, unlike extreme asceticism, does not scorn them and, unlike extreme materialism, does not overrate them. What harm is there in them so long as they are regarded as being mere accessories and not the principal end of life, minor essentials and not the major ones? Man needs them when he lacks the philosophical means of keeping his sanity and balance.

It is only when they are overdone or oversought, when they become narcotics to relieve him of the trouble of reflection about life, when they divert his attention from the tragedies and sorrows which should prompt such reflection, that they become dangerous and lead to the very insanity and unbalance against which they ought to guard him. When this happens, desire rages in the heart of the self-indulgent sybarite and disharmony spoils his outer existence. The only way of escape he knows then is to add still more to the fast-burning heap of pleasures. They may push him into sheer vice and harmful folly. When too high a value is set upon pleasure, the inner retribution is inescapable: happiness will last only as long as the pleasure lasts. The hedonists who spend their affections upon vanishing things alone, hardly conscious of the inner desolation and the fatuous aimlessness of their gilt and lacquered lives, do not realize that the leisure which might be devoted not only to getting necessary relaxation and amusement but also to fulfilling the purpose of incarnation and gaining a little understanding, discipline, and peace, is literally wasted away in a quest of idle or sensual enjoyment. But the heaviest retribution comes when the supreme Reality is regarded as the supreme triviality.

The agony of a world hurled into the chaos of a great war was not remote from such a retribution. For many men and women, before it broke out, the values of a higher purpose to life might as well have been nonexistent. They could not believe in immortal Mind, which is perfectly credible, but they did believe in perishable Matter, which is metaphysically incredible. They did not understand that in holding to the reality of Matter they were holding to the most illusory of man's conceptions. Consequently, they swung their censers of admiration before worthless idols. Such a self-deceptive outlook could only end in dangerous disillusionment. There was a grinning skeleton at such feasting, sarcastically shaking his bony hands in warning.

The dark sorrows which life may present us can and should be met with a quiet confidence in the power of the soul to conquer them either psychologically or practically or both. But this power must be felt for, found, trusted, and obeyed. If we keep our thought wise and good and brave, it will shield us, always inwardly and mayhap outwardly, from life's sharpest arrows. And this is true whether they are shot at us by harsh fate or by human malice. Even in the darkest situations we often hope for the best. This is really our faintly echoing comprehension of the higher self's message, that its bliss, and therefore our best, forever awaits us. There is a paradox here.

We begin the quest of inner happiness when we feel the deep melancholy of discovering the transiency and limitation that underlie all life's beauty and pleasure. We finish it when we discover the deep joy of the soul's everlasting loveliness that underlies the melancholy itself. We suffer today only that we shall be happy tomorrow. The Overself's tranquil smile must be earned by fighting a way through the valley of fallen tears. Our deepest wisdom confers the only lasting serenity, yet is born amid cruelest agony. The most evolved individual in any community is also the happiest one. He has renounced past attitudes and retreated from the ego and all has come right in the end. Yet, if the secret chronicle of his bygone births could be read, its great length would inevitably single him out as having passed through a full experience of anguish. All the distresses which made their valuable contribution to the development of consciousness and the expansion of intelligence, were by Nature's mercy utterly obliterated from memory in the end. When the estranged ego shattered its chains, renounced its isolation, and returned to its holy parent, secreted within and behind its own self, it found it was hitherto taught by suffering only that it may henceforth be taught by bliss.

CHAPTER VIII

THE EVIL IN OUR TIME

THE EVENTS of recent decades provide nothing more or less than a visible commentary on the messages it was the privilege of inspired prophets like Jesus, Krishna, and Buddha to deliver. The unprecedented times through which we have lived merely prove by terrible facts what such men preached by opened lips. They prove that the religious unfaith and materialistic trend of a whole generation, the hard skepticism which has degraded their values and dragged down their instincts, afford too insecure a basis for human living.

Materialism—by which is meant here not merely the openly confessed and crudely obvious doctrine which goes under this name but also its unconscious and disguised forms —has been the bane of our time. The total impression of all the forms it has taken—and they are to be found in the scientific, political, educational, literary, artistic, ecclesiastic, and legal spheres also—is a ghastly one. The end of it all is the terrifying figure and the typhoon destructiveness of the atom bomb. It is the natural consequence of belief in the final supremacy of intellectual thinking when pushed to its logical extreme and unbalanced by spiritual intuition. In war human evil always appears in its worst form and its effects in their most widespread form. With the discovery of the atom bomb the pathway leading to a large part of civilization's utter self-destruction is now wide open. Nothing in history is comparable to this terrible situation.

It is not enough to understand the tragic as well as historic significance of these world-shaking events. We must also understand their underlying religious, metaphysical, and philosophical significance. And, as mentioned earlier, this cannot be done adequately unless we let the light of doctrines like the inevitability of spiritual evolution and the factuality of the law of recompense shine down upon them. For without them, it is too taxing to explain why society today is as it is. The psychological situation which has been created by the crisis and the war which expresses itself in the tragic physical situation, can be adequately understood only by the light of these and other related truths. Mankind's own wrong thoughts and emotions, bad passions and deeds, must share the responsibility. Its civilization has indeed received the rewards of a shortsighted selfishness, for it has seen so many of the material things it strove to obtain, as well as the ideals it strove to realize, crumble away in its hands.

Most people assume that good alone has the right to be active on earth. Therefore the presence of so much that is evil perplexes their minds. It seems that such presence is too abundant and too continuous to fit smoothly into a divinely ordered scheme. The crime and violence of recent times, the horror and shock of recent history, have pushed this question of evil into the thinking of many persons who formerly ignored it. A generation which has heard wicked propaganda, witnessed wicked atrocities, and watched unscrupulous moves toward world domination would be very soft-brained if it does not conclude that some malignant influence is at work in human affairs and that some malignant forces are manifesting their disturbing activities in its midst. The existence—no less than the power—of evil has forced itself so plainly and so savagely and so insistently on their notice in recent times that those who, at the bidding of extravagantly optimistic theories, previously shut their eyes to it, have perforce had to open them and recognize it. Such a belated and bewildered act is painful.

The materialistic view of evil regards it as a by-product of physical environments and temporary circumstances, to be set right by the mere setting right of those physical things. But the type of evil which is so prevalent in our own times, glorifies brutality for its own sake, justifies oppression for the oppressor's sake, pedestals greed, ridicules religion, and derides conscience, as much for the pleasure it gets from these activities as for the rewards. The men who practice it love it as intensely as saints love God. It can no longer be reasonably maintained, as the dialectic and rationalist materialists have hitherto maintained, that external circumstances are alone sufficient to account for the unpleasant character of such noxious creatures. On the contrary, it is evident that the wrong of human conduct rises because evil is a real element in human beings, independent of human environment and circumstance. It is deplorable but it is also unfortunately true that this element asserts itself more easily and more frequently than the good. The historical perversity of human nature, its constant inclination to do wrong, too often discourages the philanthropist.

Philosophy does not regard this problem with indifference, as the London *Times* reviewer of *The Wisdom of the Overself* alleged, but rather with seriousness. Nothing that was written in that book was intended to deny the horrible actuality of evil, the constant activity of evil, its terrible havoc in human history, and its frightful reality in human lives.

That humanity should be allowed to fall into its horrible depths seems to show a lack of goodness in the divine Idea of the world. Men are not to be blamed for questioning the divine goodness and doubting the divine wisdom. They often ask themselves the question: Why does the Higher Power (which they call God and is in scientific actuality the World-Mind) which is so universally regarded as beneficent, even permit these evils and horrors to threaten humanity? But they ought also to ask themselves the further question whether the World-Idea could have completely fulfilled its lofty purpose for humanity without permitting such experiences? If it seeks to bring every human entity to full moral, intellectual, and spiritual self-consciousness, the range of experiences within which the entity would have to be free to travel would have to be sufficiently wide, and consequently sufficiently contrasting, to achieve this goal. To have limited this range to the nonevil, to have restricted the kinds of experience only to what *we* know as the good, would have rendered impossible the full achievement of human self-consciousness. That, after all, is a matter not only of morality but also of knowledge. There is indeed no other way than the existing one in which humanity could have found all the conditions necessary for the development of *all* its faculties. The mere fact that the

World-Mind suffers evil to exist should show that it has a temporary, an inevitable, or else a utilitarian place in the economy of things.

No mode of conscious life could have been devised which provided unalloyed happiness and unmixed goodness at the same time that it provided the varied experiences and diverse states necessary to develop the knowledge, intelligence, character, and spirituality of the human being. Although some facets of this development could have been obtained by a one-sided monotonous experience yielding only the pleasurable enjoyment of life, important parts of the psyche would then necessarily have been left untouched by it. Only by providing a course of changing experiences which took a wider, more varied route and also included the opposites of suffering and evil, could the full complete evolution of man have been achieved. The memory of the past darkness of ignorance heightens his appreciation of the present light of knowledge. The vivid contrast between the two conditions makes him much more conscious of the meaning and value of the higher one. Without the experiences of both to complement each other, he could not distinguish good from evil, bliss from misery, reality from appearance, and truth from falsity. How, without conditions productive of sacrifice and self-denial, for instance, could the spiritual widening of his consciousness be obtained? Good becomes significant to him only as it stands in contrast to evil, which is indeed the Not-good. The consciousness of sound as sound always needs to be accompanied by the consciousness of its opposite and differentiating number, silence. There could have been no manifestation of a universe without this play of opposites running completely through it. As soon as the One became Two, it began. Hence birth and death appear everywhere in the universe, pleasure and pain in man!

Heraclitus of Ephesus shrewdly commented that Homer was wrong in saying, "Would that strife might perish from among gods and men," that he did not see he was really praying for the destruction of the universe and that if his prayer were answered all things would have to pass away. Every biological scientist who has peered beneath the surface of things knows, what every metaphysician should know, that the world-process is inescapably an interplay and interstruggle of the creative and destructive forces. The cosmos could not be continually alive if it were not also continually dying. The struggle of these opposing forces is an eternal movement which is reflected in the birth of majestic stars and the death of minute cells. Only a static motionless universe could have avoided it. If man were not to be a mechanical robot, he had to be free in his will, within the limits imposed by Nature and by the universal purpose. He had to be given the power to choose. And if he were left free to choose good, he had necessarily to be left free to choose evil. That he would act wrongly, would clash with his fellow men, and would even match his foolishness against God's wisdom was foreknown from the very beginning, was indeed inevitable from the fact that he began his conscious life in ignorance and desire. Through experience he would eventually learn to act rightly and this dark phase in his career would disappear. Only by the experiment with evil could the value of good be adequately realized.

God has given man enough freedom to work out his own destiny and since there is both good and evil mixed into his nature, when the evil becomes great in volume and massive in strength it inevitably leads to consequences such as those which menace him today. Yet this cannot be a sole and sufficient explanation of his present situation. Since his freedom of will cannot operate within a vacuum there must be other forces at work within his environment modifying it, influencing it, and even ultimately directing it. There must be some sort of rough pattern in the universe within which his own activities must eventually fit. Unless we find some glimmering of this pattern we shall not be able to understand sufficiently why so many millions of apparently good decent people should be exposed to distress and affliction resulting from the evil activities of other men. Nay, why even civilization itself should be so darkly threatened by such activities.

That man's own free will has created so much of the evils and misery in the world is obvious. That with his own moral improvement, this deplorable situation would itself improve, is equally obvious. But the situation itself could not have risen except by the permission and within the conception of the World-Mind. Where is there more than partial freedom for a man when, at the very beginning, he is forced to accept and given no chance to select a certain race, a certain country, a particular family, a particular economic status, a condition of health or ill health, and an abundance or lack of energy, intellect, will, and intuition? Thus, much of the course and something of the end of his life is dictated by Nature, fate, or God. No human entity can determine its own course with complete freedom. No human entity can deviate from the cosmic plan with complete independence. The freedom of all human entities is limited, as their power is dependent. Man has never possessed, does not now possess, and never can possess absolute free will. Above his own fluctuating will there is the inexorable cosmic will. All his individual development is but part of, and controlled by, the evolutionary plan for the cosmos itself. It has not been left to his internal whim or external chance what the outcome of that development shall be.

If the whole cosmos is an emanation of the divine Mind which, although mysteriously transcendent is also significantly immanent, there can be no force and no entity within it that is not fundamentally rooted in the beneficence, the wisdom, and the serenity of divinity. It may have its origins obscured, it may appear, think, and act evilly, but can do so only by the permission and consent of God. Therefore, it is not only man's ignorant and wrongful use of his free will that accounts for human evil and human suffering but also the cosmic Idea itself. And this is something outside his control and beyond the operation of his will. The wrongs and pain that shadow his existence were sanctioned and included in the method of his inner development.

This is God's world; it could not be anyone else's. It must ultimately be an expression of God's wisdom. Therefore if we find in it things and people, events and sights which offend us because they are diabolic rather than godlike, the reaction of instinctive repugnance is human enough but the shortcoming is in our faculty of vision, the unpleasantness is in our limitation of the understanding, and can be nowhere else. Everywhere there are signs that the divine power is working in the midst of us. But eyes that are not spiritually opened naturally fail to see them. We would do better to complain at the presence of our own blindness than at the absence of God's activity. What we see in the world's present state and past history depends on what we are in ourselves. If we are morally crooked, we shall regard most of the people we meet as being so too. If we can find no deeper meaning in our own nature, no higher purpose in our own lives, we shall see none in the world outside. The discovery of a divine self in our own heart will be a pointing finger to the presence of a divine Mind behind the whole universe to which we belong.

As the human entity evolves in knowledge and consciousness, it changes its view as to what is or is not evil just as it changes its view as to what is or is not desirable. As it sets the different pieces of the mosaic world pattern more and more into place so that the whole becomes more and more significant, as it first controls and later divests itself of the negative personal emotions, as it develops a calm impersonal interior life, its own attitude toward the ills of life changes. The change is slowly and reluctantly made but in the end the entity is unable to resist making it. For to the extent that it deserts the ego's littleness and responds to the higher self's leading in other matters, so must it respond here. Its highest change results from the discovery of its divine Self, when this relativity of evil becomes perfectly plain and the evanescence of the ego against the background of eternity becomes perfectly visible.

If, from the highest possible point of view only, evil is an illusion and if good is the opposite of evil, surely must not good itself then be an illusion also, it will be asked. The answer is that there are two "goods." There is a relative one which is evil's true opposite, and illusory. There is an absolute one which is a quality of the One Infinite Life-Power; this is real good. Evil has no endlessly real existence in itself. In our ordinary human life, we find this statement contradicted. With our ordinary human mentality we find it incredible. An almost Tibetan solitude of living is needed to make it acceptable. What we have to learn, even though it is so hard to accept, is that the divine thought of the universe is not only perfect and good in its first as in its last stages, but also in its present stage. If we find the world in a mess of tragedy and suffering, of chaos and sin, the mess is really in our own sight, our own way of looking at things. If it is hard to comprehend this statement, it will be helpful to gain such comprehension by comparing humanity's experience of evil's reality with a sleeper's experience of a nightmare. The hideous or hateful figures that he sees therein are unquestionably present to him, the torments and terrors which it causes are very real to him. Yet after he wakes up, all these are seen for what they are worth, are recognized as now being what they even then were—merely ideas. On the immediate practical view it is quite true that evil is a real, widespread, powerful, but limited factor in human existence. Nevertheless on the ultimate philosophic view it is not what it seems to be. It certainly exists. But such existence is relative to the human body with its finite thinking. Its presence is not to be denied, but at the same time there is a higher factor behind it as there is a higher factor behind the human body.

Both evil and suffering have been allotted roles in human development from its very start. They have not appeared by accident or by any unexpected "fall." They have not been introduced against the divine will by some satanic power. The fall into sin and the experience of pain are integral parts of the cosmic Idea. They are not cosmic accidents or cosmic mistakes. The divine wisdom is as much at work in them as anywhere else. What is at fault is human perception, human impatience, and human limitation. It is his quality and degree of consciousness which makes one man perceive only evil where another man perceives *both* evil and good, as well as comprehends that human evil is both the consequence of human free will and the cost of human evolution.

It is difficult to defend the cruelties of Nature. The destruction which happens in the teeming animal kingdom and which arouses no attention, far outweighs the destruction which happens in the human kingdom during a world war, which arouses everyone's attention. But the birth of living forms on our own plane *has* to be followed by their death on that plane. Those two poles in Nature, the positive and negative, are an inevitable corollary of the cosmic manifestation. If the intellect can justify the cruelties of Nature only by divorcing itself from all the finer emotions, let us remember that it deals with the physical level alone. The intuition, operative on a different level, finds that behind all outer forms there is the inner spirit of Nature and that a living and loving presence lies beyond the thought of man. Where the intellect becomes bitter with Nature, the intuition remains sweet and serene. It concludes, and can only conclude, that if there is such goodness at the hidden heart of Nature, there must be some good purpose on the surface of things.

All seeming wrongs and apparent ills must have a rational place in the cosmic order, the sufferings as well as the joys.

The order is not the less divinely controlled because of their existence. They are not the result of an accident in the universal functioning or of a mistake in the divine planning.

The cosmos is grasped as a single whole in the infinite consciousness of the World-Mind. The latter, in its infinite knowledge, has foreseen all probable courses and possible consequences of human conduct. But it also knows that a corrupt humanity today will be an ennobled humanity in a far-off tomorrow. We would be justified in denouncing the divine thought as entirely wicked and absolutely merciless if the end of human existence were like this present phase of it, or if it were an uncertain risky gamble. But the end is glorious, its accomplishment a certainty, the process a worth-while one. For it is a genuine unfoldment from within of attributes, capacities, and states of consciousness which reflect something of the divine.

If there is but a single supreme principle of Being in the cosmos, if all things and all creatures have emanated from it, then what in the workings of this cosmos we call evil as well as what we call suffering must also have ultimately emanated from it. But this Supreme Principle being the only ever-existing one, it follows that evil and suffering in individuals are only transient appearances doomed to live fitfully and then vanish altogether. There is no pain, evil, or sorrow in the eternal essence of things itself, in the absolute unity of life, as Mary Baker Eddy rightly noted. Only when the time processes of manifestation appear and only when innumerable beings are differentiated out, does their existence become even possible. For only then does the duality of opposites start. Nothing can be brought into actuality without necessarily bringing in the possibility of its contrary also. We can form the idea of light only by forming the idea of darkness along with it. If light makes darkness possible, love makes hate, joy makes pain, and good makes evil possible. When the manifested beings are permitted to possess desire and to exer-

cise will—as they must be if they are not to be robots—then
potential strife for selfish ends is inevitably permitted too.
There will always be evil at some point or other in the manifested cosmos because there will always be a shadow in the
sunlight. No sun, no shadow; no good, no evil. These things
are presupposed and negatively present in their opposites. We
cannot have a manifested cosmos without having also this
perpetual relationship between them.

But because change is imprinted upon manifestation, it is
never the same evil that we see but only a new embodiment
thereof. Its old forms are transmuted by time and evolution
into good. Thus, in spite of themselves, apparent evil may
be productive of a change for actual good and temporary
suffering may eventually result in stable happiness. The ob-
structionist principle, the adverse force, the dead weight of
inertia against which every effort of man to uplift himself
has to contend is there because resistance to it affords the
chance to develop the good. The struggle to which he is
called against the resisting elements, however long-drawn this
struggle may be, leads to his progress. It is one allotted task
of the so-called evil forces to try his mettle by hindering his
growth, to test his character by tempting his desires and to
expose him for what he really is by opposing his efforts in
self-development. What is this opposing power, this adverse
force in the end but the personal ego in man, the lesser and
lower part of himself with correspondences in the outside
but unseen world? Its presence in his life provokes him into
either overcoming it or yielding to it. If the first, it has led
him to work for his own improvement; if the second, it has
led him to acknowledge his own weakness. Sooner or later,
the unpleasant consequences of such weakness will lead him
to grapple with it and develop his power of will. That is part
of the mission of evil, to stimulate him into its own destruction and to force him into his own betterment. Immediately

and directly, it may either strengthen him or weaken him. Ultimately, it can only strengthen him.

So far as human evil is concerned, it is useless to talk of the Supreme Power being omnipotent and therefore being able to abolish such evil at a stroke. Man could not have been granted some measure of freedom of will without being granted at the same time some measure of freedom to act evilly, if he so chose to do so. The whole idea of human evolution would have been a useless one if he were to have been nothing but a slavish automaton, utterly deprived of all capacity for self-determination. To the extent that he has freedom, to that extent the Supreme Power has voluntarily given up its own omnipotence in the individual but not in the cosmos, has necessarily self-limited its own will *in appearance* but not in reality.

The theological notion that there is a fundamental duality of good and evil running right around the tortuous pattern of the universe and through the tangled narrative of history is neither right nor wrong; it needs to be correctly interpreted. Philosophy offers such an interpretation. It does not hold that there is satanic power which is co-equal with the divine power. It does hold that God has no independent and equal rival. The parallel notion is that the world has somehow fallen into a grievous muddle, that the work of God has been dangerously sabotaged by Satan, and that this muddle can be put right and this danger can be overcome only by man's coming to the help of God. The Infinite Wisdom and Infinite Power has indeed fallen low if it has fallen in such need. Human conceit reaches the level of utter fantasy or becomes even worse by becoming spiritually arrogant when it considers itself called upon to "help God." The Infinite Intelligence is also the Infinite Power. It would be less than itself if it needed the assistance of a finite creature like puny man in its cosmic work! All that man can properly offer it is the harmony of his own purpose with the universal one. But this will be for his own benefit, not God's, as it will be for his own loss if he does not offer it.

Is it not saner to believe that the World-Mind still remains what it always has been and that the planet's history would take on a very different guise if we could see it without the limitations of our finite perceptions and finite understandings? It is human to want certain things to happen and to desire certain purposes to be fulfilled. But God is not human. The Infinite Being has no wants, no desires, and no purposes. When they appear to exist, they are for others. Let us not saddle our finite conceptions on the Infinite Being nor our human qualities on the Absolute Power.

The philosophic concept of evil is often too hastily rejected because it is too hastily studied. It will not be adequately understood unless its twofold character is understood. It readily grants a real, hidden, and widespread activity of malignant forces in human history. It recognizes their opposition to humanity's spiritual evolution. But it also holds that this activity is limited and that it still leaves the ultimate nature of evil unexplained. It says that all evil is in the end forced to serve the purposes of good. The one has only an ephemeral, the other an eternal, life. If we can rise to the level of the Real, we are no longer able to perceive the transient evil by itself. We then perceive it against a background of the final good. Because we have something of the World-Mind deep down in us, an adequate view of the problem must include both standpoints. There is a relative good and a relative evil, they being necessary opposites. But there is no ultimate evil, only ultimate good.

Have We Made Progress? A glance at the historical scene might tempt us to deny that human morality has ever made any advance and to affirm that human evil remains utterly incurable. Does humanity grow better or worse in character?

Has it become purified mentally and emotionally by the war? What has it learned from unprecedented national calamity and personal sorrow? Is there evidence anywhere that goodness is displacing wickedness? Is it harder in the postwar world to maintain moral integrity than it was in the prewar days? Has the flow of experience worked no changes in the heart of man, stimulated no lasting good will between man and man? Has the most horrible era in history taught nothing of life's spiritual significance? As the parade of contemporary life passes before thoughtful eyes, these questions insistently rise. They can be answered only at the cost of stirring up several equally difficult questions.

Man does not evolve by passing smoothly in a direct upward line from a lower to a higher point. He evolves by trudging along a winding spiral path which rises and falls and circles about itself. The course which his spiritual, mental, and moral advance takes is seldom direct but mostly zigzag. There is no straight-line progress in history. Development is effected through an ultimately ascending spiral of rises and falls. It is historically like a tide whose waters advance only to recede later. But it differs from all actual tides inasmuch as with each recession, it does not fall so far back as the previous one. The cycle seems to return on itself but is really a rising spiral.

When this conception of picturesque advance from cellular life to celestial being is first given welcome admittance into the mind, we are likely to limit our understanding to only this part of life's course, for every such phase of development is eventually succeeded by its complementary phase of disintegration and collapse. In short, progress exists in a general way but it is intermittent, and is the total result of a long series of triumphs and setbacks. There is a moment when it reaches a turning point and then the glorious goal which lures its creatures on turns out to be an abyss into which they finally fall. Despite this periodic retrogression, the spiritual journey of mankind is essentially progressive. Every rise of evolution's cyclic arc is higher than the one before.

All its future developments lie concealed in the original cell. All its physical and spiritual growth through the ages is really an unfoldment rather than an evolution. Yet this is true only of the major features of its life course. For the rest, there is a kind of uncertainty and therefore a kind of freedom.

The animal unhesitatingly obeys its bodily instincts partly because it is untroubled by the doubts and questionings of reason, and partly because it is still intellectually unindividualized. Nature guides its instincts, and they are usually correct. But man is in a different situation. He is developing the faculty of reason and also becoming individualized. To the extent that this happens he loses the guidance of Nature and has to depend upon himself. So he moves through misty uncertainties and acts upon half-blind promptings, with consequences which are sometimes favorable but quite often not. So he walks through life with faltering steps, not able for periods of time to see clearly whither he is going.

If our thinking upon this subject is to be right, it must clear up the significance to be assigned to such a term as "progress." For too long it has been rendered foolish or contradictory by our misconceived and easy acceptance of traditional nonsense. The setback given to human society by the war and its aftermath destroyed foolish notions of continuous progress which so many smug people used to harbor. They were bitterly punished for a delusive shallow optimism. As a materialistic civilization moved on apparently indefinitely toward increasing triumph, men began to doubt all the spiritual truths they had learned. But as all observers now know, it moved toward disaster instead. For it is not enough to be moving; you must know where you are moving to! Do we not somewhere read, "They that walk blindly shall perish"? We can now sit up ruefully and confess that we were fools to travel so far and find so little.

The escape from postwar troubles will not be achieved by finding middle positions between extreme ones, but by seeking new positions in preference to old ones. Modern society has to make the final and irrevocable decisions as to which direction it will take. It has to choose whether it will cling as hard as before to the materialistic and animalistic ego or loosen the hold on it. On this choice depends its fate. Its spiritual adolescence has already, and so dramatically, come to an end.

Darwin and Spencer set the ball of evolutionary theory rolling with such gusto that few departments of thought escaped contact with the doctrine. Later, even religious leaders or thinkers became jubilant at times over the law of inevitable progress. They did not even stop at making the Absolute Power progress unendingly together with its creation! With extravagant, almost inebriated optimism which alienated the more deeply thoughtful, they declared that God, man, and the universe all moved onward to perfection! The Darwinian struggle for existence is true of the animal and primitive-human kingdoms, but it is only half true. The spiritual purpose which informs this struggle and guides its course is the complementary half-truth which must be added by the human mind if it is not to deceive itself into a hopeless materialism. For the grand evolution of consciousness which is ultimately behind all this evolution of forms, ennobles the world-view where the other merely degrades it. The concept of evolution must be enlarged, elaborated, and defined.

We are not to confuse evolution with progress. This first is a permanent fact in Nature, the second a temporary phenomenon in human history.

Science, with all its wondrous machines and chemicals, has yet to solve the ancient riddles of light and life. It has discovered much about their operations and mechanisms but little about their nature and essence. The Darwinian materialists, for instance, might well be asked how it was ever possible for live entities to appear on this planet when their own science says it commenced with such fiery beginnings, such temperature as would sterilize every potential cell and germ of life upon it. Philosophy always proclaimed the fact that there is no dead matter anywhere in this cosmos. There is only living radiance, throbbing energy, informed and controlled by inherent mind and everywhere expressing the cycle of evolving life, of movement from an inferior form to a superior one and by spiral-like circuits, from a lesser degree of consciousness, intelligence, and character to a greater one.

If it be asked why the spiral-path principle of evolution should have been laid down by the infinite wisdom behind the universe, the answer is that in no other way could such a rich variety of experience have been attained by the experiencing entities. As they trace their circular course they move from one direction to its very opposite, passing through all the different regions that lie in between. They move from contrast to contrast, from gain to loss, from summer to winter, from day to night, and so on, by the compulsion of an eternal law, which exists both outside and inside themselves. The yearning after change begins to arise within them even when their experience is blissful, if this experience is prolonged so far as to become monotonous. This also explains why the experiencing entities recapitulate earlier forms of their experience, albeit briefly and tersely. For in returning upon itself the spiral-path has to repeat itself. And this repetition is not only physical, as in the embryo developing in the mother's womb, but also mental, as in the first twenty-eight years of each reincarnation.

The desire for happiness is a universal one but the conception of happiness is not. All creatures share the first, so why do they differ about the other? Why does not the same meaning arise spontaneously in their minds when they hear this word? The answer is supplied by the doctrine of physical evolution through repeated embodiments. They themselves differ in length of experience and innate capacities (and hence in their conceptions and attitudes) because they stand on different levels of evolutionary life. The grossly materialistic are on a lower level and can find their transient satisfactions only in grossly tangible things. The more refined are on a higher one and have included purely intellectual or aesthetically emotional things within their conception of happiness. There is a loftier level still, where a smaller number of men and women recognize spiritual attainments as the most precious, the most desirable, and the most durable of all forms of satisfaction.

If we look only at the past thirty years of humanity's history, we may well ask ourselves whether evolution applies only to its intellectual and physical life; whether, in respect of its moral and spiritual life, the doctrine is nothing more than a wish-fulfillment. Unless we express our meaning of the term more exactly, it is self-deceptive to assert that the world has or has not shown progress. Macaulay's essays show a thoroughgoing optimism about the millennium which science was supposed to bring to our civilization. But Matthew Arnold, looking at the development of this same civilization in the same period, wrote about it with a disquieted heart. Both were more or less right from their respective standpoints, for each had a different kind of progress in mind. The first saw and cared for physical and logically intellectual improvement whereas the second had moral and intuitively intellectual improvement in his mind.

It is hard to recognize the slow ennoblement of man if we look only to a limited period. Indeed, in certain cases we have seen the very contrary process—his swift brutalization—in our own time. We may therefore ask ourselves if we are so sure as we once were that we have progressed. The answer is everywhere evident. Our machines and chemicals have progressed, but our morals and manners have not. Our technical skills have outstripped our character. We grow worse with each generation in faith, spirituality, and reverence for the higher power, but better in reasoning capacity and mental information.

If so many outward signs show a drift not toward peace and spirituality, but toward new clashes over material possessions or outward power, it is precisely through such clashes and their ensuing educative results that we shall ultimately pass to understanding, peace, and spirituality. But the process must necessarily be a slow one. The mistakes made by a carpenter are quickly shown up by his finished work either in its appearance or in its use. But the mistakes made in the conduct of life may be attended not only with much slower results but also be much harder to recognize. This is because the truthful work of the carpenter is judged by the senses whereas the truthful understanding of the human being is judged by the intelligence. And in the evolution of man, his senses have arrived at a more developed state than his intelligence. Hence, experience alone does not bring immediate wisdom as its fruit. Only after it is well and honestly thought over, well reasoned upon, or deeply intuited in an impersonal manner, does the fruit appear. This takes time, yet it both implies and elicits growth.

Here is the answer to those who deplore the fact that men seem to learn nothing from history, whether it be their own or others', or worse still, learn entirely false lessons from it. Time brings ripeness to some fruits, decay to others, more wisdom to some men but more foolishness to others. Deceived by egoism and blinded by passion, there are those who get from experience the very opposite meaning to the one it is intended to yield, and so fall into wicked ways. But the Overself is supremely patient. It knows the hour will come when further experience itself with its errors and consequent retribution, its sufferings and consequent despairs, will confront every man with the insistent demand that he understand it. If the divine order of the universe provides him with the time and events he needs for growth, this does not mean he is left to rely on them alone; that would be too long, too tortuous, and too uncertain a road. To help him shorten the road and make it both safer and pleasanter, he is led to add to them the right use of his reasoning, the humble following of spiritual teachers, and the proper attendance on intuition.

The earthly journey supplies part of the requisite conditions for unfolding his latent attributes and capacities. He passes by degrees from ignorance through experience to knowledge, from desire through suffering to peace. The immersions in evil and darkness provide the opposition whereby he may exercise his will to the good and aspire toward his consciousness of the true. There is a power inherent in him and also played upon him by Nature, which makes both for his mental growth and for the moral improvement of his species. Life is an ordered if broken progression from the infinitesimal up to the infinite, not only in the struggle for physical existence but also in the development of creative talent, the unfoldment of mental capacity and the awareness of inner being.

Those who wish to anticipate this evolutionary advance should make the effort involved and discipline entailed in a cheerful and willing spirit. For the same truth which earlier punishes us when disdained and rejected, later blesses us when welcomed and received. The same evil which first tempts us, later tests us. Its revelation of what we are, when linked with its consequences, finally brings us to seek the good. It works by examining our right to Life's supreme treasure, the divinely rooted consciousness of the Overself, by tempting character and faith or testing motive and goodness; it enables us in this way to establish such a right. Thus, in the end, it is an instrument of the cosmic purpose for us and not, as we often suppose, only the enemy of that purpose, and nothing more. Our human perception of the life around us is limited and narrow, our conception of it imperfect and prejudiced. We see it as we see the underside of a rug in the course of being made, when it is a shapeless mass with a fragmentary pattern, which is itself hardly discernible because reversed.

Whatever catastrophe injures the bodily life of contemporary man, the advance of his spiritual life is foreordained and inevitable. If we have only to survey the bloody and greedy course of history to realize that the evil in man is as innate as the good in man, it is nevertheless true that whereas the one will grow ever upward, the other will shrink and wither to the ground. During the war, the philosophically minded were able to hold on hopefully, knowing that the rope of karma was running out and that the evil incarnate would destroy itself in the end. The mind can support itself more firmly during contemporary upheavals, and even keep itself unharmed by them, only if it seeks and makes its own by constant contemplation, a knowledge of the divine Idea back of things. This will give it the faith that the moral law must always prevail because evolution is divinely ordered. Amid the widespread darkness and tumult of the war, there was still the assurance for it that those forces which work only for evil, work in the end for their own destruction and that evil's success is always transient. In their metaphysical ignorance, the evil leaders did not comprehend the forces of evolution and destiny which were also at work, did not know that they would become the suffering heirs to their own deeds. The calamities which they brought to other people became curses which fell upon their own heads. They did not realize that every form of wrongdoing contains in itself the germ of its retributive reaction.

We live in an epoch when the powers of evil have been making their strongest bid for world domination. We have also lived to see the colossal failure of the first phase of that bid. The hour of punishment can only be postponed; it can neither be evaded nor avoided. "Not in the heavens, not in the midst of the sea, not if thou hidest thyself away in the clefts of the mountains, wilt thou find a place on earth where thou canst escape the fruits of thy evil action." Thus spoke Buddha and history does always verify these words. We may see in the outcome of the first phase not only a striking demonstration of the ultimate triumph of good over evil, but also a contemporary confirmation of the statement made in *The Wisdom of the Overself* that there are definite limits set to the activity of evil.

The atheist says that even if God exists, He is either powerless to prevent the rising of evil or merciless to permit its continuance. The philosopher says that God does exist, does possess power, and even display mercy, but that these things are channeled through a cosmos, that is an orderly regulated universe. He says, too, that the permission under which the dark forces operate has a string of limited length tied to it and that at the end of their cycle, they are either destroyed by retribution or destroy themselves.

Our Practical Duty. If there are any who object that such a conception of evil's divine sanction enervates the will to resist it, let the answer be that, if they look at it from the standpoint of the blind personal ego only, it may seem so. But if they look at it from the standpoint of the enlightened human soul which loves truth, it will not seem so. Even truth can be dangerously misapplied. This is the case when the foregoing doctrines are made, by a false logic, to free anyone from moral responsibility. Although they attempt to explain the circumstance wherein men think wrongly and act wickedly, they have not sought to extenuate it. Anybody who drew the conclusion that he is not responsible and therefore not punishable would draw an unphilosophical, misleading, and dangerous conclusion. Nothing that is written here is a defense of tame submission to evil-doing. Nothing here puts the murderer on the same level as the saint. Anyone who still thinks so has merely read, but not studied, these words. The triumph of evil is only a seeming triumph, for it is a limited power. If the sinner were *compelled* to commit sin by the divine plan or the divine will, if he consequently were to think that he could perpetrate any crime because it is God ordained, then the foundations of morality would collapse and the belief that we are free to choose between righteousness and wrongdoing would become illusory. This would be inconsistent with the ethical teaching of all great prophets.

Although at the level and from the standpoint of ultimate reality, the infinite wisdom and love reign supreme, if we descend to the level and standpoint of the phenomenal world, we have to admit the existence of malignant entities and hostile forces which thrive on hatred and wrongdoing, on falsity and evil. We are here only in the world of appearance, yes! but to creatures whose perceptions are limited to that world these are terrible realities, whose interferences we must fight and whose solicitations we must resist.

Philosophy does not deny evil's existence but only its absoluteness. Philosophical ethics always oppose it but at the same time point out its relativity. We are never at any time under a necessity to do evil and may only at certain times let it be done to us. And when philosophical knowledge teaches us that it is a form of error, we inevitably seek to do good always, however lamentably we may fail occasionally. It is a fallacy to think that because all is perfect in the World-Mind, it is consequently perfect for human beings. To the divine wisdom, the evil in the universal movement is something which flows out of the very nature of separative existence, for that eventually takes the shape of aggressive self-assertion. The man who can rise to this understanding is not thereby exempted from his human responsibilities, nor granted permission either to proclaim every happening as *equally* divinely willed or to forsake his personal duty of resisting mental evil. Because it is said that the evil in man is due to his ignorance and consequent misplacement of forces which are not evil in themselves, such as intellect, energy, and emotion, let this not be mistaken to mean that the presence of evil is consequently to be denied. On the contrary, because it is a feature which transforms life into an arena of unending conflict, it should specifically be acknowledged, faced, prepared for and struggled against. It is not a contradiction to struggle sternly and unceasingly against evil in practical life while at the same time philosophically recognizing the part it unwittingly plays in the World-Idea.

A man may never come to understand why things should be as they are; he may have to leave the riddle an unsolved one, but this need not interfere with his practical attitude. Evil develops his moral muscles each time it is resisted and overcome. Nothing in philosophy should encourage any wrongdoer in the continuance of his misguided course. On the contrary, he is warned that suffering awaits him and that there will be no peace for him until he repents. The recognition of divine will back of things does not and must not be allowed to lead anyone into an irresponsible attitude toward life and a lethargic tendency in conduct. When destructive thoughts have overwhelmed a man's feeling and obsessed his mind to the extent of making him injurious to his fellows, it is a proper duty of society to defend itself by taking preventive measures against him. The pessimistic outlook which stifles initiative, acquiesces in immorality, and bids tormented men be contented with their lot, may serve to confirm their tormentors in their own wrongdoing. Thus it may promote crime and increase the world's evil.

The attitude of fatalistic resignation to evil events because they are believed to be the expression of God's will, is sometimes a heroic one but sometimes a cowardly one, sometimes wise but sometimes foolish. A proper judgment would require a knowledge of the invisible factors as well as the visible ones involved in each particular case. The attribution to God's will does not in any way shift the responsibility which properly belongs to human endeavor. The fallacy here is to make man the doer of actions and yet saddle God with the responsibility for them. It rises from confusion of thought. Only after we study evil from the religious, metaphysical, and mystical standpoints combined, after philosophy illumines this confusion by its penetrating analysis, can we get really clear ideas about it. In the result, it advises the aspirant to accept evil metaphysically but to resist it practically. He has to do the one because of the divine origin of the cosmos and the other because of the imperfect state of humanity. From the practical standpoint there is no alternative but to see evil as evil or as ignorance and deal with it as such.

The outlook which would ignore the evil in men and gloss over their wicked deeds by pretending a large angelic charity is unphilosophical. Although not less charitable, philosophy does not buy its virtues at the cost of losing its balance and shutting one eye. It prefers to stand on both legs and open both eyes. It acknowledges the good in men as part of the same picture as the bad in men. Because it understands, it never condemns.

In the realm of conduct, evil is no metaphysical illusion but a practical fact. We find it here in our midst every day and have to deal with it as best we can. We cannot reconcile ourselves to it, much less collaborate with it. We should always remember that metaphysical reconciliation to the presence of evil is not the same as practical resignation to it. We see that it is an inevitable accompaniment of the earlier phases of personality in the universe, but we should also see that it is only a temporary accompaniment. It may be there, but we do not have to co-operate with it not submit to it. If we understand its limitation, it need shake neither our faith nor our nerve.

Thus there are plenty of reasons why would-be philosophers, as well as laymen, should strive to overcome evil by personal example and thus try to elevate the character of mankind. It is true therefore that the practice of nonresistance might so surprise the evil-doer as to disarm him of his wrong outer attitude. That would be well. But it could happen only in certain cases. In most cases it would tend to produce the same effect upon his inner attitude, his conscience, but that would be very slight and quite subconscious.

It was said in *The Wisdom of the Overself* that the most excessive form of the animalistic evil in humanity is being brought like scum to the surface during the present epoch, in order to remove it more easily. All the selfish killing tendencies, the violence and greed, the hate and spite, the anger and suspicion, the resentment and revenge which have had their worst manifestations in the two world wars, find in the tremendous explosive force of atomic bombs their final expression. Beyond such murderous violence mankind cannot farther descend. Humanity's blind adherence to its animalistic fighting and killing propensities manifests itself in two terrible deeds—the avoidable taking of men's lives in war and the needless taking of animals' lives in peace.

We need not ignore the evil in our fellow men, for we have to deal with them in a practical world, neither should we ignore the soul working silently within them. The evil will go eventually; the good will remain permanently. If we have to enter into relation with them, we must perceive what is wrong in them but we should do so impersonally without ill feeling. The human weakness which returns one wrong for another, which seeks to retaliate or to revenge itself against the wrongdoer, is unacceptable. We must do what social responsibility calls upon us to do in such a case. But we should not sully ourselves with lower deeds.

Now should we ever indulge in the useless but common habit of condemning those who have committed offenses against us. Jesus has explained one reason for this counsel:

"Father, forgive them for they know not what they do." And Epictetus has pointed out how the man who cultivates his power of looking beneath appearances, will not find fault with others. Their evil conduct rises out of the imperfections and limitations in their psyche, out of its unbalanced or undeveloped condition. They cannot help doing what they do because they cannot help being what they are. And this in turn is the inheritance of all their past experience, all their past thought. Time will teach them. Life will instruct them. Suffering will drive the poison out of their system. The law of recompense will take them in hand and discipline them. When they become acutely aware of the mischief wrought to other lives and the harm wrought in their own, they become truly penitent and more discerning. This requires much time and many births. Meanwhile, we humans may learn to forgive what life itself may sometimes forgive. There would be little hope for humanity's eventual escape from the thralldom of evil, if God's grace did not enter into its evolutionary life at some point or through some blessed man. And this does happen, bringing redemption, liberation, and illumination. There is love at the heart of things. There is forgiveness for repentant man. There is forgetfulness for his forsworn sins, but only to the extent that their causes within his character are removed.

The merciful remission of sins, the compassionate granting of pardon is a fact in the relations between human beings themselves. How much more should it be a fact in their Divine Father's relations with them! Forgiveness of sins is a fact, not merely a hope, but it is a fact only for those who learn and apply the lessons of their sufferings. The others must bear the consequences of their wrong conduct, otherwise karma, the law of recompense, would be an erratic and unreliable law and the experiences it brings would be valueless. This remission does not become operative until after the repentance of sins and the actuality of reform. The belief that he too, depraved sinner though he has been, may also expect forgiveness and attain to goodness, is a true one even for the worst of men, if only he becomes deeply repentant and changes ignorant living habits, character, and conduct.

The law of recompense (karma) is not a vindictive one. It does not, as some believe, express the Hebraic "eye for an eye, tooth for a tooth." If it did there would be no hope that humanity could expiate its dark karma or escape from the tangled web which it wove around itself in the past. The actuality is that as soon as it comes to the full understanding and deep conviction that wrongdoing must be abandoned and as soon as its character, conscience, intelligence, and balance are sufficiently developed, it frees itself from the consequences of its mistaken past. In other words by changing itself, its mentality and its feelings it creates a new and powerful cause, while the law itself produces the new effect of that cause, which is to bring an end to the dark karma inherited from its ignorant past. In this sense there is a forgiveness of its sins, which is a different sense from the merely sentimental form of wishful thinking that, in religious circles, misuses the idea of forgiveness.

The forgiveness of some sins does not mean with ordinary humanity the forgiveness of all sins. The past cannot be totally wiped out, even when its legacy can be modified. With the aspirant, forgiveness applies only to a specific sin or a specific group of sins. With the adept, it applies to the totality of all his sins. For the first is still carrying his unfulfilled self-earned recompense entwined round his neck, because he is still carrying his ego. But the second is liberated from the burden because he is liberated from its hidden core, the ego.

In dealing with those people who have fallen victims to the suggestion of malevolent forces, whether continuously or intermittently, we must remember not to condemn, resent, or hate. We all carry a load of wrongdoing out of the far past yet we are always ready to seek forgiveness of this heavy recompense. If we are not ourselves prepared to forgive those who wrong us, we have no right to expect the remission of our own sins. This in fact is a spiritual law. All those who seek forgiveness for themselves, should follow the rule of forgiveness in their dealing with others. Every time they have to endure hatred from men, they are given the chance to learn good will toward men. Where others find only poison, they are to find its antidote.

But these are not the only grounds for such an attitude. There is another and one not less solid. Each man's thought contributes its little mite to the world's store, makes it better or worse. He is responsible for his own thoughts and if he is on the spiritual path he must try to keep them constructive, positive, and harmonious, not destructive, negative, and discordant. Darkness has no positive existence in itself. It is simply the lack of light. Just so, ignorance is simply the lack of knowledge and evil is simply the lack of good. And just as the only way to get rid of darkness is to bring a light into it, whether by switching on a lamp or opening a window, so the only way to remove evil from the world's thinking and eliminate the ignorance that promotes it, is to bring more good thought and spread more spiritual knowledge in the world.

As man unfolds his diviner characteristics, he sheds his grosser ones. By his own labors in self-improvement, he prepares the way for the entry of God's redemptive grace. When he discovers his real self, whose first attributes are love and wisdom, he discards evil and error. In the moment that he casts aside the shrouds of ignorance, he sees through the evil values and turns to the good ones. To know himself fully, he will have to know himself as a ray of the divine sun, shedding light and expressing goodness. To understand evil fully, he will have to love the pure truth rather than pleasant illusions. And then that same evil which was formerly a dark and tragic riddle to his lower perceptions, vanishes as such before his higher ones and becomes transmuted.

This quiet confidence in the ultimate goodness of the universe is based on a finer perception and is not to be mistaken for the unbalanced optimism that is based on a boisterous emotionalism. Man is himself led to reflect it through spiritual guidance by revelation from without and by intuition from within. This helps his evolution toward it but does not guarantee it. For that look to one fact alone—the presence in every heart of the Overself, whose patience will outlast a thousand reincarnations of denial, whose power will master all animal impulse and calculating worldliness in the end, whose magnetism will draw him irresistibly through countless pains and raptures, for it is Love itself.

There is an Idea implicit in the very orderliness of the cosmos. Science has begun to get some dim glimpses of little fragments of this plan. The last value of science is its revelation of the presence of law in the cosmos. For law presupposes mind and infers intelligence. Even so far as man's present knowledge of the laws of nature extends, some kind of unifying mind is evidenced behind them. That it is not indifferent to his development is also evidenced.

Nothing and no one has ever been, could ever be, outside the Infinite Being's infinite field of awareness. Moreover, no event could ever happen except within its infinite field of law.

If all men knew how much perfect wisdom, intelligence, and orderliness have gone into the cosmos, all would fall on their knees every day in deepest reverence before the Power behind it. Let us derive from every intuited fact the firm assurance that a divine law holds all the processes of the universe in its power, and a divine mind exists behind all the innumerable human minds and is their source and goal.

If anyone sees only a universe governed by blind chance that is only because his own eyes are myopic. It was Remy de

Gourmont, a distinguished French literary critic who wrote: "Truth is an illusion, and illusion is truth. Humanity has never lived except in error, and besides there is no truth, since the world is in perpetual change. If you succeed in building up a true image of the world, it will cease to be true to your grandchildren." If de Gourmont had addressed his words to those metaphysicians who acknowledge no higher guide than what the intellect can ascertain, they would have been correct enough. But his overanalytical mind inevitably missed the one fact that defies all analysis, the fact that there is a hidden reality which manifests its existence—although not its nature—through the world's appearance, *and an eternal law which governs these endless changes.*

We learn from philosophy that the life of the whole universe, no less than the life of every man, is ruled by order and not by accident, by law and not by chance, by intelligence and not by senselessness. There is an intelligent direction behind every phenomenon of life and Nature in this cosmos. There is no event, no creature, nothing in the whole universe which is without significance. This is so and must be so because the whole universe is the thought of infinite Mind. Everywhere and always the universal intelligence is ever present, unceasingly working. Nature's laws are really its laws. And this still holds true even where man's limited power of sight sees fault because of the presence of evil and death. The chaos and confusion, accident and chance, the pain and misery in human existence are only passing appearance, not durable reality. Even where we cannot know or see, as is mostly the case, we may believe with confidence that a higher power is activating the world process for what will ultimately prove to be the best interests of all creatures and things within it. To the persevering student of philosophy all the pieces of this mosaic pattern which individually seem so meaningless and unrelated, gradually fall into place and reveal the wonderful significance of the whole. There is wisdom and goodness at the heart of things, and we may walk with faith even when sight is denied us.

The divine Idea is the outcome of divine wisdom and perfect understanding. Therefore it is the best possible one. And it could not have been other than it is without the divine Mind being other than it is. The universe too cannot be other than the best possible one. If we fail to perceive this, we fail because finite mentality cannot comprehend infinite existence. If, in this matter, we begin by doubting the wisdom of God, we shall have to end by accepting it. Such conscious acceptance of the divine order of things does not come easily to most men. Indeed, it comes only long after their reason has first complained and their emotion has first rebelled against it. The ego must first be laved with grace before it will submit and accept. Even in its spiritual aspiration, it is forever looking for quick results; the higher self, for durable ones. Hence, the eternal patience with which that self gazes down on its offspring's sufferings and waits for its reclamation. Many may deplore this awe-inspiring patience. Yet in no other way can it really promote and guarantee the genuineness of the ego's evolution. For every upward step the latter takes will then be a spontaneous one, elicited from within itself by its own experience and observation. Its growth will not be artificial and dubious but natural and sure. The ego has the right and freedom to make its own mistakes and involve itself in consequential suffering, because it must become thoroughly integrated with its parent-self by a process as natural as the seed becomes a tree.

It is not for weaklings or cowards to take such an impersonal view of the universe, to see its Idea as wise and its processes as good. A man must call up the hero within himself to be able to do this. The heroic attitude is indeed the price he has to pay for truth, that truth which brings peace in its train. He who takes such a long-range view, he who formulates such a large-based conception of existence, will never yield to despair over mankind's present misery or contemporary darkness, chaotic unrest, and seething tumult. *He knows that holy forces will interpose themselves more and more into their history, despite all temporary lapses or partial retrogressions.* For everything and everyone dwells inescapably within the principle of beneficent being.

Bitter and brutal experiences will not be glossed over, for he may not try to shut his eyes to the evil forces and chaotic morality, to the tragedy and degeneration in the world around him. Indeed, he will see them even more clearly and more alertly for what they are than other men, because he will see down to their very roots in human nature. He will never pretend with the softer idealists that they are not there. Yet the consciousness of these harsh realities can never intimidate him or disillusion him. He knows that they will one day arouse more men to seek for the only power by which they may be overcome, and meanwhile, until they are so wakened, he himself must hold aloft his own guttering candle of inward light. This is his responsibility and he will not retreat from it. This is what he can do for humanity and he will certainly do it.

The ugly side of life need not be ignored, as some mystics and yogis in the East and certain cults in the West ignore it. Such evasion of its existence is either a moral cowardice or an emotional narcotic or an intellectual befuddlement. Philosophy faces this side, with all its evils and horrors, and does not deny it. But neither does it accept it.

Let those who wish serve humanity by the means within their power, let those who can seek to distribute the spiritual waters of life and the material bread of man. But, this said, let none of them fall into gross error of believing that the laws of the universe are all wrong, that the powers of evil are almighty, and that unless they personally interfere with the course of events the outcome will be most deplorable. This is not so. The universe will still carry on, whatever they do. Its administration is still in capable and beneficent hands. God is still the Supreme Authority and does not require or ask anyone's help.

The vague feeling that, despite all the suffering and sin, the outcome of this drama of the human race will, in the end be a blessed and happy one is correct. Where today we see evil in a man, an event, or a place, it is rather the absence of good, just as cold is the absence of heat. For the good rightfully belongs to the inner nature of things, and can never permanently vanish. The surest guarantee that good is destined to triumph, however deferred the hour of that triumph may seem to us, is to be found among the attributes of the Power which sustains all existence. One of these attributes, as sensed by all mystics who have approached the divine, is love. To know, to feel, or believe this is to know, feel, or believe immovably in the ultimate rightness and beneficence of things. The philosophical mystic affirms that hatred is not a permanent reality but only the temporary absence of love, and just as darkness vanishes when light appears, so will these negative emotions vanish when evolution forces men to waken and admit the love which is inherent in their deeper self, the Overself. The philosophic conception of life sees in the presence of a divine soul in man the further guarantee that his feeling nature will one day experience such true happiness that his intelligence will know and understand it, and that his character will finally evolve into a state of truth, goodness, and beauty. That is why it is exempt from the melancholy experience of an H. G. Wells who had to replace in old age his earlier tremendous "scientific" optimism about humanity's future by an equally tremendous "scientific" pessimism.

Earthly experience is not an instrument of human torment but a device for human education. Its lower values are transmuted by time into higher ones, its evil values into good ones. The immense multitude of human beings which has passed in procession over the face of this turning globe for unknown millions of years, has not passed in vain. The mysterious laws of this cosmos will not and cannot allow an ultimate triumph of forces or entities which violate their inward essential beneficence. If the appearance of individual evil is an ordained phase of human development, the liquidation of individual evil is equally ordained to succeed it. This is the paradox, that although evil is present everywhere, it will prevail nowhere. Analysis of what it is shows it to be a set of values and qualities, not an eternal principle. That a cosmos divinely born and divinely sustained should illogically contain such evil qualities, is something not to be understood at first thought or judged at first glance. Instead of seeking their origin in the universe without, we ought to seek their origin in our own consciousness, within. For they represent a corruption of human values, an alienation from the higher self, and a misdirection of free will.

The evil man writes in water, the evil being is a track in the sand. For the destiny of the one is to be transformed, and of the other to be forgotten. Somewhere in the exercise of human free choice, a cycle of sinful thought, feeling, and action came into being. But as it had a beginning, so shall it have an ending. Since it starts afresh in each individual, it ends there, not in the species. The sinful kingdom of hell is within us. The sinless kingdom of heaven must therefore be found by each for himself, and it must be found within himself. That sinners may one day become saints, that the evil life may one day be transmuted into the good, is not only a possibility we must admit but also a truth we must recognize.

If the present situation of humanity depresses us and if the prospect of its future situation frightens us, still we must not desert our belief in the eventual triumph of right over wrong and in the eventual destruction of the forces of destruction. We are not merely to believe this because we wish it to be so but because it is so. We must never forget that the advances and victories of the dark powers are only illusory; they seem to be real but they are not real. If there is evil in the universe, nevertheless the universe itself is good. If ordinary men have to look to the far-off future for the transformation of the darkness of the one into the light of the other, the sage finds the light *here* and *now*. He sees the menace and danger of our time for what it is, but he knows that he will be as secure later as he is now, because he, the true self, cannot be touched, cannot be reached by any menace or any danger, but dwells beyond them. The universe which he sees is ever shining. His higher consciousness has put such a different aspect upon it that he is reconciled to it as it is today, and not only as it will be one day. He knows well enough that if so many of the creatures within the universe have to pass through an evil phase, the Supreme Being behind the universe never does. Insofar as he has brought his own mind into harmony and unity with good, he perceives how it will forever be more than evil.

Thus in the end every man will have to solve the baffling problem of evil for himself. Nobody else can solve it for him, for he must penetrate to the very depths of his own consciousness, those mystical depths where the Overself resides, before he can possess himself of its true solution.

The true philosopher is conscious of one fact, taught him perennially by his Overself, that truth will triumph in the end, that good will outlast evil, that tolerance and kindness will overcome persecuting cruelty and that the spiritual tendencies will outlive, outweary the materialistic ones. If the realization of these things is not for his time, if they are hidden in futurity, he learns to acquire Nature's patience. If the earlier development of the human entity seems to necessitate the bringing of evil to the surface of its life, the further development equally necessitates the banishing of this evil from its life.

Even within the next two or three millenniums civilization will shed so many of its evil characteristics, including wars, and acquire so many finer ones, that it will be blessed by a veritable new and joyous epoch in comparison with its present state. Just as the dinosaurus and other reptilian monsters died out when the planetary conditions had nothing further to express in that way, so the tiger and the vulture will die out at the same time outside man as Nature and inside him as passion and greed. Just as every night is followed by a dawn, so the dark period of materialism which now is culminating with its worst features will be followed, first by a short transition, then by a dawn period when the bright rays of a better age for man will manifest themselves.

CHAPTER IX

GOD IS !

WHAT CAN BE WRITTEN in these pages possesses its own importance, but what must perforce be left unwritten is of even greater importance. Since so many of the foregoing statements depend on the single affirmation of God's existence, and would fall down with the unreality of that existence, it becomes needful to speak a few words on behalf of the Speechless.

If, as Bacon says, anyone merely scratches the surface of philosophy he may become an atheist. But if he digs a deep shaft into it he will become completely convinced of God's existence. Since a crystal, a flower, and a human body all follow the same law of development by stages, and since these stages and their forms show an intelligence behind them infinitely beyond that of man's, he who denies its existence is emotionally prejudiced rather than intellectually penetrative. If he could consider without such prejudice and deeply enough the nature and usefulness of the four seasons, the creative power of the sun, and the travels of the planets, he would have to add law to this intelligent rulership of the universe. There is no chance in all these things. If anyone considers all the evidence of intention of life here and on the stars out there, and fails to come to the belief that a higher power directs all, if he comes only to atheism, it is because the mind with which he considers this evidence is already closed by bias or ill-balanced by emotion or upset by suffering or too extraverted by the body's senses or faulty in some other way.

The world is not bereft, like a corpse, of life and sense. It has both. There is within and behind every bit of it, even when undiscerned by us, a directing Mind, a governing spiritual principle. This everywhere-present principle of life and the creative cosmic power are one and the same—God. In both stars and men we see the sign or evidence of its incomparable intelligence and unbelievable omnipotence. Its laws are ever present but human sense knows them only by the effects they produce in this world of form, time, and space. If the universe were quite lawless, if universal events and movements, such as the sun's rising and the seed's growth, happened in a merely haphazard way, it could hardly go on with its existence. Even those microscopically tiny organisms we call cells, out of which plant, animal, and human bodies are built up, contain latently and will develop eventually the mentality and characteristics of man himself. And this they will do in conformity with a perfect pattern, by orderly stages and through millions of rebirths.

Nothing that has happened in the world's history could ever have happened except by the ulimate sanction of the will and wisdom of the Universal Mind. Without this key to guide the reason, human thought would have to attribute what happens to mere chance. The universe would then seem senseless, fortune appear grossly unjust, and living itself mere folly. Life in every kingdom of Nature would then indeed be the play of brute, mechanical, and blind forces, as the materialist thinks. But with this key we can discern amid all this chaotic turmoil, that there is a divine purpose behind human existence, a rational order within the universe itself, and a beneficent Mind as the real ruler of both. With it we can find some meaning in all existence and still more in human existence. This will no longer look like an insignificant speck of transient foam on the ocean but rather like the first faint glow of an eternal light.

Let no one impugn the infinite wisdom of the universal Mind merely because it is beyond his finite understanding or because evil and pain anger him. Could such a one have predicted, after seeing under a microscope and without prior knowledge, the minute piece of protoplasmic jelly, that it would grow into an adult man possessed of the capacity to think, to love, and to worship? Yet every plant, every living animal shows forth the presence of cosmic intelligence in the progressive stages from seed to flower, from fetus to full-size creature. These stages are too wisely and obviously organized with and for the end in view to be the result of mere chance. The evolutionary process is as inevitable, however slow, as the sun's return. Nothing is, or is to be, left out, for every atom is alive and has the germ of self-consciousness. The old sharp division between dead inert matter and living active cells is out-of-date and dissolving in the new knowledge of electronics. There is no energy anywhere and no object which is not in essence a form under which the World-Mind's Life Current appears. The material of our fleshly robes was once mineral, later plant and animal, and is now human. Man's body is Nature's crucible; his thought, her transmuting power. Unfoldment from the physical to the spiritual states necessitates passage through these three kingdoms, through different planets and through the human form, where the fires of self-consciousness lit in prior evolutions work their wondrous magic. Even more, just as the cells in his body are affected by what he does to and with it as well as by what he thinks mentally and feels emotionally, so man himself is affected by what the planet is doing to him. For it has its own individual goal toward which it is evolving, and because of which it slowly or abruptly changes the conditions for the living forms in all kingdoms dwelling on and in its body.

The life-force in man could not have expressed human intelligence if there were not universal intelligence behind it, nor human spirituality if there were not a universal spirit to prompt it. A leading British biologist, Sir J. Arthur Thomson, affirms, "After a long circuit there is a return to the old truth: in the beginning was Mind." As the philosophic seeker's knowledge increases so his religious worship intensifies. He becomes more and more convinced of the ever-presence of infinite wisdom in the universe, more and more lost in contemplation of the wonder of its infinite life. It was not metaphysical theories or visionary dreams or mystic intuitions or pious feelings but personal first-hand practical observations which forced Professor Geley, the brilliant French physiologist, to exclaim: "Doesn't this whole conglomeration of facts, brought to our attention by different scientists, give proof of the extraordinary, amazing, incomprehensible, I would say, miraculous, *intelligence* of Life?"

No man has ever shown the same degree of intelligence and artistry which Nature shows. The technical skill which has gone into the building of the human body is something to be wondered at, first in awe and then in reverence. Whoso calls this skill "blind force" and does not perceive the living intelligence behind it, thereby reveals his own intellectual blindness. The infinite intelligence reveals itself on every side to seeing eyes and thoughtful minds. Medically trained men need never have become the agnostics and atheists so many of them formerly became if they had observed more intuitively the numerous signs of a supervising higher force in the birth of the human body, the evolution of the human fetus, and the activities of the human blood. They had no right to assume, for instance, that because the involuntary events which occur in the nervous system lie outside the field of personal awareness, they must therefore lie outside the field of all possible awareness. The reactions to danger; the reflexes and movements such as gland secretion and stomach digestion, which are supposed to occur in the world of mechanism; the automatic workings of internal organs (like the heart) which maintain the body; the activity which tries to repair internal and external injuries—all these are manifestations of a rational directing intelligence within the body itself. Countless, complex blood cells are born, mature, and soon die in every human being. They live active, purposeful lives. Yet each is unaware that there is a common entity called man behind the whole group, just as he himself is never aware of the processes whereby the white and red corpuscles of the blood carry on their work. So mind contains physical awareness but may not be limited only to one kind of it.

Why is it that plants find their nourishment, animals their food, and man his subsistence and clothes—all out of the body of this planet? Why is it that Nature provides so unerringly for their needs? The answer is that Intelligent Mind is the underlying basis of everything, the activating force of the universal event. Only when this idea has been thought through on every level does it become clear enough, its importance vivid enough, and its implications visible enough. It leads directly to two other ideas.

First, the World-Mind is the origin of all existence. Just as it is in the very nature of the sun to radiate light, so it is in its very nature to manifest the cosmos. Second, all things have God as their essence but no thing reveals God as the essence. The immensity of the universe is unimaginable. Our earth, despite its continents and oceans, is less than an atom against that astounding vastness. Yet we come closer to the truth when we understand that although the entire cosmos is an inevitable expression of the World-Mind, it is still a most limited expression.

We may be assured of this—whatever those unreliable witnesses, our senses, and that erratic pupil, our intellect, may say to the contrary—that there is a cosmic order, a hidden Idea behind the world process. But we, too, are parts of this order, this process. Hence the Idea exists within us also as the divine soul.

What the senses tell us about the world is always reversed by what the soul tells us. The senses tell us that their experience is real, but the soul tells us it is illusion. The senses tell us that we are nothing but bodies; the soul tells us that there is something godlike in each of us. The senses tell us that things happen by the accident of chance; the soul tells us that things happen by the wisdom of God.

The World-Mind is all-conscious, all-knowing, and all-present. It is impossible for man to know all the truth about any single fact, only this Mind can do that. Nor can any human being ever comprehend all the particulars of past and future as it can comprehend them. All possible kinds of existence are grasped together by the World-Mind. Thus its consciousness is truly cosmic in a way no finite consciousness could ever be. All points in space and all moments in time are held within the World-Mind. Such an infinite capacity of experience is utterly beyond the immediate comprehension of the finite human intellect.

And yet men everywhere try to drag God down to their own littleness! They have attached their dubious and false imaginations to the word, or used it in different senses. The meaning here assigned to it is that of a supreme imperishable Power which is both in the world (and hence in us) and yet transcends the world.

What is that Power? Is it a Thing or a Person? It is neither, and those who think otherwise are deceiving themselves. Philosophy holds that Mind is this one ultimate reality. God is Mind, and is everywhere. Only an impersonal Mind could be everywhere present in such a boundless cosmos, sustaining every kind of personal life as it does. God's creatures could not be other than personalized; but God Itself could not be. If it were, then the planets would not rotate under universal law but under personal whim.

Last century's scientists, in their cold scorn of emotional conceptions, called an anthropomorphic God what religionists in their genuine need of inner comfort, called a personal God. By such an anthropomorphic Deity was meant an outside power which is completely apart from man himself and to which he ascribes somewhat similar, although greatly enlarged, attributes to those he himself possesses. It has been his common error to father his own higher—and even sometimes lower—emotional attributes upon God, and then forget that they are still human attributes which could not possibly belong to the one, infinite, omniscient, and universal Mind. This error arose because he could not worship such an impalpable and impersonal God, could not even grasp intellectually the concept of It. So religion allowed him, either as a concession to his incapacity or as a dogma of its own actual belief, to worship It in forms whose existence was easily brought within the sensual imagination or the intellectual grasp. It was easier for both to present him with a conception of Deity which merely enlarged his own human self and reduced his limitations, because the thing which he knew best was his ordinary self.

The demand for a personal God is really the instinctive attempt of the personal ego to drag God down to its own level, the natural longing of the human entity for a glorified human Comforter. Man is a person and feels the need of personal relationships. This is quite pardonable and proper in all his human activities, including his religious ones. But to introduce it into his attempt to penetrate metaphysically to the inmost secret of his link with the infinite power, is to remain in the nursery and to refuse to leave the elementary stage of the spiritual life. It is to insist on spelling over and over again the first words of wisdom in the school primer of life.

The suffering man may say hard things about the austere indifference of God, even about the puzzling and implacable cruelty of God, just as the happy man may say pleasant things about the gracious benevolence of God. Both men know nothing about the real nature of God and are merely investing impersonal being with personal human attributes enlarged to a cosmic scale. It is a God made in their own image. All our reproaches upon God for having made this or that faulty part of the universe, or having permitted this sin or that misery are based upon our primal error in thinking of God as a man. A humanized God is no God at all. Men can more easily understand the concept of a Deity who is somewhat like them, who is capricious, temperamental, revengeful, and biased, who is open to, and desirous of, flattery. They cannot so readily understand the concept of a Deity who is too impersonal to be affected by such personal approaches, too impalpable to be reached by ornate pageants.

Wherever and whenever these pages have criticized the dogma of a personal God, they have done so with the thought in mind of the glorified and magnified man, of the arbitrary, jealous, revengeful, unfair creature who is to be flattered by praises or swayed by fears. The power sustaining the cosmos, the mind behind it, is infinite, ultimate, and eternal. How can it ever be personal, when a person may think of objects outside himself whereas such a power could never do so? The glorified man of exoteric religion is a finite God, whereas this absolute being of esoteric philosophy is an infinite one.

Yet those who passionately believe in a personal God have an uncriticizable basis for their criticizable belief: those who fervently feel His presence are not mistaken in their experience. That basis is the Overself, the root of that feeling is the Overself too. To think of the One Infinite Life-Power as the All, is to think of God; to think of it as oneself, is to think of the ego; to think of it as that in which the three states of waking dream and deep sleep merge, is to think of the transcendental Overself.

Just as man feels an ego within himself, so this personal ego in exalted moments may feel a living Entity behind and within it. In that sense only is this Entity its personal God. It was to this Entity that Jesus addressed the opening sentence of the Sermon on the Mount, "Our Father, which art in Heaven." The word Father indicates and expresses some kind of a personal relationship here. This is therefore the paradox, God is both personal and impersonal, appearing in their own minds as the former to those who need him as such, but being the latter in essence.

So long as man looks for a God made in his own image, he never finds God in reality. The human mind creates its own gods. They are in the end only its own conceptions, but behind them all still exists the reality on which they are based. Growing intelligence and evolving ethics yield an ever higher idea of God.

Until man can realize within his own consciousness his nearness to God, whatever idea he forms of God will be a useful help, if not a practical necessity, to inspire his efforts, influence his motives, and guide his attitudes. He must love this Idea if one day he is to love that which is beyond all ideas, the Absolute which is beyond all relativity.

Sir Arthur Keith once complained that when he read the words "God is a Spirit infinite and eternal," no visual image appeared in his mind, and that when he heard the words "the Holy Ghost" he tried in vain to grasp the mental image held by the clergyman who pronounced them. But how could an abstract conception assume pictorial form? How could imagination probe into mysteries where the senses can register nothing at all? Only the metaphysical faculty can even approach them, although it too cannot go far into them. And Sir Arthur Keith's complaint revealed his unfortunate deficiency in that faculty, his brilliant, one-sided scientific specialism limiting and trapping him.

In the very act of revealing its own existence through the universe, the World-Mind hides its own truth. When the Deity begins to look like any form we know or imagine, it is no longer Deity. When God begins to appear, he disappears. Every artistic picture, every verbal metaphor which may be used to represent the Real, only misrepresents it. Even the nearest and truest human conception—that of an utter emptiness, of formless Space—may easily be misunderstood. The "Supernal Empty," as Oriental mystics call it, is nothing more than a help to point the mind in the right direction. Every symbol is only a servant of the Divine. No servant should be mistaken for his master. Formerly it was hard to believe that the whole of this vast and varied cosmos could be traced back to a state of apparent no-thing-ness. Now atomic energy research has made it easy to believe that the Void may be the opposite of what it seems, may indeed be the Real. No scientist has ever seen a single atom, for his eyes are too feeble. But his delicate and ingenious electronic instruments are not. They tell him indirectly of the presence, and show him photographically the path, of tremendously dynamic and mysterious energies within the atomic structure where his senses report blank nonentity. In the attempt to relate the two together, he uses his powers of imagination to construct explanations and his powers of reflection to construct mathematical equations. To that extent and in that way he is forced to expand his outlook and become metaphysical.

Some may incline to doubt its existence, others may flatly

deny it, but no one will ever be able to strip the Infinite and Absolute Origin of its mystery. There are some truths which grow stale by reiteration but this is not one of them. It is the Unknown because it is the Alone, the Unique, the One without a second. There are not two realities, hence we read in the Bible "He is God; there is none else beside him." If the first cause of this world were itself born of something else then it would also be the second cause—a numerical reckoning which is mathematically impossible.

Men have only touched upon its appearances and never grasped its true and essential nature. To bow the head in confessed ignorance of the real nature of that Power is something which the greatest sage must do just as much as the most untutored savage. It is not only a dignified humility, it is also practical wisdom which makes him do this. He knows that even the best of human perceptions are too narrow to take in what must forever remain outside them, and therefore it is more profitable to apply them where they can hope to gain knowledge. It could not be what it is—unique in every way—if it could be directly known and brought within the range of personal experience.

We call the ultimate principle of all being MIND. We call the ultimate principle of this manifested world of things and creatures, the World-Mind. But whereas the first is beyond intellectual expression or reach, unique, unlimited, absolute, and ever still, the second exists in relations with the universe and with man. It is qualitatively describable, individual, and ever active. The word GOD to the philosopher means the first, to the theologian and mystic it means the second. MIND stands alone in its uniqueness, whereas the World-Mind is forever in relation with the world which is its product. The second is an aspect of the first, a timeless God in time and for a time, but MIND is a God forever out of time and space. Yet, except for human thinking about them, the two are not totally distinct entities.

We shall never understand the true intellectual concept of God unless we first understand the twofold nature of the divine Mystery. It is in its most abstract and most remote aspect, the immeasurable all-transcending Void, to which no attributes or qualities may be stated. Yet it is also, in its more concrete and nearer aspect, the animating everywhere-immanent Life and Mind of the universe. Thus God is both the No-thing and the Every-thing.

"I am that I am" was the answer God gave to Moses on Sinai when His name was asked. This phrase is puzzling until we see that it tries to say God is beyond telling, beyond description and definition. It really means: "I am the Unnameable!" "ı ᴀᴍ!" The declaratory answer which Moses received is the only positive statement about God that could be ever made; *God is!* All other statements must necessarily be expressed in negative terms, all others can only tell us what God is not.

Time and Salvation. Mind, the Godhead is beyond all thought and outside all imagination. We can have no correct conception of it other than the one we can form by analogy from our own human experience, the concept of endless time and boundless space and of a Mind coexistent with them. We ordinarily think of time by putting it into three separate compartments—past, present, and future. The common idea makes it a continuum, and pictures it under the form of a straight line, coming from the past, running through the present, and continuing into the future. The correct idea of time is a relativity and the correct picture of it is the circle. In a circle there is no absolute past, no absolute present, no absolute future: they will be entirely relative to the point which we take as the beginning. Again, a circle has no absolute beginning and no absolute ending; it is as relative as time is relative.

Everything from microscopic cell up through man to gigantic sun is following a preconceived pattern of this circuitous development rising spirally to ever higher levels. And this is true not only of its outer body but also of its inner life and consciousness. When the implications of the tenet of the beginningless and endless character of the cosmos are adequately understood, it will also be understood that our historical era of a paltry few thousand years is to be set against a prehistoric era of millions and millions of years. Because the planetary cycles which preceded our own have passed away under conditions of vast and destructive upheavals of Nature, their events have been forgotten and their records obliterated. Yet, we, in our ignorance and arrogance, continue to estimate evolutionary values on a most insufficient basis. The perplexing tale of time which is told us by those tear-stained records which so inadequately and imperfectly pass as history, perplexes us only because we do not know how man lived and thought and felt in the far past before that tale was written down. Even suns and stars will pass away: everything is ephemeral. Only that mysterious No-thing out of which they came, will remain. For God alone truly *is*.

The series of cosmic cycles is an endless one. The infinite Mind did not suddenly decide to become creative. It always was and always will be so. All the infinitude of this cosmos is a kind of mirror reflecting the infinitude of the Godhead whence it comes. All Nature is but a parable of the primeval reality which transcends it.

A cosmic Mind holds the thought of the world. We humans are part of that thought and, to a limited degree, somehow share in thinking it. The universe is an idea in God's mind. But it is also an idea being tried out in an infinite variety of ways for an infinite length of time. Each living entity is therefore different from every other entity—whether it is a plant in the ground or a human being on the ground. Consider that each face is individually shaped, that no two faces in the whole world are alike. In the whole of Nature there are no two things alike, no two beings alike, any more than there are two thumbprints alike in the whole gallery of human thumbprints. Is it not astonishing that, whereas the experience of every man who realizes his Overself, is identically the same, the entity he discovers differing in no way from that which all others discover, no two men have been formed by Nature from the same pattern? In body and mind, in physiology and faculty, in hand-palm and foot-sole, in emotion and thought, diversity rules the more than 2,000 million human entities on this earth! There is no form in Nature which exactly duplicates a second form, no happening which exactly duplicates a previous one. This shows how infinitely varied is the attempt of the Infinite Idea to express itself and its infinite existence through man and the world.

From the human standpoint the most important characteristic of the World-Mind is its creative ability. We see the infinite and boundless cosmos consisting of universes, galaxies, and solar systems coming into existence by its means. It has been explained in *The Wisdom of the Overself* how this creative ability is inherent in the very nature of the World-Mind. Both are in fact so inseparable that it constitutes an eternal and unchanging law. This creative ability is also the most important characteristic of the human being. It manifests in a variety of ways, whether through the half-blind act of self-reproduction or the fully conscious act of logical intellectual creation, whether in the inspirational production of an artist or the mechanical ingenuity of an inventor. The creative energy displays itself also in the human being's destiny which, for better or for worse, it is making every day. Whether he remains in darkness and ignorance or whether he enters into light, peace, and power, lies within each individual's own hands.

The manifestation of the cosmos recurs infinitely and eternally as a reflection of the infinite and eternal nature of World-Mind. The world is limited and finite whereas World-Mind is unlimited and infinite in nature. World-Mind could not do otherwise than fulfill the law of its own mysterious being. It unfolded a *hint* of its own infinitude in unfolding an infinite universe, and of its own timelessness in unfolding an eternal one. Hence we must not mistake the concept used in mathematics of a tedious and endless repetition of the finite for the true Infinite. It is not time's endless continuity but its utter absence that is the true eternal. Whoever imagines that the infinite is a grand mathematical totality to be reached by piling up one incredible dimension after another, errs. For all dimensions, all figures are concerned with measurable space or time. The true infinite is spaceless and timeless. Mind in its pure essence cannot be brought into the category of space because we cannot measure its dimensions, nor into the category of time because we cannot measure its duration.

World-Mind never loses any part of itself when it projects the universe. Nothing is really taken away from it and nothing is really added to it. This is because it is truly infinite. Through a universe of finite forms, the infinitely Formless can only hint at but never achieve adequate expression. Therefore there is nowhere where it is not and nowhere where it really is. This is a paradox. But if we want to get an intellectual understanding of World-Mind we are forced to think in paradoxes. Hence the various forms of this world contribute toward the form of the whole cosmos but cannot of themselves constitute it, for even their totality falls far short of it. The Infinity of all infinities has a value all its own, which transcends every possible gathering-up of lesser values —however complete it be.

Infinite Duration alone is real. The planet's circling movement and the clock's ticking changes merely measure time but do not make it. Waking time vanishes in dreams as though it were a mere nothing, for the events of a day are there lived through in a flash. The experience of time's succession is made for us by the mind; therefore time itself must be mental. We see objects distributed in space and experience events ordered in time. We do not know that our sense organs impose the particular nature of this experience because of the way they are themselves constructed, that our world-consciousness is entirely relative to them.

There is something terrifying to the ordinary, self-centered city-born and city-bred person in the thought of the procession of eternities moving endlessly through Infinite Duration. He finds it almost impossible to grasp the meaning of Infinite Duration and Infinite Space because he lives from moment to moment in a constant quest of movement and activity amid a curbed and circumscribed environment. The meaning dawns almost imperceptibly and quite naturally to a more mystical person who has been reared in immense desert spaces or vast open wildernesses, because the tremendous stillness and silence react upon him.

When the human mind will solve part of the hieroglyphic mystery which governs its own relation to time, it will solve, at the same instant, the linked mystery of religion. The Overself is not in time although it co-operates with the time-consciousness of its offspring—the person over whose existence it presides. That a part of the human being can exist simultaneously out of time, is a statement which is not intelligible to the human mind. It is unlikely that this idea can even begin to penetrate the consciousness of more than a few in our harassed age. It is hard to receive this truth that beneath the century's horrors and agonies, there is a divine life of bliss, serenity, love, and goodness. For the eyes cannot see its beauty, nor the ears hear its music, nor the hands touch its reality, nor the intellect easily reason out any relationship between the two orders of life.

Mind ever was and ever will be. The body is here today and gone tomorrow and those who foolishly insist on identifying themselves with it alone must change from day to day and finally perish along with it. But those who wisely identify themselves with Mind also, share in its infinitely continuous existence. What did Jesus mean when he said: "Before Abraham was, I am."? He meant that in identifying himself with the Christ self, his higher Self, his eternal Self, he identified himself with something that ever was and ever would be, with timeless and deathless being. He meant that those who could only personalize him, who could think of him only as the human Jesus immersed in time and dying with the body, could not understand and did not know him as he really was in his higher Self.

"*Now* is the day of Salvation," announced Paul the Christian Apostle who had never met Jesus the man, but who had met Christ the Overself that illumined the man. That salvation lies not only in the timed future but also in the timeless Now —which is not the same as the timeful present. It is gained by effort spread over the years, but its happy culmination is entered suddenly and effortlessly. At such a moment the entrant may well smile at himself as he comes to realize how his quest has been for something which he already possesses and has indeed always possessed. He comes to perceive that the timeless Now of what perpetually *is*, is somehow inexplicably related to the shifting "now" of what perpetually flows; that appearance is so sacramentally and so intimately in communion with reality that the two are, in their mysterious embrace, as one.

"I am all that is, that was, that will be." These words, reflecting the grandeur of Eternity meditating upon itself, were honored by the Egyptians, who carved them over the shrine of the temple of Sais. They were honored by Beethoven who wrote them on a card which he framed and kept always on the table whereon he composed his immortal music.

There is a valuable practical lesson to be drawn from these facts. Man should endeavor to gain a fuller view of life by gaining the viewpoint of this higher observer in addition to his present one. Such an alteration of standpoint would enable him not only to be an actor on the stage of life, as he is at present, but also a spectator. He would thus fulfill a double role, paradoxically and simultaneously being the observer of his world and the observer of the observer of his world! The first observer would react to his surroundings but the second would merely see the reactions. The first is the ego, the second the soul. The first is active in evolving through the pattern set for it by the second, and thus unwittingly points to the latter's real existence. Hence it is a salutary and necessary exercise for the aspirant to the philosopher's goal, the mystic's attainment, or the religious devotee's crown to practice constantly, taking up the disturbing, exciting, important, or joyful events of his life as they occur, and to regard them from a standpoint quite different from that which the unaspiring man habitually regards them. He should do so both impersonally and as if they already belonged to the past, as if they were mere memories only. He should aim at the serenity or security with which he is ordinarily able to regard only long bygone years. Let him remember and apply the mentalist doctrine that time is meaningless when taken away from the succession of his thoughts, that it is only an idea imposed upon his consciousness and that he may put forth antennae to the source of this idea, to that which itself is out of time. If he is to free himself from the domination of all time then he must necessarily free himself from the domination of the present too. What is required of him is to rise calmly—inwardly detached and sublimely poised—above its evanescence.

If this exercise in imaginatively converting the present into the past is done twice during the day, that will be enough to produce good fruit and yet not be enough to interfere with the day's duties. An essential point is that it should be begun abruptly; it should have the force of unexpectedness. One practical result will be to impart under all his habitual dwelling in time, the sense of an immense power tirelessly supporting and sustaining him from underneath. This victory over himself will help also to free him to some extent from the misleading rule of the ego. It will tend to exalt him above the distractions of his earthly existence and to fix his thoughts on a higher order of being altogether, where peace eternally reigns. Although this order seems so remote from him, it is nevertheless not beyond his reach. By setting his thought perseveringly in these attitudes and holding it steadily in their truth until its liberating significance permeates him thoroughly, little by little their tranquilizing effect will saturate his whole being. Playing the witness of his own life, he begins to find what inner peace really means. Then, if he joins the exercise to certain disciplines of the passions and denials of the body, he will cease to imagine that he lives only wholly in time, for the glimpses of his real self that will come to him will reveal that there is no time for it to live in.

The man who does not tire but carries this quest of the ego for the Egoless through to the end, discovers that while his body is acting busily in time, his mind is standing profoundly still in the eternal. This new awareness remains with him all his days. His experience tells him that this is the meaning of the *New Testament's* solemn declaration that "there shall be time no longer." So, being already in possession of the future he does not need to plan it. Having mounted on the step of the past to the platform of illumination, he does not care to descend to it again. Seeing the present like a dream, he does not let go of his wakefulness. Here he finds the healing Ever-Now, the liberating Ever-Free. Here time-bred cares are stilled and place-caged lives released. Here is happiness without external cause, love without persons, truth without thinking. Here is the native land whence all men first came and to which they still secretly belong.

The whole planet becomes an image to the man who understands. Its grand natural landscapes become an emblem of the divine beauty. Its heaving seas and flowing rivers become a reminder of the protean power of the One to assume every imaginable form as the Many. Its blue sky becomes a hint of the utter formlessness of the Absolute. Its ceaseless rotation of days and nights, seasons and years, suggests the eternity of the Overself. Thus earth, water, air, planetary and solar motion speak to him of That which transcends them.

God and Man. No one can measure the infinite power and no one can weigh it. No one can touch it with his hands or see it with his eyes. Yet something that emanates from it mysteriously takes form in and as our experience. This is the real reason why men in every age and land have given themselves the trouble, and imposed on themselves the sacrifice, of engaging in the quest of this power. The philosophic doctrine of the Being of God rests upon the solid foundation of the statements of those in East as well as West, in antiquity as well as modernity, who have succeeded in this quest and come closest to God. Its truth has been known to, and verified by, the wise, the mature, and the inspired of all periods in all parts of the world. What they have done and known points a path for all other men to do and know. It may be hard, it may call for many lifetimes of effort, but it is not their special prerogative alone. They stand out as symbols for the whole human race, telling us what we really are and whither we are really going. If people will turn to their writings and profit by their counsel and apply what they learn to their own lives, the result will be that instead of troubles destroying faith, they will deepen it.

Like millions of trees which are all rooted in one and the same earth, so millions of human minds are rooted in one and the same universal being. Everything and every creature that is in the universe owes its own being to the undifferentiated Being, Mind. If then we declare that there is something god-like immanent in all men, we are not guilty of declaring an absurdity. It is not enough for anyone to look at his body and say he has seen a man. He must look also into the mysterious depths of his mind. Just as the Ordered cannot come out of the Chaotic, so the Conscious cannot come out of the Unconscious. If the first truth means that the universe is divinely governed because its orderliness bespeaks divine ever-intelligence, the second truth means that man is divinely rooted because his awareness bespeaks divine all-knowingness. The last truth of human life, as of universal existence, is that it is merely the echo of a whisper uttered by the unique and unseen power—God. All that anyone can know of God is what he can find in himself, in his essence.

God is so interwoven with man that the two cannot possibly be separated. It is not only for entranced mystics but also for ordinary men that the poet Tennyson's phrase is true: "Closer is He than breathing, nearer than hands and feet." Every time they hear or see anything, touch, taste, or smell it; every time they remember or reason about it, it is in the mind that really does so. And this, when traced analytically to its ultimate character, is rooted in the universal basis of all experience and all thought, all life and all existence —God. Their sensations and thoughts may be associated with materialistic beliefs about the nature of mind, but this does not alter their own fundamental nonmaterialistic character. If they doubt the divine existence, they are able to do so only because they employ what is in reality a divine power! The internal thought of self and the external experience of the world could not arise if there were not this fundamental principle of Mind at their base. The very thinking power by which they deny God is itself a manifestation of God within their own selves. The denial is paradoxically possible only because God does exist. What they really deny is merely a creature of their own imagination. How forces which are themselves unintelligent can produce intelligent beings; how energies which are themselves blind can produce purposive ones: these are questions which such materialists cannot answer satisfactorily.

It is reasonable for a reasoning being like man to demand a reason for his own existence. But those who have been led by atheism into denial of their spiritual nature have been deluded. They mistake the mind's first exercise of its own power for its ultimate mature capacity. Without that capacity such men cannot be blamed if they come and tell us that the spirit is a delusive mirage. Yet we should not believe them. If that were true these pages would never have come into existence, for there would have been nothing about which to write. Nor would hundreds of mystics' writings rise out of the past to silence the error upon their lips. Hundreds more will yet rise out of the veiled future.

The question why man was suddenly endowed with soul at a certain stage of evolution is one for the religionists. Their statements created it so they must answer it. Mentalism does not consider he was ever without a soul. Wherever there is life there is mind. And life extends from the mineral upward through every kingdom of Nature. The birth and death, the coming and going of every individual creature within Nature is governed by a higher power with which it is inseparably linked. Generations of beings have followed one another like waves on the ocean. Whither? All this impressive movement of cosmic life, all this tremendous interaction of countless creatures on countless stars has but a single ultimate if unconscious direction: the rediscovery of self as living and having its being in God.

He who can truly think, in the profoundest sense of the word, comprehends that there must be one infinite source of all the universe, and of all the life in the universe, and of all the consciousness in that life. The troubles of suffering man rise ultimately from the fact that he has severed himself in faith and awareness from that source. When he no longer worships God, he worships his own little ego. His failure to connect the two makes him suffer from the antagonism of Nature. He imagines in his blindness that he stands self-sufficient—he does not see that the moment he tries to do this, he antagonizes the very power upon which he is dependent. This ignorance becomes insanity. His interest in life ends with the ego, which becomes the center of his universe. He misunderstands himself as well as his experiences. He is beset with troubles—many of them avoidable—all the way from birth to death, thus paying the heavy price of his disruption from the source of his own life and mind. In exalting his finite ego, in separating himself from its infinite source, he commits his greatest blunder and pursues one illusion after another.

Such is the condition of man today. Although the reality behind these illusions is all around and all within him, his relation to it is like that of a blind person to the glamorous luster of a row of pearls which lie in his own hands. The personal and physical ego comes to believe that it is all that there is in him, thus falling into the greatest of illusions, when all the time the Overself's life and consciousness are the root of its own existence and expression. It is this terrible fact of spiritual estrangement which is at the bottom of most human sin and misery. After all, how can there be peace for anyone if his lower nature still enslaves him, still disturbs his relations with others or disrupts his relations with his diviner self?

It is only the sun that can bear the fittest comparison with the Overself. It can never really be covered by darkness or brightened by another orb; and similarly the Overself is never really covered by the person's ignorance of it or brightened by the person's knowledge of it. The sun lights up everything else and thus makes every other object known; similarly truth is, as Sanskrit texts say, "That which when known, all else is known."

In the divine soul of every human being there is perfect peace and unalterable goodness, even when in the person there is a diseased body and a wicked mind. In the higher self there is always sweetness and love, even when in its projection there is sometimes avarice and hate. The feeling of man may surrender itself wholly to such evil passions but the innermost being of man never does. It remains inviolate. His thoughts may be overcome but his real self is untouched. The rule of evil pertains only to the level of transient appearances, not enduring realities. If we could pierce *deep* enough into a man's soul—however bad he is—we would find that he is fundamentally good. The basis of everyone's nature is goodness. Evil is just a thick layer of thoughts and tendencies superimposed upon it. The man he appears to be is one thing; the man he really is beneath it is another. Coordination of the two, as expressed in the statement, "I and my Father are one," brings harmony and happiness. With it the person enters the kingdom of heaven.

The whole orbit of man's life is haunted by a terrible contradiction. On the one side he sees that everything and everyone is fleeting and perishing. On the other he is pursued by the hope that life has something more hidden beneath its veil. He feels forever impelled to seek this More. The explanation is simple. Both sight and hope are true; each explains the other. For the world and man *are* finite manifestations of Infinite Being; consequently the part ultimately seeks its source as water seeks to rise to its own level.

How necessary to remember the fundamental principle and not lose sight of it amid all the pressing trials and personal burdens of today! How essential to remember, when contemporary events dishearten us, that in our innermost being there is the real, unaffected, serene, and sublime Overself! It requires our love and offers in return great benefits in peace, assurance, understanding, help, and strength. Even when, during the war, mankind was working out its bloodiest destiny the eternal Witness still enfolded it and there still existed within the hearts of all combatants That which is the essence of all pity—the blessed benign spiritual presence which shall ultimately redeem its prodigal children.

If the cosmos is in some fashion the expression of an infinitely wise Mind, it cannot be other than good in its central meaning and final outcome. For where is the wise man who is not also a good man? And if such a limited finite entity as the human is good at its best level, how much more beneficent must the unlimited infinite entity, God, be! In his highest perceptions of the universe, the mystical seer finds that the guiding idea behind it is a meaningful one, and that the guiding presence within it is a friendly one. He finds that neither he nor any other man is utterly alone. There is a divine presence which exists, knows, and cares. There is a Power, invisible and universal, immortal and original, ineffable and transcendental, which surrounds and supports everyone, through its representative in him—the Overself.

The masses are victims of this restless and troubled civilization and cannot read the real meaning of their lives, but the illumined seer, who sits with quiescent attitude of mind by the beautiful pool of his inner being, reads it in a flash. Philosophic awareness of humanity's corruption is always coupled with reassuring awareness of humanity's evolution; its sadness over widespread evil always mingled with its hopefulness over ultimate good. If it is excellent and even essential to ask the question, *What am I?* it is better still to add the question, *What am I in the world for?*

When we have seen the last city and toured the last country; when we have wandered the streets of every historic place and well-nigh circled this planet, then we shall still have perforce to return to the question: "What is the meaning of our life in this world?" The circumferential motion must cease for a while, the restless feet must halt. For the years have been largely wasted which have not been spent in traveling toward the true answers to these questions; which have been given wholly instead of partly to this earthen globe and not to the serious reflection why we were born upon it.

Unless we understand why we are here on earth at all, we

may blunder badly. We spend our energies wholly on physical needs or animal appetites, on social trivialities or evanescent amusements, on intellectual curiosity or futile aims; or on endless labors whose rewards are used only to gain these things. We spend and strive to gain a healthy body, a well-nourished body, a finely dressed body. This is good but are these goals ends in themselves? Will the clothes, the food, and the stamina always keep us from stupid mistaken or criminal courses that end in sorrow or disaster?

We are not here for the body's sake alone but much more for the soul's sake. We have to feed, clothe, and shelter the body only that it may be instrumental in the attainment of the diviner consciousness. Indeed our physical existence is spent in less than one-tenth the period of our superphysical existence. We have to work for the money needed for the body's food, clothing, and shelter only that in the end it may carry us along the road to God. The flesh is indeed busy for the sake of the soul. Earthly life provides us with conditions whereby the ego can strive to rise beyond itself. When we remember that this higher self's vital importance is usually underassessed and insufficiently understood by politics, economics, and sociology, we may realize how incomplete must be their understanding and consequently how imperfectly they can fulfill their tasks.

Men who have no interest in higher aims, no faith in spiritual ends, no reverence for the uplifting ideal, must necessarily fall into the moral offense and intellectual defiance that is materialism. Materialists may say what they like but without a spiritual ethos, a worth-while civilization cannot be built up successfully. Freedom from the miseries of economic want may be good but without freedom from the miseries of materialistic blindness it may fall into the ditch of peril. The organization of human life overlooks the ultimate aim of human birth, which is to realize the divinity in each heart, only by endangering itself. This is why it is one duty of a human entity to discover his place and meaning in the planetary Idea. For its basic outline is unalterable by him. Even his so-called conquests of Nature are themselves really part of that Idea, although he does not know it. Much of his vaunted free will is a myth. Nevertheless the belief that the universe exists for the individual's own evolution is only partly wrong. If it exists primarily for Nature's purposes, which the individual is forced to subserve, it is his own ultimate and willing co-operation with those purposes which brings out his own best potentialities and leads them to magnificent efflorescence.

This question of what relationship his personal experience bears to the total human experience, of which it is only a part, needs asking and answering. He has to take the long view and understand all mankind's role and goal on this planet, if he is to understand his own. He has to take the large spacious view of particular events and relate them with the impersonal operations of universal law, thus giving them a pattern when they would otherwise be meaningless, and finding them a place in the universal order of things when they would otherwise be insignificant, unjust, and unreasonable. He has to see the ultimate direction of his own efforts as well as of society's efforts. He has to see an impersonal picture of it all, a world picture. Life then ceases to be chaotic, personal fortunes cease to be confused, and experience becomes orderly and even holy. For it is God's order. To understand life is to perceive this order. To be happy is willingly to co-operate with it.

The human being plays the part of a mere cell in the Planetary Mind's consciousness and life. There are millions of such "cells" within it, within this soul of the universe. But within his own body there are as many tinier beings playing a similar part toward himself. Nature's creative ability is thus ever and everywhere at work. This infinite variety of life, mind, movement, and activity all directed toward rational and purposeful ends, is God in self-expression. Its very infinitude speaks to him clearly of the infinite nature of God. Its endless operation speaks to him of the inexhaustible creativity of God. What is the meaning of these biological facts? It means that every thing and everyone stands in relationship to something or someone else, that the correct nature of that relationship must be found out before it can be successfully achieved and that until man finds out what is his relationship to his Overself on the one hand and to his underself of minute micro-organisms on the other, he will live in disharmony with himself and at cross-purposes with the universe.

The personal first-hand knowledge of these facts provides even amid twentieth-century evils and horrors an unshakable hope for humanity's future. Unless its educators and leaders, its guides and rulers learn to see their frightful problems by the direct or reflected light of such knowledge, which Jesus saw and Buddha reasoned, the solutions will all too often evade them as they grope in the dark. It is not of use only to lazy drones and mere dreamers. Correctly expounded and properly understood, it can be brought by everyone into relation with the strifes and strivings of this harsh world. It has direct practical value for that world, inasmuch as it offers the only principles upon which right action can be based and true prosperity achieved. Its practice abases selfishness and exalts virtue, pacifies violence and dissolves hatred. It is a solace to those who once played with life when it was kind to them and have since been shown its second hideous face.

The situation of the human race today seems so dark that pessimists ask the questions, "Where is God?" and "Is God really interested in mankind?" Everyone may attempt to answer these questions on the basis of a surface view of the world. But only a few are qualified to answer them on the basis of having explored the innermost recesses of their own psychological being and discovered their kinship to God. They are the few who have the perfect assurance, through the witness of their own experience, that this innermost self is divine, is linked with God. Through that self they are able to discover some little part of God's intentions toward the human race. Consequently they possess also perfect assurance that those intentions are beneficent ones despite all appearances to the contrary. To those who have lost faith because of the tragic course of world events, their answer contains hope.

The divine power is not absent from the world nor from any situation which can develop in the world. The divine laws control every situation. It is true that there are evil men among us and evil forces working in their background, but they can never really rule the world, never completely determine the course which mankind's life shall take. God's will has always been done and always will be done. No lesser will can triumph. And it is God's will which has set a course for mankind leading from darkness into light, from ignorance into knowledge, from wickedness into goodness, from helplessness into power and, above all, from junglelike animality into rational humanity, and thence to intuitive spirituality.

CHAPTER X

THE PROPHET'S VOICE

THE INTELLECT, working apart from intuition and divorcing itself from conscience, held down by desires, passions, and egotisms; swollen by pride into self-deception about its own vaunted powers; picturing science as the Messiah walking hand in hand with psychoanalysis, led too many prewar sophisticated men and women naturally and inevitably into a cynical materialism and a pleasure-seeking "liberation." They thought that social circumstances and bodily emotions were the supreme forces to which human life responds. They thought that human character was mainly the product of physical environment and heredity. Religion was despised as being only an incident in, or merely a caprice of, the history of the human mind; metaphysics was turned into a handmaiden of their own bleak, blank, amoral world-view; and mysticism was ignored altogether. Yet to live, asleep in the ego's ignorance, to exist without the faith or understanding that a divine soul was at their root, to continue smugly satisfied with the common heedlessness, and to repose in such fancied security, was to lie already stretched out in a kind of spiritual grave. Those who could not understand this, who could not understand the deeper meaning of their own experience and their own self, either laughed with ridicule or looked with indifference at sincere attempts to reawaken the intuitive divine sense in mankind.

They received a tremendous shock when contemplating the enormous areas of pain and depths of wickedness which the war brought into being. Here was a phenomenon before which their complacent theories had to withdraw in uncertainty and bewilderment. Here was a civilization, based to a large extent in practice upon materialistic sanctions, which had brought on itself a crushing disaster. The war showed up the insufficiency of all materialistic views which ascribed the existence of human afflictions solely to bad economic conditions or simply to psychological repressions, frustrations, and perversions. These causes could account for some of the evil in humanity, but they could not account for the monstrosities of cruelty and criminality on the immense continental scale in which they then appeared. The utter failure of modern society to keep the peace, the pitiful inability of modern civilization to keep human beings from becoming ravening beasts, humiliated and depressed many of them. But it also instructed some of them. For only then, when the painful consequences of a materialistic world-view and the misguided actions which flow out of it came home at last to roost, did such people begin to reflect upon the insufficiency of the one and the foolishness of the other. They found that they had become so absorbed in earthly business that they forgot there existed a transearthly one.

Was it true, after all, that unguided by God and unstrengthened by divine forces, man could only make a bad mess of things? Could it be that the traditional religions of all peoples during all times were not fooling themselves and others, but really did contain some truth? Thus the more intellectually humble began to turn contritely back toward ignored paths. Thus a new spiritual urge was awakened out of their sense of the colossal failure of unaided human wisdom. And thus they expiated their sins, educated their minds, and sanctified their hearts in a far truer sense than the orthodox and conventional one. They saw, at last, that if the mysterious unseen realities of existence are left out of sight, they could not hope for the best, and must expect the worst, from existence itself. This vindicated the philosophic dictum that "materialism may capture man's thought and feeling but it cannot hold them." Such is the spiritual history of a limited number of persons only. If it had been the history of all persons, how different their future would be today!

It is not enough that humanity's leaders concentrate their time and energy on overcoming the military, the economic, and the political crisis. They should not make the mistake of ignoring higher principles and neglecting to seek divine aid. And because it was the moral crisis which produced these outer ones, men and women need more spirituality, that is to say, more religion, more mysticism, and more philosophy, not less in the name of pseudopracticality. They need one or two or all of this trio, because out of such sources flow the moral sense, the consciousness of a distinction between right and wrong, the felt duty of self-control and noninjury toward their fellow creatures, and the compassionate feeling for others. They need them, also, to redeem faith and restore hope.

Spiritual truth is, in the end, an essential part of the cure for the maladies of disillusionment and discouragement, of unhappiness, worry, and sin, which have descended on the world. This fact has been overlooked because of competing issues or overlaid because of human exploitations. Its appeal ultimately rests upon intuitive acceptance felt deep down in the heart, its endorsement must be found there because the Overself is there. The religious instinct has been an elemental and therefore persistent one throughout man's enormously long history. It has been covered up and disguised, put aside or apparently suffocated at times but it has never been really killed. How could it when at the very center of his being there always exists the godlike spirit within man which guards and guarantees his ultimate redemption!

If there were no divine soul within him, his ideals would be meaningless and useless. It is this that gives secret reality to his strivings for self-improvement and to his yearnings for social betterment. There is an undisclosed mystery in the heart of the worst individual. For everyone embodies a ray of the universal Mind, which pervades all men even while it also evades them! It is the presence of divinity within him, however covered over and however deeply hidden it may be, that gives some sort of an ideal in his better moments and that makes him dissatisfied with what he now is. It is this presence which causes him to assign different values to different things and to different moods as he unconsciously progresses nearer to awareness of it. Above all, it bids him follow religion.

It is needful to say what is meant by religion. It could mean membership of a historical public organization like the Church of Rome, or accepting a system of doctrines about God, man, and the universe like Hinduism, or experiencing an emotional state like the conversion to Methodism. Or it could mean an unattached individual's private faith in God. For the purposes here, it is enough to say that men feel its necessity when they seek to travel beyond the first sense impressions of their existence, that pure religion is the belief by man in a secret and invisible power higher than himself, that popular organized religion ought to mean such belief made simple and suitable for the masses, and that no one is under any necessity whatever to express his faith by joining any organization if he does not want to. The proper functions of religion are: first, to instill into its believers faith in a higher power, and to sustain it; second, to bring them into communion with this power, and to inculate worship of it; third, to make them better in character and nobler in conduct; and fourth, to relieve emotional misery.

Any public religion offers the first step to bringing people into a life of supreme significance. Its benefits reach all classes. The simple and ignorant have as much right to be served as the evolved and learned. It is indeed established primarily for the benefit of the multitude. Its work teaches them not only that God exists but also what is their relationship to God; it not only explains the psychological consequences of this relation but also inculcates a morality necessitated by them. Religion is the most widespread, the most popular, and the most elementary source of righteous conduct. It is consequently the most valuable means of uplifting society. If it does nothing more than offer a serviceable bulwark against the remnants of man's extreme beastliness, it remains necessary and justified. This is its inescapable duty, for a faith in God which does not yield this much at least, can be only a hypocritical one and consequently worse than useless.

Those who say that religion has failed, on the ground that it has failed to prevent war, pass too quick a judgment. For what would man's behavior during the years of peace have

been like if the moral restraints of religion—however weak
they may be—had been totally inoperative? Let us admit that
some failure is plainly there, but justice asks us to add that it
is only a partial one. If the world has seen, in the tragic events
of our time, how unheard-of forces of evil raged for a while
in triumph upon the planet, and if we examine into the causes
of this partial failure, we shall find that the first one is that
religion has not been true to itself. Its real functions have been
too often contradicted by its traditional offices. It is a fact that
sincere religion teaches its devotees to forget prejudices and
to overcome animosities, certainly not to remember the one
and nourish the other. Mohammed, for instance, democrat-
ically preached the brotherhood of all men. Most of his followers unworthily accept the brotherhood of Mohammedans
only. Thus his teaching degenerated with time. The history
of every other religion—be it Christianity, Judaism, Hinduism, or Buddhism—is deeply and darkly stained with unreli-
gious thought and unfaithful practice.

A second cause is that modern people, and especially the
younger people, want to investigate for themselves, to use
their own judgment and not blindly accept as religious truth
whatever they are told. The day when tribal theologies could
satisfy them is fast fading before our eyes. Such things cannot
cope with the needs of growing mentalities. Two tremendous
factors have more and more entered the past hundred-year
scene: science and democracy. Modern man's mental characteristics have inevitably been affected and altered by them,
while his outer life has been helped in some ways and harmed
in others. He both wants to understand things rationally and
he wants to understand them for himself. He is better able to
receive and understand a faith when it makes less demands
on blind credulity and more demands on rational intelligence.
He is breaking away from outmoded conceptions and crystal-
lized forms, as those conceptions and forms themselves break
down under the inability to adapt themselves to the period's

need. The influence of ecclesiastical hierarchs has been waning and the power of pious authorities has been fading. Scriptural promises no longer attract the young and sacerdotal threats no longer intimidate them. They may be quite foolish but they even ridicule the past because it had no automobiles and no radios! Hence, beliefs and dogmas, institutions and offices, which depend on the past for their sanction, automatically come in for a share of this ridicule.

At a certain stage of society's religious history, humanism and rationalism liberate it from the superstitions, corruptions, and degradations of degenerated religion and thus act as retributive factors. It is not at all essential to anyone's salvation that he should believe the earth and he were made by God in six twenty-four-hour days. Nor is it essential for him to try to feel sincere reverence when rituals have become empty, dogmas senseless or grotesque, liturgical intonings mechanical, and moral codes fossilized. Indeed it is his right and duty to resist the hierarchical exploitation and to recognize the easy lapse into hypocrisy which mars religion's history.

Let it not be thought that these criticisms come from a sneering enemy of religion. On the contrary, they come from a sincere friend. Even Jesus did not think it either wrong or a waste of force frequently to denounce the rabbinical hierarchy for their hypocritical ways, nor Buddha the Brahmanical hierarchy for their superstitious practices. But because love of God and not hate of men motivated their criticism, it was always constructive.

As soon as it has fulfilled this corrective need, the opposition to religion becomes a retrogressive factor. The same faculty of critical reason which leads man out of gross superstition and thus gives mental sight also leads him into scientific materialism and deprives him of intuitive sight. It is an effective medicine when his religious faith gets diseased, but he cannot live by medicine alone. No one is really healthy who is physically robust but spiritually feeble, who is emotionally vigorous but ethically paralyzed and who is alive in his animal nature but dead to his angelic one. When he declares, as Freud declared, that "God is an illusion, religion a disease, and the religious sense a pathological neurosis," then he himself must be treated as one suffering gravely from delusions and neuroses. In losing that quality upon which rests the very purpose of his earthly incarnation, the quality of feeling veneration for something beyond his own little being, he is losing the sense of a higher existence being possible for himself and of a higher power being present in the universe—only to gain a blank, bleak materialism.

If the dangers to the human entity of this spread of materialism are paralysis of intuition and restriction of consciousness, the dangers to human society are loss of moral impulse and deterioration of moral conscience. So far as the old religions support and promote these things, they help people, especially the common people. So far as they have now lost ground, and the influences replacing them neither support nor promote moral values, the state of affairs is anarchic, regressive, and dark. It is a historic fact that religious collapse in signaled and accompanied by social upheavals. When irreligion flourishes and morality vanishes, when the human aspects of society deteriorate even though its technical innovations multiply, no real peace and no lasting prosperity are possible. We have only to imagine what would be the condition of a country if all religion were eradicated from it, to understand its necessity. With all its defects, abuses, and insipidity, an organized popular religion does do enough good, usually does have enough beneficial influence to justify its existence. When moral principles are no longer binding on conduct, when the ethical appeal is thrust aside as an antiquated nuisance and its religious basis is denounced as a narcotic drug for the masses, a dangerous situation opens up. The effects of disbelief in the existence of a divine power show themselves in many different ways, but worst of all in the moral chaos and confusion which then prevails, in the brutality, selfishness, and falsehood which become acceptable when it is thought that there are no retributive principles governing the world. This, in turn, rises out of disbelief in any other reality than that of Matter. Man pays a heavy price for such one-sided development of his own thinking powers.

Pure religion itself is divine and enduring, but religious institutions, dogmas, and hierarchies suffer from human frailty and time's deterioration. The historic forms which religion takes may be infected with gross errors, polished superstitions, selfish exploitations, and ancient hypocrisies, but the pure and permanent essence which it holds justifies its existence and imparts its best influence. The devotee may dispense with these forms, but he cannot really dispense with this essence. The skeptic who loses faith in erroneous teaching about God and the soul, undiscriminatingly or unwittingly loses faith in the true teaching that goes along with it. In turning aside with disillusionment from the slavish veneration of ecclesiastical authority, he is turning aside from humble veneration of the higher power itself—which is a profound and dangerous error. It is well that he is tired of being irrational. It is not at all well that he should therefore become irreverential. He falls out of the danger of being led astray by others into the danger of being led astray by himself.

This is why his repressed aims, his secret purposes, and his half-banished aspirations continue to torment the man who is not utterly bestialized or materialized, but caught in the steel-trap mechanism of modern civilization. But they operate indirectly, they are the mainsprings behind emotions and activities which seem to be of a quite different character. Whether it be through drink or through sport, through the cinema or through sex, the hard-driven human cog of an unbalanced machine age seeks for an escape from the tyrannic ego. How many men and women are in the unhappy state of yearning for spiritual life unconsciously through not understanding their own yearning! Modern civilization has tended to suppress these vague yearnings, or at best to leave their existence and importance in a half-acknowledged state, so that they have lain like soft arable earth beneath congealed volcanic lava.

Religion Should Broaden Out. Where the representative of official religion has failed his people, his place is taken by others. The inspired poet was one of the active preachers of last century, as the illumined artist was one of the missionaries of recent times. The metaphysically bent scientist is being looked to for light more and more in our own epoch. All this is doubtless quite good in its way, but poetry, art, and science are not religion. Each is capable of giving man some inner support for living, but none can give precisely what religion alone gives. Scientific facts and scientific abstractions cannot of themselves nourish the soul of man satisfactorily. The modern intellectual, or his proletarian echo, is left half-starved by such a diet. He seeks the missing pabulum in art, pleasure, entertainment, or sport. These certainly help him and indeed he often considers them sufficient to fulfill his want. But the transcendental needs of his soul being what they are, they can never really be replaced by any substitutes.

It is needful to develop a means of giving satisfaction in a modern way to the sense of reverence. This would not necessarily mean the creation of a new religion or the adoption of some exotic one. It could mean nothing more than a new and enlarged understanding of the old religions. The West could save its perishing inner life by getting back to what Jesus really taught. Christianity, properly understood and correctly expounded, is somewhat different from Churchianity and certainly more inspired. Such is the common slavery to phrases and words, that any reference to religion is at once turned into a reference to rigid orthodoxy or narrow sectarianism. Yet the great conventions of the religious life, its traditional ideas, methods, and forms, are not forever bound with iron chains. Man may shape them to suit his place and time. The religious attitude and the religious goal cannot be altered and must remain the same for every people and every century. But their ways and means may alter and cannot remain unaffected by changing circumstances.

Religion will begin to demonstrate its usefulness on the modern scene only when its sponsors begin to make it relevant to the modern age, adequate to the modern need, open-eyed to the modern crisis, and open-eared to the modern tragedy. This done, it will again fulfill its beneficent function. It must become a flexible institution and should progress with the life and mind of man himself. In no other way will it best serve humanity. Unfortunately, past history and present signs show that those who should be the first to comprehend this are usually the last. The lesson being disagreeable to them, they are disinclined to receive it.

A graver error made by these official orthodox representatives is that they are often the first to oppose and the last to accept any manifestation of the living spirit of God among men. If people are forced to look elsewhere for religious sustenance, if so many of them feel the need of something new, it is because they can find help nowhere else.

We moderns pride ourselves on having developed far beyond the narrow, ignorant, and superstitious mentalities of the past. But these were after all the defects of certain virtues and in getting rid of the defects we have also got rid of the virtues. For the narrowness came out of a misplaced religious faith, the ignorance out of a too stubborn recognition of the limitations of the human intellect, and the superstition out of an uncriticized intuition that the physical world was not the only world of being.

It has been suggested that either a union of the traditional old faiths or the imposition of a single new one is the best solution of modern man's religious problem. Here sentimentality has mastered reason and the wish is father, mother, uncle, and aunt to the thought! Humanity is so variously constituted that this would be more of a hindrance than a help. The temperament, which finds emotional satisfaction in the impressive sacramental forms of Roman Catholicism, for instance, will find emotional starvation in the bare, inward formlessness of Quakerism. And what has the savage, with his taboo and dance and magic, to find in fellowship with the Quaker, with his silent seated worship of the Invisible Presence?

The spiritual requirements of different grades of humanity are so varied, owing to their imperfections, that it is better to wait patiently their natural growth in mentality and character than to force all grades within a single iron frame of manufactured unity. Schisms into parties and divisions into sects will continue to occur anyway. This is because faith may wander with the creator of one group as widely as imagination may travel with the creator of another: rarely is intuition upheld by investigation or divine inspiration kept free from human opinion. The ego creeps in here, as elsewhere. These separatist tendencies need not be deplored and so long as they exist they must also be recognized. A mechanical conglomeration of the old existing religions is impracticable on any large and therefore useful scale, and could never satisfy all tastes.

The attempt to force an artificial unity upon rival organized religions would be as unwise as it is likely to be unsuccessful. Let us not become futile dreamers and demand from humanity a unity which its own variety could never give. Let us not expect it to subscribe to a single universal religion which would displace the necessity for all other religions, nor ask it to live in a universal brotherhood which would be attainable only after the prior attainment of a superhuman, moral perfection. The belief that to bring such a new utopia into being it is needful only to do some quite simple act or make some overnight gesture or join some spiritual movement, is an intellectual error which besets the path of those who would improve mankind's lot. Such excessive idealism is not their strength, as they think, but their weakness. The desire for fraternity between the faiths is much wiser and more praiseworthy than the desire for their unification.

If spiritual harmony between men is certainly part of the ultimate goal, it is essentially an inward, not an outward fact. It must exist within or it does not exist at all. No organizations, no institutions can make it so or are at all necessary to its own existence. Therefore, it can be truly found only in the individuals. To be real, it must grow by itself out of a wakening to the fact that disharmony is the cause of constant trouble and suffering as well as the effect of spiritual ignorance. Meanwhile there is need to emphasize inward holiness more than outward observance, to have the largeness of mind to recognize that there is more than one bible and more than one spiritual leader. The study of comparative religion does much to wipe out bigotry and soften bias. By its means the tenets common to most religions—and therefore the truest ones—are brought forward and their universality proclaimed.

If religion, whether embodied in the old familiar creeds or the new unfamiliar cults, is to become morally powerful, it must absorb some Asiatic knowledge. The nineteenth century, which saw the expansion of capitalism and transport, the development of machinery and commerce, saw also the introduction of Asiatic thought into Europe and America and of European thought into Asia. Man's general situation is so tragic that it is time some of the more vital Oriental ideas should cease to be regarded as strange, abnormal, or exotic plants. His need of their fruits, in the reorientation of himself, the reconstruction of society, and the reinterpretation of his scriptures is urgent and profound. For only a shift in his thought and values can bring him the betterment that will be most worth while. From the East, he can learn emphasis on two ideas which show that ideals of self-discipline and self-improvement are indeed practical, sensible, and necessary. First, that the law of recompense (karma) will eventually bring back to him whatever he gives out; second, that the divine soul is not only ever present in him and everyone else but can be known. If accepting the second truth, he thinks of God as being not far-off and remote but here and now within himself and within others, then he is more likely to improve himself and ennoble his worldly dealings. And once convinced of the first truth, aggressive peoples will tend to abandon the false conceptions which lead them to believe that they could really profit by making war upon others. Because so much poison has been poured into the human mind for so many years, a counteracting serum is urgently needed. These ideas uphold the dignity of human life, proclaim the divine potentialities which it contains, and inculcate the reality of the moral order.

The struggles of war have tangled the threads of Oriental and Occidental karma. The thousand-million population of the Far and Middle East have come into a contact of communication, whether hostile or friendly, with Western races to an extent never before historically known. The consequence of this is not only that the white peoples have to make some effort to understand the yellow and brown ones, but the latter have to make the same effort to understand them. However fumbling, an approach toward such understanding must inevitably be made. The student of comparative religion, who studies the culture of the Orient side by side with that of the Occident, tends to free himself from environmental bias. It is necessary for the whole world to broaden its religious outlook. The Occident must one day make its salaam to Oriental wisdom, for its elder brother has a heritage of spiritual lore which it must learn to respect and

revere. The admirable mind exemplified in the writings of
Plato, in the questions of Socrates, in the thought of Spinoza,
and in the plays of Sophocles, is not dissimilar from that exemplified in Oriental culture at its own best level.

It would seem that just at the time when there is real need
of expanding the Western outlook in these matters by accepting loans and gifts from the Eastern, just when the West's
own repressed longing to balance its high practical development with an intuitive-mystical culture has been precipitated
by the crisis into the conscious mind, the Orient is itself yielding more and more to the bewitchment of material progress
and consequently sinking more and more into materialism.
This condition has been brought about by its great age. For
it is not enough to display great books written thousands of
years ago; there should also be displayed a great civilization
today. The contradiction between the East's sublime literature and backward physical condition is a tragic one; its
amendment is a necessary act but the manner of amendment
too often injudicious.

We Westerners should avail ourselves of what the finest
minds of the East thought, taught, and knew; should help
ourselves amply and humbly to their wisdom, for that will
enrich our own store and enlarge our outlook. But we should
do so without illusions. Although such a broadening will help
our civilization and not weaken it, as bigots assert, it will
not be enough of itself to renew our civilization spiritually.
That will be possible only if it really wakes up, if it listens
to the voices of its own living prophets, and if it follows a
modern version of the age-old religious quest livable amid,
and in touch with, the realities of its own situation. Such are
the dangers of this situation that it would be well to start a
new living tradition rather than get entangled in an old de-
caying one.

The modern seeker, born in a Western land and brought
up in its individual atmosphere, finds himself pulled two con-

flicting ways. There is the attraction of the Orient, where the traditions of mysticism are as rich and its sources as developed and alive as nowhere else. And there is the attraction of his own native Occident, whose scientific rationality and physical practicality he has learned to take for granted as necessary to civilized living. These pulls from different directions tend to split his will or confuse his mind. What is his spiritual duty? Wisdom answers that there is no need to surrender to either of these two pulls but rather to set himself creatively to work upon both of them. Life itself has today given him the task of putting them smoothly together in such a way that each rounds out the other and contributes toward the final result.

Divine revelation is as available today as yesterday, as free to the West as to the East. No particular race, no particular nation holds it in sole possession. It is universally potential and, if he sets about the task in the right way, the inhabitant of the western hemisphere may convert it into an actuality, although maybe a little less readily than the inhabitant of any Indian monastery. Let him not be cramped by those who insist on a merely local tradition, a specifically racial expression, a historically limited standpoint, or a rabidly sectarian partisanship. That which is everywhere present cannot be the monopoly of a particular race, people, or sect. The Occidentals can find their soul's root in God—although perhaps not as easily as the Orientals—if they want to. The Overself reveals its presence to all alike. The fact that men such as Socrates, Lao Tzu and Emerson, living in such widely separated lands as Greece, China and America got this same blessed revelation means that the truth is just as accessible in one place as in another, that no one is under any real necessity of traveling to the Orient to find it and that if he will set about looking for it in the right direction—within himself—he can stay at home and still find it.

Nevertheless it would be a grave mistake to believe that philosophy holds one religion to be as good as another. It does not. It admits the differences in the intrinsic truth of various religions, but says we have to ascend beyond the outer forms of all religions for the pure truth. Moreover, it tolerantly and pragmatically holds that there is usually one religion which is best suited to a particular man in his particular stage of development, although it may be ill suited to another man. Whatever method or idea or institution effectively helps a certain type of individual to adopt a spiritual life, cannot be dismissed as worthless by a different type of individual merely because it does not attract and cannot help him in any way. He should be tolerant even though he turns indifferently away, remembering that it may still speak usefully to another.

This much-needed universal tolerance is beginning to manifest itself, albeit faintly, as a result of the unbiased study of comparative religion, itself the child of the earlier study of Oriental languages in Occidental universities. Its study has favorably altered the attitude of intelligent Westerners toward other faiths. The latter are no longer arrogantly denounced as being wholly false. Moreover, a nobler concept of divine beneficence and justice has led to the realization that other peoples could not have been left—in an orderly world—without light, help, revelation, or guidance. It is, however, only the philosophic student who can come to the study of comparative religion in a genuinely unbiased way. For it is only he who comes with prejudice cast out of a disciplined intellect and favoritism held away from a purified emotion. The reward is his discovery that the ultimate source of all authentic religious truth is one and the same—man's higher self—and that this explains why the best ideas of such truth are common to different peoples and different epochs. In the fullness of its own time, with the growth that follows his efforts and the maturity that solidifies his experience, this fact establishes itself in his mind as being so utterly obvious that he may wonder on occasions why everyone else does not see it. It teaches him to hold all religions in esteem, no matter what particular one he ties himself to or sets himself free from.

How few ever stop to think that the religion they hold and believe to be true might have taken another shape had they been born in another country! How few think that the same comfort and help, the guidance and support which they have derived from their own religion, have also been derived by other people from other religions!

How many millions have only a census-paper connection with their professed religion! Of what use is it to point to the large number of members of this church and that church; rather let us ask what is the faith of these so-called believers? Is it a vital faith which strongly influences their thoughts, feelings, and actions, or is it an empty faith, merely nominal and mostly dead? The complacent inheritance of ancestral views, however limited, deficient, or even false they may be, is perhaps more noticeable in the sphere of religion than in any other. No man can become a real Christian—or Hindu or Buddhist—by the accident of birth or by the formality of baptism. He can become one only by thinking it out, feeling its reality, and obeying its moral injunctions. All the rest is a vast social suggestion which, however much it fools mankind, has never fooled the witnessing Overself. It is not his opinions so much as his actions, not his belief so much as his character which evidences the acceptance of religion by any man. Society is easily deceived in this matter, but not the higher laws and forces. Reason should tell us that whatever powers there are, will not judge us by our formal professions of religious faith but rather by our thought and conduct.

The Mystic's Light. We have earlier written that the partial failure of religion happened because it was not true to itself. But such infidelity, in turn, happened because it ceased to understand itself correctly and luminously. This point must be clarified.

Most of the world's wickedness rises out of the tragic ignorance of men and not out of the repulsive badness of men. This ignorance rises, in turn, out of their habitual identification of self with the body alone, utterly ignoring its larger and diviner side. The separation which exists in consciousness between the ego and Overself is a fatal one. It is the root of all man's sins, ignorance, woes, and evils. To counteract this ignorance and gradually to remove it, religious, mystical, and philosophic teachers are in very truth sent by God to enlighten the three different strata of the human race. Left to themselves without the guidance of spiritual instructors and divine awakeners, men would lie in the torpor of ignorance and die in the baseness of animalism. It is not enough for experience alone to form their characters and sharpen their intelligence. Their experience must be explained to them—something of its inner significance must be revealed to them. Their suffering must be solaced by compassionate words and their vaguely felt faith supported by given instruction.

In the appearance from time to time of a spiritual teacher, a religious prophet, or a divine healer, we may see one source of such instruction. Out of the divine silence there intermittently issues forth the Word. It is spoken, not by the sky but by the lips of a man. It is not only a heard sound or written document; it is also a creative and transforming power. He who speaks or writes the Word becomes the founder of a new religion, the prophet of a new uplift. His part is carefully to decode, if it may be put in that way, a message received in transhuman cipher and to fit language to it. Such is the supreme intelligence which holds the world within its grip, that its operations help mankind by bringing about his birth, as, when, and where needed. Sometimes he comes here, as Jesus came, from a higher evolved planet. Such an individual is like a general in the war against evil. He works for its defeat. His appearance among us at periodical intervals is as wise as it is necessary. Neither this nor the eventual spread of his influence is accidental or dependent on anyone's personal choice. Both are divinely ordained through the forces guiding human evolution and the law of universal recompense.

The prophet or the seer may expect that his counsel will be rejected by all except a few but he may yet be guided to express it formally. If he is, then such expression has more than a personal value. It will stand in symbolic relation to the unheeding people. It will be a two-edged sword, which could have saved them but will be used to judge them. His work may be ushered in quietly at first—it may even escape notice for a time, as the work of Jesus escaped every contemporary historian except Josephus. He himself collected a few hundred followers, and Buddha only a few thousand, although their teaching fed millions in later centuries. Confucius was largely ignored although his teachings became part of the Chinese educational system for two thousand years. During the first ten years of his prophetic mission, Zoroaster could find no other disciple than his own cousin, no larger following than a single person.

The real disciples rather than the nominal followers of the world's great Messianic leaders were always a negligible minority. This was partly because the meager means of transport and the primitive means of communication did not formerly allow a divine message to spread otherwise than slowly. Today it may spread much more quickly and to the whole world. Nevertheless it is still needful to realize ruefully how impossible are those dreams of a miraculous overnight conversion of all mankind with which the uninitiated and the sentimental like to play. What Jesus could not do, what Buddha failed to accomplish, could certainly be done by nobody else. Those great lights in human flesh moved the terrible spiritual inertia of mankind, it is true, but they moved it slightly. The sensitive few responded powerfully, as ever, but the matter-minded many were barely touched.

Few people understand that the work of a prophet is essentially accomplished within a limited period after his own appearance on earth and does not endure for all time. For his primary task is twofold: to plant something in the hearts of men, a gift of his grace, which shall be transmitted down through some centuries in ever widening ripples; to speak or write a verbal message which prudently caters to the needs of the moment, to the thought-forms of the people, and to the historical background of the era. The force thus spread reaches its zenith and then begins to weaken and ebb away. At its zenith the spirit is triumphant, but at its nadir the letter rules. In the first case we have true religion and men feel its inspiration, but in the second we have often its mockery and men feel its emptiness. The prophet truly possesses the power to bestow grace, whereas after the lapse of centuries many who speak in his name mostly lack it. This is one reason why religion evaporates during the long lapse of centuries so that what people mostly get then is merely its last residue.

Today, the original principles of the great religions have been so altered, their moral effectiveness has been so markedly lessened, their antimaterialistic influence so sadly enfeebled, that the need of a vast inward renewal throughout the world and among all classes is incontestable. When man's professed credo is no longer a flamelike conviction but a cold convenience, the need of a new dynamic is unquestionable. Yet it is a common error to take for granted that this kind of interest is the business of specially pious, eccentric, or solemn people, as if the pitifully minimum common attention given to spiritual matters is a sign of healthy normality and excellent balance. After all, it is not the disciple of the Quest alone who is called to the seeking and finding of the Overself's happiness, but everybody else. Only, with the latter, the call comes as from afar off, and being only dimly heard, its place of origin is wrongly judged.

God has laid down an evolutionary path for man that leads from the basest in his character upward to the noblest and that is destined to raise him far above the level of unconscious animality. He must travel it in the end; so far he has no freedom of choice. But ordinarily the pace is to a large extent his own, he can make it as slow or as swift as he likes. Religion is a first step in this right direction, but sooner or later he must continue his journey and go all the way along this road, which means that he must next pass through the phase of personal and inward mystical experience. The first and final demand which religion makes on mankind is faith—simple and unquestioning. There is nothing wrong in that. Every mother rightly makes the same demand on her little children. The religious man believes that a divine power exists and sustains everything. But his faith may change, slacken, or even vanish altogether under the hard pressure of unfavorable events or skeptic arguments. The mystic is not satisfied with such a situation. He sees the need for a more intimate relation to God. And through self-denial, self-discipline, and meditation he realizes it, finding a reflection of the divine power deep within his own self, its existence clearly proved by his own intimate experience. It does not depend on the appeal to any externals to convince him, but works entirely within his thought and feeling for its truth. Where religion derives its chief sanction from outside authority, mysticism derives its chief sanction from first-hand experience. That the passage to it is an upward and progressive one is unquestionable. And this is the passage which numbers of people need to make in our time.

Valuable and necessary though religious knowledge and its preparatory efforts certainly are, they leave still unfulfilled the highest object of human existence. The somewhat limited circle of those who are not satisfied with a merely preparatory knowledge of the higher life but want to acquire its truths through their own inner realization, as well as those who feel strongly the urge to climb from a lower stage somewhat nearer to the summit of spiritual attainment, may get their aspiration fulfilled if they agree to pay a higher price in the coin of self-training and self-discipline. Thus they make themselves worthy of fuller and personal illumination by the Overself.

When people of every level of character and intelligence, conduct, and intuition are thrown together in society, the problem is created of reconciling a simple faith for the masses with a complex one for the few capable of absorbing it. The majority cannot go beyond this simplicity but they should not stand in the way of those who can. On the other hand, the latter should not turn mysticism into an aristocratically exclusive affair for some privileged persons, depriving large numbers of people of its higher benefits. If it is wrong to proffer knowledge to people faster than they can absorb it, it is equally wrong to refrain from proffering it to the extent that they can do so. The solution of this problem calls for a filtering process, which would provide every opportunity for those anxious to progress but yet not confound those who are not.

The sages start religion as a school for the spiritual uplift of man. The sacerdotal caste tends to turn it into a prison. It is instituted to advance him slowly yet gradually. Human organizations later begin to use it to keep him down subserviently. The evolutionary experiences of life give him more and more inner responsibility, that is, individualize him mentally. Yet certain shortsighted ecclesiastics think they can keep his intelligence and character in artificial clamps. Life seeks to transfer him from stage to stage of spiritual perception. Yet they seek to limit this holy aim to a single stage. The religious devotee should be permitted and even encouraged to take the step into mysticism, to change from worship of a remote anthropomorphic God to communion with a heartfelt divine soul within, as soon as he feels quite ready for it. Instead, he is usually hindered from taking such a step. That is because it is not understood that true mysticism is not inimical to religion. It is an advance, but it is not an advance away from true religion.

When institutional religion can achieve the largeness of heart to keep itself open as a door to mystical religion and not wall itself in as a jail, everyone, including itself, will be helped by the renunciation. Contemporary needs especially call for it. The strain of these times is such that even the proud and sophisticated as well as the sensual and ignorant are unable to cope sufficiently with it. The necessity of something that can dispense peace, hope, strength, and light to their confused inner selves is beginning to make itself felt.

Philosophy does not call men by asking them to cast religion aside, nor to scorn it by asking them to treat religion as useless. Religion is for everybody, including philosophers. But philosophy does ask men to extend their religion beyond sectarianism, to purify their practice of it, and to deepen their understanding of it. It crowns what mysticism sets forth and consummates what religion promises, yet at the same time it corrects the errors and eliminates the limitations of both. It never opposes itself to religion—how could it, when genuine religion grows out of its own soil?—but only to the degeneration and corruptions of religion, just as it never disparages mysticism—whose meditational practices are part of its own lifeblood—but only the extravagant and foolish forms which mysticism tends to assume. Since finality and perfection belong only to the standpoint of the unachieved Whole, it says that all earlier standpoints were useful as provisional ones only and become imperfect as final ones.

Because comprehension grows as the point of view rises, a religious teacher explains experience in an elementary way and a mystical teacher does it in a more advanced way.

Within the conventional surface of religion and covered by its imposing rituals, there lies hidden a mystical content. When elementary religious tenets are put forward as ultimate mystical truths, the results are lamentable. They wax gradually from misunderstanding and superstition to absurdity and intolerance. This rises because the uninitiated uncritically confuse levels of intellectual reference, because they fail to make the clear-cut division between what belongs to the sphere of outer observance and what belongs to the sphere of inner life.

But even more unfortunate than what religious believers have done to mystical fact is what would-be mystics and unbalanced mystical teachers have themselves done to it. The cautious student who wants to keep his mental sanity and arrive at true knowledge must be warned that the realm of mystical studies is fringed with occult bypaths clouded with silly superstitions. Truths have been taken from it and associated with much nonsense. The mixture has been propagated by fantastic movements, silly cults, charlatanic leaders, and dubious secret societies. Those who have never undergone any intellectual discipline, whether during the course of formal education or of self-development, may easily tend to believe in what is merely fanciful or to fall into the bog of religious mania. The intelligent seeker must walk warily in these fields, for noxious weeds thrive luxuriantly there. Let him always remember that if he wishes to accept the belief in a higher power, he may do so without having to accept along with it a host of dangers, superstitions, charlatanries, and delusions. Only by holding fast to the scientific test of *practical observed fact* can he even begin to thread his way safely through the glibly spoken theory.

No ridicule will kill the farfetched pretensions, the folly or fraud of such cults. Their credulous addicts take themselves too seriously for that, so seriously, in fact, that they soon lose their sense of humor. "Nothing succeeds like excess," was the airy advice of Oscar Wilde. They take it to the full. Are they then mere simpletons whose critical faculties are still ungrown and who swallow every fantastic tale and tenet? The paradoxical answer is both yes and no. Many are but others show some intelligence in professions and businesses, and become amusingly naïve only when they listen to pseudomystical lectures or read seminonsensical psychological literature, or study under Indian "*gurus*".

These teachings contain a curious mixture of truth and fancy; hence there is sometimes difficulty in appraising the movements behind them. One of the reasons why they get a hold on the minds of people is that, along with, and in spite of, their exaggerations and falsifications, they often have helpful elements. Some are the inevitable result of man's straining to escape when the bonds of religious orthodoxy become intellectually painful.

Many join these cults through hope, and remain through habit. Others are merely gratifying their passion for sensation, and imagine they are gratifying their passion for truth. When the miracle prevails over the mystical, there is risk of losing the latter's real worth. When mystery predominates over mysticism, difficulties are invited and dangers are fallen into. When the mystical good degenerates like this, it leads not to the splendid enlightenment to which it could lead but to a stunted life, a shriveled heart, a moral helplessness, and an intellectual atrophy.

It is not surprising, therefore, that so many intelligent, educated, or practical people smile in derision or sneer in contempt if anyone mentions mystical ideas, and especially Oriental ones, for these are invariably associated in their minds with queer fantastic groups or gross charlatanic exploitations. Nobody who has moved amid a larger circle than the narrow one of these small sectarian cults may justly deny this, as nobody who has traveled in the wide world may fail to observe it within his own experience. Nor may he deny that there exists a rabid half-lunatic fringe around the following of these cults which is sufficiently large to draw them into this ridicule. True mysticism has indeed suffered from the generally disreputable status which is indiscriminately attached to it. The contempt or indifference in which mystic, occult, and yoga studies are held by so many; the derision to which the teachers, organizations, and prophets are subjected; the charlatanry and exploitation practiced by not a few among them upon the gullible; the failure to influence, guide, or direct public life for the better to any marked degree; these are facts which have an obvious lesson for the open-minded. They indicate that something is wrong with many of the leaders as well as with many among their flocks. They reveal that it is foolish to accept uncritically every fantastic concept or exaggerated claim promulgated in the name of occultism, mysticism, or yoga, and that everything is finally to be tested not only by its intellectual truth but also by its moral and practical results.

Not a few mystical writers of antique or medieval times, and not a few of even our own times, have cultivated the art of letting their fancies run wild. The intent in some cases was, no doubt, simply and well meaningly to impress their readers and arouse their interest or, in other cases, to express symbolically what would be difficult for immature minds to comprehend literally. But their writings have an unfortunate effect, in places, upon those who are still medievally minded or intellectually immature. For if we apply the various tests of credibility, such as critical analysis, rational plausibility, past experience, or scientific knowledge, we are forced to recognize that although great truths are to be found in these writings, great nonsense is also to be found there, especially when they are supposed to describe historical events quite literally. However, those who wish may continue to read and study such literature, for it still holds a precious content, but they should do so with caution.

All this is regrettable but it does not make what is true in the mystical ideas less valuable or veridical. It should put students vigilantly on their guard. Even more should it point to the need of finding their way to surer ground. This is provided by, and can only be found in, philosophy. Here they are taught to cultivate deliberately the qualities of a just mental balance and a proper emotional equilibrium. This results in swift repugnance to immoderate exaggeration and instinctive rejection of wild unqualified claims.

Religion is best suited to the masses just as mysticism, its higher level, is best suited to more sensitive people and just as philosophy, its highest level, is best suited to the most sensitive and intelligent people. The wise men, who devised systems of religion and techniques of mysticism, did so with the ultimate purpose of leading the human adventurer step by step from lower to loftier stages of spirituality. Although man's higher life begins and ends with religion, it mounts to mysticism and proceeds still farther to philosophy, before finally it returns on itself and renews afresh the humble worship of God. Philosophy includes and contains religion, as a cult of worship, but is not itself limited to religion. Its frontiers are much wider, its explorations much deeper. Religious faith cannot do the work of mystical experience nor that in its turn of philosophic insight. The three are not on the same level. This may be better understood if it is said that a man may be religious without being mystical. He may even, though more rarely, be mystical without being religious. But he cannot be truly philosophical without being religious as well as mystical at the same time.

If religion engages man's faith, metaphysics his intellect, and mysticism his intuition, philosophy not only engages his whole nature but also engages it at its highest pitch. Religion presents truth pictorially, mysticism presents it intuitively, metaphysics presents it intellectually, but philosophy becomes the truth in every part of being and life. The religious code of conduct checks and disciplines the baser passions, aggressive instincts, and selfish desires of man, but does not adequately overcome them. Only the philosophic code, which includes a training of the whole being, including the bodily being, can do that. The scientific method questions Nature by obervation and experiment. The religious method reveres Nature as the handiwork of God. The mystical method introverts the senses and ignores her altogether so as to see God. The metaphysical method indulges in abstract reflection about her. The philosophic method holds, completes, and balances them all, adding the unfoldment of a transcendental insight and a divinized activity.

Philosophy rejects proselytism. It accepts no converts. Men are slowly educated into its outlook by their own intuition, their own thought, and their own experience. When they hear their growing unformed ideas stated by it with clarity and expressed with authority, and when the utterance has the accent of truth and the appeal of affinity for them, they are ready for it at last. It is only when their outward experience and inward growth have been formed enough that it begins to serve their need. Hence the philosopher does not propagate his ideas. He merely shares them. They usually find recruits among those who are not afraid of new standpoints and who feel invigorated when gaining fresh insights into the course of events and the nature of things.

All this does not mean that everyone travels to philosophy by one and the same described route. That was the traditional one until the modern age but the uprush of intellect and the quickened individualizing of the ego have brought about some change. Although the ancient and medieval approach through religion and mysticism is still made by most people, an increasing minority enters the philosophic portals from widely varied directions: from science, atheism, psychiatry, health regimes, naturopathic and faith healing systems, etc. To some extent or in some way such an approach has purified them physically or healed them emotionally or prepared them mentally, which in turn has made them more receptive to, and readier for, philosophy's voice. It is possible for our era to bring about a balanced combination of science, religion, metaphysics, mysticism, and the healing arts such as no earlier era could attain. With its basis on the philosophy of truth, it would be something on which humanity could finally depend, for that basis has been tested since the hoariest antiquity and has emerged triumphantly from the scrutiny of many a century. The wisdom of the sages is the wisdom of the ages. It can never perish. Why? Because all human thinking, all human feeling, all human experience, when led to their farthest end by the spiral evolutionary movements, return and must return to it.

What the most illumined men of history found in the innermost depths of their being, may be found again in our own being. What they learned, we can learn. Their efforts did not exhaust, their discoveries did not end, human possibilities. We must believe this, not merely because it sustains us in a weary and disillusioned epoch, but because it happens to be true. Not one in a thousand follows their example today. That is no reason why the few who appreciate it at its true value should not attempt to do so. We need to be reminded that God did not die with the past but lives today: that the voice of those who come back from God's presence can be heard from living lips, and not only from the dead ones which the past honors; that no period has ever had a monoply of divine revelation, inspiration, and illumination. Every book that helps us to perceive spiritual truths is a scriptural book, no matter if it was written in the twentieth century and no matter what conventional or self-interested or unreflective persons may say about it. Those who refuse to attribute authority and holiness to the living present, thereby betray a spiritual pessimism which is unjustifiable and unjustified. That which taught the most ancient peoples is with us still today and can teach us too. The World-Mind is as much behind our finite minds now as it was then. History cannot limit its working to a particular period or a particular individual. It is present in all men and, therefore, accessible at all times.

Let us make our worship of this Mind total, intelligent, pure, and direct. Total, because every moment is henceforth a holy one. Intelligent, because there is clear understanding that the divine life is not alien and apart but dwells at the very root of the worshiper's own life. Pure, because no personal benefits except of a spiritual kind, are asked for in return. And direct, because the ceremonial symbols and intellectual draperies, the dim intimations and human intermediaries of public religion, are displaced by a sacred private insight.

If there is any single message which philosophy gives the wayfarers on earth it is that there truly is this World-Mind in which our own little minds are mysteriously rooted and which is the inspirer of all that is benign and noble, serene and beautiful in our thoughts and feelings; that the full reverent awareness of its presence and conscious co-operation with its will, fulfill the ultimate purpose of human life and bring the extreme measure of human happiness. Once this message sinks deeply into his heart and once he takes it receptively into his mind, man finds that hope, meaning, and worthwhileness are gloriously restored to life. Like a great star blazing alone above the darkness, it is ever there to lead him where others wander without directive purpose or stumble and fall in the unmapped night.

CHAPTER XI

OUR INNER RESOURCES

DEEP WITHIN its peaceless heart humanity is frightened by the specter of the atom bomb. To an indeterminate extent, it takes, however, the conventional path and conceals from itself the extent of its fear. The consequence of this deceptive pose is the breeding of nervous strain, psychoneuroticism, and even physical maladies. The number of those who suffer from serious neuroses does not run into hundreds but into millions, is not limited to a single class but spreads over all classes. The continued state of public alarm and private fear during the bombings of war and the bickerings of peace has also affected the sanity of weaker minds.

Fear is a negative feeling, and therefore not one to be cultivated, but it does have some usefulness if it succeeds in arousing people to their need of facing the calamitous situation which creates it and if it forces them to do something about it. As a warning of the necessity of action, its voice should be heeded. The cheap psychology which, although preaching a fearless life, smothers that warning under a spate of unrealistic optimism and ungrounded confidence, renders only a disservice. Just as a man struggling for life in fluid water appreciates intensely the value of solid earth beneath his feet, so the tranquillity of a period of true peace between the nations is appreciated most intensely when the products of scientific warfare belch forth their ghastly horrors. The chance of a new peaceful world could come only out of a changing reflective humanity, keenly aware of the lessons of the wartime sufferings of its recent past. It is then that the leaders and the led should look deeply at their situation and resolve firmly to seek out the real causes of such recurring wars and take the correct action to eliminate them. That this has not been done enough in the past, or done rightly, is plainly evident today.

People do not know and need to be instructed that what is happening all over the world is a picture, in exaggerated degree, of what is happening inside themselves to a varying degree. Some have more, others have much less surrendered their inner lives to the rule of conjoined animality and materialism, yet do not know it. So the same rule, but in a more blatant and crueler form, is ruthlessly trying to take over their outer lives. They have brought over the remnants of powerful propensities from the animal stage of their existence, and added to this a cunning misdirected egoistic intellect derived from the present human state. Animals kill for hunger but men are worse, inasmuch as this possession of the quality of cunning leads them to kill or torture for other reasons also. Violent energies and explosive passions make much noise in their hearts. Down-dragging desires grip them between sharp fangs. Aggressive instincts roam like tigers and gloomy suspicions crawl like snakes within their conscious or subconscious minds. Selfish greeds have a firm habitat in their attitudes. Hates and bitternesses and lusts stir from within and are fomented from without.

Inevitably and inescapably such bestial thoughts take external form and historic struggles appear. How can real peace come into the world until the jungle-struggle mentality goes out of it? No law, no government can do more than curb to some extent the active expressions of this mentality. The statesman can regulate them within certain limits but not farther. Whenever they are able to dominate, they not only poison the inner being but also contribute toward the outer experience. The anger which is felt today may manifest itself on the physical plane tomorrow as an accident in which its owner falls and hurts himself—this is only a small incident illustrating the importance of self-control and the value of right thinking.

Wherever people have to live together in a home, or work together in a field or factory, an office or a business, the presence of even a single undisciplined aggressive personality among them is enough to bring trouble or create quarrels. From this we may see what benefits the insistence of all spiritual guides on self-training and self-improvement can bring to social living. It teaches men to lift themselves up to their higher nature and to keep down their lower nature. To the extent that they are able to do this, to that extent, society benefits along with them. But to the extent that the warnings of the prophets are disregarded and the wisdom of the philosophers is unheeded, discord, strife, and war show themselves.

When emotion runs out of hand in the wrong direction, be it in anger, lust, hatred, or pride, it is also apt to run away with peace and happiness. It becomes a danger to person and property. The most predominant among the evil complexes which, under the law of recompense, bring suffering when activated are the aggressive, violent, explosive, and selfishly passional ones. People who want to keep these causes of their troubles simply because they are natural or familiar, but do not want to experience the troubles themselves that inexorably follow, have an attitude which is illogical. Until angers and greeds, hates and lusts die out in men's hearts, conflict and contention will persist in their lives. And such a death to the primitive passions comes only with total surrender of the ego to the Overself. Those who seek this are not many: those who attain it, very few. Peace on earth is a noble dream; its full realization is far off (although its limited realization is not) until more people come to its quest in this, the only true and lasting way. Each individual must deal with his lower nature for himself and in himself, must pit intellect against it, instead of letting intellect serve it. This done, not only does he profit but also his people.

Humanity must learn to discipline and rule its violent negative passions, its aggressive emotions, and antagonistic destructive thoughts, must begin to fight itself if it is ever to refrain from fighting others, must grow out of adolescent emotional immaturity and move upward from infantile, wholly ego-centered attitudes. The search for peace within itself must precede and thus inevitably create peace in the world without. The world-wide unbalance is partly a result of the failure to recognize that being physically mature is not enough, that it is still needful to become emotionally, intellectually, and spiritually mature.

It is a plain fact that the spiritual life is outside the vision and beyond the power of so many today. If we inquire into the causes we find that they have become so enslaved by their lower natures, so responsive to materialistic outside suggestions and environments that only the things which they can touch and feel and see with their bodies have any reality or meaning for them. Only those things attract them, not the finer things of the mind and the heart, not the sublimer ideals of the intuition.

What wisdom dictates and experience endorses is that if a better world is to come to humanity, better thoughts and feelings in humanity must be the prelude to that desirable condition. The notion that it can have a better order of society without troubling to better itself first, is an idle one. Reform must start with human character, if it is to make a real rather than a sham start. For out of its own long past it has brought over a residue of murderous qualities of feeling which belong naturally to the subhuman kingdom, to wild ravening jungle beasts. It is their combination with cold ruthless intellect which has produced megalomaniacal, inordinately ambitious men who in turn have led so many others down roads of strife, selfishness, and atheism to what can only be disaster and doom in the end.

The suspicions and fears exhibited by such leaders, who represent the evil forces in our time, the psychotic intensity of their hatreds which are partly the result of the contemporary situation and partly contributory to that situation, are instinctive if unwitting recognition of the ultimate defeat and doom of what they try to express to the rest of the world and to impose on it. What is lacking in their views of the situation is not only faith in higher values but also faith in the idea of higher powers. They are, for so long and so deeply, drunk with the success of material development and achievements in apparently mastering Nature, that they have become the victims of an inflated ego, the proponents of the complete capacity of the human will to flout ethics and deny spirit when moving on toward its goals. But the dramatic events of the twentieth century will show them what a tremendous delusion this vaunted capacity really is, for our planet is not a dead thing, but a living one. It is the visible body of a living intelligent and potent Mind. It eventually shakes out of its system and off its surface the moral and mental poisons which threaten to become utterly self-destructive to its own children, just as a human body throws up and throws out its own poisoned blood through skin eruptions. Those who refuse to permit themselves to be infected by the negative characters and adverse forces of our time, who seek the knowledge of, and obedience to, spiritual laws of being, provide for themselves in this way part of a form of protection against whatever dangers such forces may seek to involve all mankind in.

The tragic helplessness which the lone private individual feels as the tide of events moves grimly onward, the apparent uselessness of striving against such happenings, crushes emotion and taunts any concern for personal fate. In the face of this formidable drift toward self-destruction, a man in his aloneness and unimportance seems to count for very little. He can hardly be blamed for raising his hands resignedly as he comes to the pessimistic conclusion that whatever he does the outcome of the world events will remain unchanged, that however much he or his like try to influence them, the extent to which he can do so is too small to count and that even if he does the utmost that his situation and status permit him to do, he will find that it is only a small effort with a very limited range at most.

Since it is manifestly impossible for governments—with all their admirable efforts—to exercise the protective power of gods, each man should seek for himself his own additional sources of help. However necessary their political and military defensive preparations may be, his own spiritual preparations are not less necessary. Would he not be more prudent, more farseeing to widen his supports and make his own extra and personal effort to safeguard himself? Should he not develop his individual resources and find supplementary ways and means to take care of himself? If outer national events are beyond his control, his inner private life is not. Here at least his choices and his checks can rule, here he has personal and immediate freedom. If his outer destiny seems rigid his inner destiny is not. Where the world's trouble is so increasingly beyond control even of those who are in a position to contribute to public affairs, an unimportant individual who feels he can do nothing about it, can still do much about his personal reaction to it. He can take *that* in hand and mold or modify it. Mentally, for certain, and physically usually less so, it is still within some measure of control. He can regard it as his creative opportunity to do some much needed work on himself. If he can do little to bring peace to the world, he can do much to bring peace to himself. He cannot by himself save civilization's outer life, but he can by his endeavor save his own inner life. If he cannot bring tranquillity to society, at least he can try to bring it to himself.

Our times are a challenge to each individual to save himself, an enforced command to seek out his inner refuge and not helplessly to stake his all only on political and military protection. Each must make an external and internal change in his way of living regime and no longer look solely to others to take care of him and bring him safely through this crisis. Each man has to bear the deepest part of his anxiety alone. No one can bear it for him, or even help him to do so, however much he may delude himself that this is being done. Life, the great tutor, places him in such isolation to show him the face of his own psyche. He is a wise man who will profit by the revelation, and see his own weakness and strength, ignorance and knowledge, frustration and sufficiency.

One often hears of the idea in religious circles of some new mass approach, or some special national prayer, or some general call to repentance. The idea is good but it is not enough to meet the crisis. Each individual must still equip himself. He must start by waking himself and accepting some portions of elementary spiritual *truth*. He does not have to join any group, institution, creed, religion, or organization to do this, nor on the other hand does he need to leave whatever group, organization, or religion he now belongs to. Such changes are less important than his belief that a good life is somehow the way to satisfaction, and wrongdoing somehow the way to suffering. If he can bring himself to believe in this law of recompense and in the existence of some Higher Power behind it, and if he will make some effort to improve his character and unfold his inner resources, all this will be arms and armor for his defense in the crisis.

It is imperative for the discerning ones to learn some self-reliance and to begin the development of their own resources. Such individualists have the better future for only they can recognize the true call to salvation. But the others, who have become firmly lodged in their little grooves, are likely to accept a truly spiritual counsel no more than theoretically.

Many of them will hardly want to apply its practical measures to their own personal lives. Therefore, they will tack adjustments on to those injunctions which feel uncomfortable and make reservations about those ideals which are disconcerting. Only a few will have the moral courage to turn away from the attractions of heavy bourgeois sensuality and comfort, which hypnotize a whole civilization, and reject the self-admiring smugness which paralyzes true spiritual intuitions or perverts them into pseudointuitions.

He who wakes to the fact that the contemporary challenge is primarily an individual, and only secondarily a social, one, may not at first be able to devise a means of molding his outer life more in harmony with his life ideal. But if he will weigh what he wants against what he must sacrifice to gain it, he will often find that he has fallen into the common error of mistaking the habitual environment for the indispensable one. The average man is quite unaware how complacent is his outlook just as he does not know that this complacency offers resistance to mystical intuition from within and to truth teaching from without.

It was quite customary until recently to relegate the votaries of mysticism to the asylum of gullibility, fraud, and even lunacy. In a number of individual cases the critics were perfectly justified in doing so, for when the would-be mystic loses his straight course, he easily deviates into these aberrations. But to make a wholesale condemnation of all mysticism because of the rotten condition of a part of it, was unfair and itself an unbalanced procedure. The so-called sensible, normal, and practical people of the world are really less able to meet the crisis than some of the so-called silly, abnormal, and impractical dreamers, dubbed cranks, fanatics, and eccentrics. And yet this is not so strange after all. When men like Jesus, Buddha, and Socrates first appeared, they and their followers were similarly dubbed. They, too, were the heretics of their day, simply because they refused to congeal into the self-destructive materialism of conventional society.

Social pressures may prevent a man from living in conformity with ideas that run counter to them. He must drop his ideas, modify them, or hide them, if he is not to quit the community. Such a compulsory adjustment is neither good for his nerves nor for his character. It is an ironic comment on the nature of our civilization that so much that is of everlasting truth in mystical ideas and so well known to ancient Asiatics, will strike many moderns as being so new, either because they never heard of it before or if they did hear of it, because they ignored it completely.

Strange and unfamiliar ideas of this kind, which collide with those long held by the society around or upset those received by convention, come up against human nature, whose first and instinctive answer is to contradict them. This still remains true even when there have been established solid facts, proofs, and evidences. Such is the power of life-long habit and the strength of preconceived opinion! The reformer who seeks to overcome them climbs a steep hill. Only the so-called fanatics and eccentrics will listen willingly to him. The others who also listen do so unwillingly, when desperate in mind or broken in body.

It is not pleasant to swim against the current of society in the name of a mystical individualism; indeed it is sometimes heroic. The thought of changing the routine habits and getting rid of the acquired tendencies of a lifetime appalls and irks most people. They have become victims of the habits prevailing in their surroundings and the tendencies themselves have assumed psychological as well as physical existence, having become deep-seated fixations within the subconscious mind. Yet suffering awaits these victims if they insist on remaining prisoners of their own worn-out past and will not accommodate themselves to the different outlook now required. Why should they obstinately continue past conditions of thought or ancestral patterns of response wherever these have shown themselves to be unable to meet present requirements?

Each man is under some degree of tutelage to the mass. Every moment he is acted upon by suggestions from the crowd. He is more or less a slave—slave to social forms, slave to established institutions, slave to conventional codes, and slave to public opinion. Although this slavery was far worse in former times, even in our own time hardly anyone thinks, feels, and acts quite fully and freely out of his individual will alone. He is more likely to think, feel, and act largely out of what has been suggested to him by other people. Hence, he hardly ever lives his own independent life or obeys his own inner self but, with everybody, lives the crowd life. Even if some part of his attitude toward life is innate, the larger part is not. It is imposed upon him by the instruction and the teaching he has received, by the environments from which he accepts influences, and by the conventional standards to which he conforms. When a world outlook is so largely fashioned by external suggestion, the need of thinking for oneself becomes both a primary virtue and a necessary factor in mental health.

The human multitude is emerging from adolescence and here and there, half-consciously, preparing for its coming of age. New realms of experience are opening up for it. It must accept some of the responsibility of thinking for itself, which comes with the approach of maturity. It stands today in an intellectual position which is very different from that in which all its forebears stood. It is no longer the simple infant holding onto the garments of authority and blindly following its leader. Today it must begin to see its way for itself and understand why it is going that particular way. History has entered an age when the masses must begin to find for themselves and in themselves the truth which in former ages was handed to them and, quite rightly, accepted by them in blind trust from other men. Now they must prepare to pass out of this adolescent leaning upon others. Destiny will no longer permit them to depend unduly on the shelter of external authority alone; they have to learn also to depend on their own growing intelligence. A child which is always carried by its mother from infancy to maturity will never learn to walk, will indeed become too weak to stand on its own feet. It has to try and tumble and even fall sometimes before its limbs come into effective use.

If life becomes exclusively authoritarian, if mass man submits to having all his thinking, response, and living done for him by others, he will eventually become too enervated or debilitated to think, respond, and act by his own capacity. For when he is unable to hold a thought unless he has received it from outside, when he does not make a single decision of his own but runs to others to make it for him, how can he grow? Everyone has now to begin to free himself from the racial suggestions imposed upon him, has to start establishing by effort his individual attitude toward life. It is time for him to show, however vaguely, some of the attributes of dawning maturity. He must begin to cast aside passive unthinking acquiescence and become more responsible for his own beliefs and his own life.

One of the first things the philosophic student discovers as a consequence of his semantic studies is the tremendous influence which suggestion plays in human life and one of the first problems which faces him is to separate the habits, the thoughts, and emotions of other people from his own. Yet this is hard because they are almost indistinguishable from his own—both play together within and upon his heart. Ideas and impulses which are native to himself have to mingle with those of outside origin or even be submerged by them.

No teachers are really indispensable, although all are always helpful. Life and its experiences, Nature and her

silences, reflection and its conclusions, meditation and its intuitions will supply the seeker with what is needful. He ought
to find in the struggles and difficulties of life a gymnasium
in which to exercise his reason and add to his capacity, not an
excuse on which to flee to the second-hand comfort of a society upon whose shoulders all burdens are laid. For he is here
ultimately to unfold his *own* faculties of intuition and intelligence; he is here ultimately to gain an understanding of existence for and by himself. Moreover, he ought to comprehend
that the pains and sufferings of life help to purge him of his
attachments and to draw forth his latent knowledge that this
world of becoming must forever be imperfect, so that he may
turn his face toward that world of being which is forever
perfect.

Evolution is both a tremendous fact and an ever pressing
force. It impels all life onward and upward. But this twofold
movement cannot actualize itself without overpassing and
denying its earlier stages. Hence, man has to free himself
from ancient enslavements. He must begin to seek in himself,
in his own latent and wonderful resources, the help he needs.
For all this is the first step to the final one, to finding the divinity within himself, which after all is the ultimate and grand
object of his earthly incarnations.

It is necessary, however, not to fall into error here. What
is meant is that, whereas the ego's selfishness has now to be
attenuated, the ego's capacity for individual judgment has at
the same time to be increased.

Where Is Man's Fortune? Morally, every man is free to use
the menace of possible early annihilation as an excuse for
slipping into debauchery and inebriation, but he is equally
free to use it as a spur to higher endeavors which will equip
him with inner armor. This age, more than any other, has
heaped up external human pleasure with all the aid of science
and yet it, more than any other, has ironically felt the loss of

human happiness. The desire for frivolous pursuits which is so widespread today would be healthier were it balanced and moderate. But when it becomes, as we so often see it become, unbalanced, inordinate, and quite extravertedly escapist it is unhealthy. It is pleasant to enjoy and be entertained, but it is not enough by itself to constitute the purpose of life. Without a higher aim to redeem it, such a life is really a wasted one.

Our age does not wish to arouse itself to the fact of human suffering as being an inevitable eternal fact, stamped in the character of all human existence itself, and not merely appearing occasionally. For if it did so arouse itself, it would consequently have to arouse itself to the need of finding a method of *inward* escape from suffering's outward domination. All its upheavals form a poignant reminder that this world is but a passing camp and not a permanent home. A sad recognition of the transiency of earthly life and the insufficiency of earthly values forms part of the attitude of the individual who does arouse himself. From this stems his decision to limit his ambitions, to simplify his desires and question the habits of his environment. From this he begins to make the momentous about-turn, looking inside himself at last for help, peace, stability, and freedom. For what is the use of possessing so many things when he does not yet possess himself, of owning so many outer resources but so few inner ones? What is the use of rushing agitatedly hither and thither but never going in quest of his own soul?

Such is the insecurity of the present-day era that only the few who have found their own soul and with it inner peace, have found authentic security. Anyone who is willing to take his chances in the world's rushing life in the belief that he can find lasting happiness therein, is quite deluded. What he can find is passing happiness and temporary satisfactions.

This belief that if they can fill their lives with things and persons and happenings they will have fulfilled the object of life and consequently attained happiness, is the error which underpins so much social activity of the modern Western peoples. Being mistaken in what is their true good, the end of all their efforts is inevitably frustration, discontent, or disillusionment. Neither a multitude of things—however useful or mechanical—nor a host of persons—however rich, loving, or important—can be enough to give the heart what it really if unwittingly seeks. Those who have enough of the things for living or those who have made an easy passage through circumstances, may for a time be sufficiently satisfied with themselves and with the external world, but it will be only for a time. Others are running from one different alleged but disappointing satisfaction to another, beginning each experience under the pathetic delusion that it is the ultimate one, and ending it with the rueful knowledge that it is not. They are unable to listen to the voice of a wisdom immeasurably older than themselves. But those who have suffered frustration, deprivation, and misfortune, whose hopes have died and whose courage has departed, whose disappointment is deep and permanent, may want to escape from themselves or the world. It is they who most often have ears to hear and who will listen more readily to the voice of this ancient wisdom.

That some people are aware of spiritual emptiness within themselves, although their rooms are crowded with furniture, their closets with clothes, and their larder with foods, is true. Yet they are so unindividuated that they go on multiplying their material wants at the bidding of suggestive voices. The idea of pausing amid this feverish and illusory activity which brings no real happiness, and starting to take at their word the numerous inspired spiritual teachers who have pointed the only way to such happiness, is a mere idea in a vacuum. It is not applied to the everyday routine of life. Others have suffered more and possess less; hence they are somewhat more aware of inner need. Nevertheless worldliness rules most continents today to such an extent that they have little use for any exertion which does not offer quick gain and which does not show itself to their personal advantage. The exertion inculcated by an ideal whose gain is far-off and whose advantage is merely inner welfare seems unattractive.

Yet individuals here and there are beginning to wake up to the fact that modern Western civilization, with its endless multiplication of wants, is less conducive to peace of mind than the simpler ancient Oriental one, with all its admitted drawbacks and disadvantages and inconveniences. How can people know inner peace when they helplessly and continuously succumb to the suggestions pouring from every direction to increase their desires? Below a certain maximum and above a certain minimum of possessions, there is no real need for them. Inner peace is possible only for those who despise not only the poverty of pauperism but also the riches of superfluity.

People who are dazzled by the ownership of things while neglecting the ownership of themselves show they are emotionally and intellectually ungrown-up, a race of spiritually small boys and girls preoccupied with small toys. They display their spiritual adolescence as they let themselves be carried away by activity, possessions, excitement, external achievement, and worldly success. They overvalue these things, and in their struggle for them lose their chances of gaining peace of mind. They are continually overjoyed by each gain only to fall later into fitfulness and dissatisfaction, into disharmony and agitation. It is not pessimism or defeatism to point out the inadequacies of such a way of life. With all their doing and getting, what is it that they have really done: they have built up a civilization which is threatened from every side, as well as from the inside; and what have they really got: they have got a world of increasing frustration and greed, chaos and violence, envy, hate, and unrest.

They amass possessions in which they take pride and to which they become attached. The pleasure felt at such acquisitions soon turns luxuries into necessities, which is at least arguable as to wisdom, but also turns sound moral values into false materialistic ones, which is not. The more they yield to the suggestions implanted by their surroundings, the more their hearts fill with desires and become restless. The complexity of modern life, especially modern Western life, has made its victims lose the capacity to discriminate between the merely superfluous and the really indispensable.

The meaning of this goal—which has nothing to do with heroic asceticism—must be carefully specified. Desire is the driving force of life. Its manifestation and development within the human entity are part of the evolutionary plan for that entity. It is needed in the early and intermediate stages to bring out various latent capacities. It is needed in the advanced stages where it assumes the forms of personal ambition and cultural aspiration, to bring out still further capacities of a subtler kind. Its place in life is not an evil, much less an accident. During the stages of man's development of the personal ego his desires for the things which hold it are right and natural. He has to make use of them, attach himself to them, to satisfy needs and fulfill ambitions. But when, during the later stages of his planetary appearance, he discerns that he has not been set down on earth only to achieve physical improvement and bodily comfort, but also to achieve a higher goal and fulfill a higher destiny—spiritual realization—the higher and consequently more important purpose of that appearance must complement and modify the lower and preliminary one. Before, these things, attachments, and desires were useful and necessary to him. After, they are so only to the degree that endless wants are differentiated from essential needs. It is inevitable that a time should come when, with the maturest experience and the ripest reflection on the one hand and the bitterest suffering and keenest disappointment on the other, his desire-nature is forced to devaluate its objects and consequently to check its own activities. This does not mean it is to renounce them outwardly, but rather to discipline itself and its attachment to them.

A life of simple tastes in and of itself tends to foster inner tranquillity. Only by beginning to simplify, can man come back to a more natural existence and consequently a more spiritual and healthier existence. Beyond the degree of real need, things may become hindrances and he may have to begin to withdraw from them. He must examine his life and question his desires, to see how far any of them interfere with the realization of spiritual aspirations or take up time which he requires for exercises in relaxation and meditation. This will inevitably need to be followed by an ascetic readjustment, a learning to do without and to let go. Life is too short to be worth spending in bodily comfort but in spiritual stagnation, if examination reveals such to be his situation. At some point a man has to detach himself from attachments, has to say to things and even persons claiming entry into his heart; "Thus far and no further." He can train himself to become inwardly disassociated from relationships without becoming outwardly frosty toward them. To feel inwardly free and detached and not to be owned by things or people is a condition few Occidentals understand, let alone experience.

It is not necessarily the things from which he is to separate his heart, but the dominating desires for those things. Such a change of attitude may or may not lead to a casting out of possessions. His inner leading and outer circumstances must determine whether this is necessary. The need to simplify his life by managing with less things may rise within him, or it may not be possible, in view of his station in the world, to do even that. It does not matter. What matters most is what keeps him imprisoned in the ego; the thoughts and feelings expressed in desires that are always demanding more and more and are never satisfied with, or resigned to, what they already have. Property may be left as a chain clanking around his ankles or converted into a power for self-improvement and larger helpfulness. It is not what he owns but how he thinks and feels about what he owns, that really matters. Therefore it is not so much through the outward gesture of renouncing things that he makes genuine spiritual progress as through a change in the inward attitude toward those things.

To become detached from the world does not necessarily involve the emotions, although it most often does. One may still feel certain attachments and yet be really detached, provided one acts so in will and deed.

Those who talk of sacrifice and detachment but have never had any possessions or position to give up, talk too easily. This is why such opinions as the following are widely and firmly held: "I think it an impossibility to obtain philosophic tranquillity without riches; and I ridicule the opinions of those philosophers who boast of internal peace, in the midst of penury: and I listen to their assertions with incredulity." These words were written more than a century ago in Italy by the Marquis Francesco Guasco. How could anyone have removed the skeptical nobleman's doubts? No argument is so solid and convincing as that of personal experience. Nothing else can bring a man to believe that those sages and mystics who felt and proclaimed this mental peace, despite their poor external conditions, were neither telling lies nor suffering from delusions. They had found true inner felicity and the incredulous would be talking better sense if they objected not to its feasibility but to its difficulty.

Philosophy teaches that the supreme fact of any man's existence is not his circumstances or his fortune. It is himself. Environments come and go like the tide; the winds of fate and fortune rise and fall resistlessly; but through all change the thought of the "I" dominates everything. And the primary business of human life is to build character, enlarge knowledge, expand consciousness, unfold conscience, and above all recognize itself, its "I," as rooted in a higher state of being. Its secondary business is to gain experience. It feels pleasures and pains, acquires money, and rears a family really as a means to the primary one.

The only peaceful individuals are those who have inwardly withdrawn themselves—and sometimes outwardly too—to follow a better way of life, who have refused to submit to an activity which has no higher goal than its own mere self-continuance, who have set up a goal of spiritual attainment inside and outside the goal of physical attainment.

The Occidental worker should not be asked to imitate the Oriental fakir and seek the state of utter desirelessness. He wants to live well and so must have some desires. Desire, as was earlier said, has its proper place and usefulness in life. Nevertheless, he should recognize the transitory nature of worldly things, pleasures, and possessions, and consequently seek also for That which alone gives durable satisfaction. He should not limit his desires only to those things, pleasures, and possessions but should also add the desire for spiritual attainment, self-improvement, and inner peace. Tired of the contradictions inherent in sensuous aims, he should begin also to cultivate supersensuous ones. He should enter on the quest of spiritual self-realization, a quest whose goal is a unique and incomparable state. This alone yields the peace that passeth all desires and that comes from rising above them. St. John refers to it in 4:14: "whosoever drinketh of the water that I shall give him shall never thirst." This cannot be attained, however, unless he lives not only for the real necessities and disciplined enjoyments of the body, but also for the intangible values which cannot be measured by earthly standards. He may rightly appreciate and enjoy owning a radio and an automobile, if he wants to, but he should not become so infatuated with these merely physical appurtenances of living as to mistake their value and place when compared with spiritual things.

A suffering and tormented world needs the silent message

of this wisdom, yet only a humbled world is likely to listen to it sufficiently. It needs it, yet only a few see that philosophy is not something fit for dreamers only but is adequate to survive all the tests of all experience. A striking lesson of the catastrophic war and chaotic peace is that security and peace must first be found within ourselves. If this is done, we can then carry them with us whatever happens externally.

These are anxious and difficult times for which we need an inner support independent of external circumstances. We must ask and get assistance from the divine part of our being. For we need the extra power to be obtained from higher values and better principles, if we are to pass safely through this difficult period. There is ready at hand an unfailing resource, there is always present a beneficent power. If we believe in the reality, the higher consciousness, the intelligence, and the grace of the Overself; if we believe that these things really exist and are not mere intellectual concepts to play with in a game of speculation, then we must also believe that the Overself can help us in our hour of need. To discover whether this is so we must proceed to make the experiment. We must place our fullest faith in it and make our deepest appeal to it, which must be in deeds as well as prayers. We must turn our face homeward. We must stop looking to, and leaning on, those who are themselves in difficulty, and remember that everything human may fail us in the end, whereas anything divine is forever a rocklike authentic refuge. The best which we seek is within our grasp because the Overself is within our self. It can hear our sincere prayer and it can grant its benign grace. We must make the effort, therefore, and rely upon our own inherent diviner qualities, our own sacred potentialities, and our own mystical selfhood.

If we believe that God is greater than man, we must also believe that the spiritual self, which is our link with God, knows all about man. Since our own knowledge of life is admittedly inadequate and imperfect, would it not be wise and sensible to refer our basic problems to this higher being, to the Overself? So long as we act solely upon our own initiative and by our own feeble light, we have only the limited and often deceptive resources of the false outer self to depend on. As soon as we humbly acknowledge this situation and cast ourselves at the feet of the higher power, seeking communion with and guidance by it, we call its greater resources to our help. It is needful to be forewarned, however, that the answer to such a call may not come all at once but is often revealed little by little through the months or years, that we may have to wait awhile as call after call perseveringly goes out from us. But it is worth waiting for and is indeed the only thing so much worth waiting for in life.

Through the adoption of such attitudes we acknowledge the existence of a higher power and invite its help or even protection, during our difficulties. There are hundreds of thousands of soldiers, sailors, airmen, and civilians who found themselves during the war in dangerous situations where violent death or horrible mutilation seemed highly probable, and who turned to the higher power in prayer or resignation with an earnestness they had never before felt. They knew their helplessness as individuals and discovered what it meant to have faith, hope, and trust in the Mind behind the universe; some of them learned for the first time how valuable was the inward support that could be derived from it.

Every crisis which shows vividly how miserably small is human understanding, every catastrophe which reveals plainly how pitifully feeble is human strength, is an opportunity to turn in prayerful humility toward the higher self for help and guidance. To those who have looked out over the world and seen only its strife and chaos, philosophic ideas may bring renewed hope and confidence in the eternal sureness of the working out of God's purpose. To those whose lives are full of difficulties and discouragements they may bring new guidance and help, or at least the faith that there is a divine ordering of the universe. To those who are willing to accept the liberation it offers from fear and hate and other negative qualities, it shows life on earth no longer as a patchwork but as a pattern. To all it affirms that the movement of the human race is, despite appearances to the contrary, an adjustment to good in the end. Although it utters a warning message to the contemporary world, it also proffers upholding thoughts and practical counsel. To the extent that anyone informs himself about its enunciation of the higher laws and keeps within them, to that extent he protects himself.

CHAPTER XII

THE QUEST

IN THAT HIGHER WORLD of being where the Overself dwells, no evil can penetrate, or passion agitate. We descend from its absolute goodness to the darkness and turmoil, the sinfulness and violence of this earth, as from paradise to purgatory. The tremendous contrast between its moral sublimity and such moral degradation would doom us to perpetual sadness if there were no link between the two. But the link truly exists. Each human being may find out and follow the age-old Quest and thus ascend to awareness of his higher self.

All people are engaged upon little quests which have trivial or serious objects as their goals; only the man who has embarked the ship of his life upon the Grand Quest has nothing less than the fulfillment of God's purpose for him as its goal. When a man wakes up at last to the fact that his life has been an endless struggle with himself and continues to remain so, he may begin to inquire why this should be and what he can do to end it. Such an inquiry will lead him eventually to the Quest's gate.

There are those who have never formally heard of this mysterious Quest but who will nevertheless get some or even much of our meaning, even when they will not be able quickly to consent to its truth or yield directly to its monitions. Yet in another and larger sense, that will be enough. The challenge will have gone forth. One day, whether late or soon, whether in the flesh or out of it, there will surely be remembrance.

What it means then is this: that the seeker forestalls the evolutionary processes by doing for himself as quickly as possible what Nature will do for other men as slowly as possible. He practices self-sculpture along the lines drawn for him by intuitive guidance and outer revelation until the Ideal becomes the Actual. He labors at shaping himself, just as a sculptor labors at shaping the rough marble into an expressive statue. He knows the truth of what he has been taught by both intuition and revelation, as well as by the wide oscillations of experience, that the happiness and character, the insight and strength which give life its real values, he himself must create from within. All these qualities already exist there latently but he has to bring them forth by willed effort. He sees in his wiser moments that he must stop waiting for happiness to come from outside himself and that if it is really to come, it must come from inside. And he finds that to make this possible he must strive perseveringly with the chaos of contradictory feelings which interpose themselves between him and the Ideal.

It is clear enough that action expresses thought. It is not so clear that doing is also the completion of being, that what we do is the consequence of what we are. Those who believe that real philosophy is lost in dreams or immersed in abstractions are wrong. It not only asks the question "What is truth?" but also "How shall I live?" and what question could be more practical than that one? The European-American is essentially a practical man and if he finds that a certain teaching is not merely theoretical but also quite applicable to his everyday routine, that it not only gives its adherents an understanding of the inner purpose of life and an uncommon peace, much power over self and some over environment, he is more likely to look favorably upon it. Here, then, is its historic opportunity, for not only is it incomparably superior to all others, but it can particularly encourage, fortify, and guide him during these crisis years in whose swirling vortex all mankind is now inexorably caught.

The discerning man should need neither bait nor reward to live as he ought to do, for by this his external well-being and internal welfare are both helped, his true happiness built up or extended. Philosophy is not just a theoretical matter. After he becomes acquainted with the principal teachings, its student has to make an effort to apply them in his everyday living. He discovered these truths by the use of intuition and reason. Now he must test them by the scales of experience— emotional and physical alike. To accept them is one thing, to make them work in himself and his life, is another. Until they move from his lips into his living, they are only images reflected in a mirror. All this superb discipline, which he must patiently work out, will be devoted to the endeavor to better himself.

Of course, if he were to accept the conventional and worldly standards of thought, feeling, morality, and conduct, certain problems might not rise for him. But he has set himself a much higher ideal. That he will occasionally fail to live up to it is most probable, for he is human, but he must not accept his failures with smug complacency. On the contrary, he must try to wipe them out by wiping out their inherent causes and unfortunate results. This demands the discipline of self and sometimes even the endurance of emotional pain. Whatever is gained too easily may go too easily. This is true of the worldly pleasures and satisfactions. But the spiritual ones, which come from self-mastery in thought, emotion, and body, and after long struggles, efforts, and toils, stay and do not pass away.

He who stretches out his hands to the glowing peace of the soul does not stretch them in vain. But he may not feel its warmth at the first movement, nor at the tenth, unless he is willing to work for what he wants. Whoever accepts this knowledge will not need to be told that whether soon or late, whether little by little, or by a revolutionary spurt, it must manifest itself in a corresponding practical readjustment of everyday life. Out of the hallowed moments of intuition, prayer, or contemplation should come active inspiration for living, and out of the studious moments of metaphysical reflection should come right principles for living. In every situation he should try to hold to these principles and apply fundamental truths, and so acting, he will have no cause for after-regrets.

To find out their higher purpose on earth is one thing, to dedicate their life to that purpose is another, but many people refuse to do that because it seems impossible for them to realize such lofty ideals. The path is long and unfamiliar, its end seems an inaccessible pinnacle, and the obstacles *en route* plentiful and formidable. As the aspirant gazes at it, his sense of inferiority may well up, he may become discouraged and feel that the journey is beyond his modest strength and short lifetime. He may doubt whether he has enough capacity to climb the upward course which is before him, as Tao Yuin Ming doubted, when he sorrowfully exclaimed fifteen centuries ago, "Heaven is beyond my hopes."

But such pessimism is too extreme, unwise, and unnecessary. Even if man knows that he will most probably never reach the Ideal, this ought not prevent him striving to actualize it. Even if he has no startling attainments to show for all his

258 *The Spiritual Crisis of Man*

efforts, even if his advance is so slow as to seem disappointing, at least he has this gratification, that his face is turned toward the correct destination and that his feet are already on the way to salvation. If he finds the right direction and keeps his face toward the goal, he need not get discouraged at the slowness of his progress. Thomas Carlyle wrote in a letter: "Let a man be true in his intentions and his efforts to fulfill them, and the point is gained, whether he succeed or not."

All men, by setting a goal, can make some little progress toward it during their lifetime. The benefit and reward attendant upon the advance are not without worth. If they do this, they will have the satisfaction that they can take the worst that may possibly befall them at least measurably better than if they do not. Let those who deem self-betterment as beyond their capacity at least attempt it hesitatingly, step by step, rather than attempt nothing at all. If they will take the first few steps patiently, perseveringly, and correctly, they thereby express their interest in the Overself, and the Overself will then express its interest in them. They may be of good cheer. There are still other goals on the way to the highest one. It may well be that few can ever reach that, but it is certain that many can get worth-while benefits by trying to reach it. Even though they may never feel they can stand on the peak of attainment in this incarnation, they may, though only for moments, get into its beautiful atmosphere. Even this is of great worth.

Hope is the power which persuades a microscopic protoplasmic cell to take its chances in the evolutionary game of life, and lifts it eventually into the form of a huge elephant. It is the mysterious breath of magic which takes a failure and transforms it into a success. It is the incoming breath of a babe and the outgoing breath of a corpse. It is the transfiguring ray of sunlight which redeems the triviality of the meanest existence. It is the last asset of man, but among the best, for he who possesses hope finds fresh strength from inner fall and outer failure.

Lastly, those who look as from afar off at the Quest, who regard its attainments as something they cannot hope for, its labors as something beyond their strength and circumstance, may yet profitably study and familiarize themselves with the teachings. If they have faith in the ideas and accept them sincerely, this is not without some present benefit to them, while it lays a foundation in this life for discipleship in some future life.

What does spiritual progress mean? Does it mean to have more and more visions, raptures, or strange happenings? No! It means that every year a man shall feel more control of himself, more improvement in his character, more watchful of and obedient to his intuitions, more devoted to his higher self. Once he has set up his ideal, the aspirant will be called upon to judge himself from time to time. He knows well enough that he cannot at once fully live up to it, and for aught he knows, he may never in this lifetime ever fully live up to it. Nevertheless, he must present to himself periodically the thought of what needs to be done, for in this way he will help to keep complacency and vanity at a distance.

The stretch or even opposition of worldly experience, its trouble and distresses, no less than its joys and attainment, afford a strict test as to how far and how seriously he regards the philosophy of truth as a practical guide in life. Even the first strong wind of unexpected circumstance will do that.

The Quest mostly winds its way across a long, flat plain, but other times it courses up lofty, difficult mountains. It is not hard to mistake the path or difficult to take a misstep. The traveler may have to pass through states of temptation and struggle, trial and defeat, combat and triumph. He may have to negotiate his way around or over the boulders which are placed at certain stages of his path. He should be prepared to endure recurring disappointments of exaggerated anticipation and to experience inevitable frustrations of premature hopes.

If it is asked, "How long a time will it take to follow this Quest until the goal is attained?" the answer can be only that so long as the Overself is only an idea, not known and not experienced every moment of the day, awake *or asleep,* so long must the Quest be followed. To measure this period on a scale of years must necessarily vary with different individuals. They all start from different starting points, from different levels of their present condition. It is not possible to set any period. Men are to be seen advancing for a time, stopping for a time, missing their way for a time, and renouncing the Quest altogether for a time. Or they move forward slowly at some periods and quickly at others. So much is asked of them that it is understandable why so few do realize the goal.

Man brings into incarnation a number of subconscious as well as conscious driving urges, but they do not make their appearance all at once. They begin to influence him at different ages, so that his character, intentions, and actions seldom follow a single line throughout the course of his years. It is in middle life that the buried spiritual aspirations of those past embodiments, as well as of early manhood reappear and demand satisfaction. Consequently, a large number of aspirants for the Quest are drawn from the ranks of those who have reached or passed forty or fifty years of age. It is often true that the man in middle life may be filled with poignant regrets that he has started on this Quest too late to make much difference in his experience, too late to hope for successful accomplishment, too late to have the strength needed for creation of new habits of thought and action. The sadness of frustration may settle upon him. Nevertheless, he ought to recognize that middle age has also brought him some valuable qualities which he did not possess before. It has brought him some equilibrium between passion and reason, between emotions and thought, between body and mind, and between ideals and realities. It has brought him wiser discrimination in dealing with ideas, attitudes, people, events, and environment. It has brought him an all-round revision of values and experience, a habit of taking second thought and a clearer recognition of the dreamlike, and therefore the mentalist, nature of existence itself. All this will help him in the Quest. Few young men have it. If he has no adolescent enthusiasms, no juvenile excitements, no hysteric infatuations, it is only because they are replaced by something better—calm appreciations, fair, sane, and balanced admirations. The Jesuits do not trust a man with full membership of their Order— and consequently with the knowledge, power, and responsibility that go with it—until he is forty-five years of age. With age, the passions lose their strength in ordinary men or submit better to discipline in aspiring ones. This change comes as a tragedy to the former, but as a relief to the latter.

There still remains the beneficent but mysterious factor of the Overself's grace, which no symbol can adequately represent. Its operations are unpredictable, but its factuality is certain. By effort of the right kind, along with prayer and service, it is possible to invoke this grace. Thus, it is not alone upon his personal strength that he has to rely. He may receive inspiration and assistance to do what he could not do otherwise, if only he will look in the right quarter for them. Lastly, if he has been lucky enough to give his loyalty unceasingly to someone who has himself closely approached or successfully realized the Overself, but who has not lost his compassion for others in the process nor shrunk from the sacrifices involved in chaining his feet to humanity's service, the reward is then *ultimately* sure. The master's grace will not be withheld but the conditions for its reception must first become suitable.

Wholeness and Balance. It is not only part of the Quest's goal to make a man wise, disciplined and, in the truest sense, a practical person, but also both a whole and a balanced one. This is indeed highly important. The direction in which life is moving us is the attainment of wholeness—body, mind, feelings, and intuition are to become a harmonious channel through which the Overself can express itself unobstructedly. Among those who follow mystical teachings, there is a substantial number who show, by the lack of balance in their character and in the way they conduct their affairs, that they are really psychoneurotic cases. As such, and for a time, they need the services of mental and emotional therapy, which might indeed prepare them for, and make them better able to profit by, the services of philosophy. It is really distressing to find such cases quoted in adverse criticism and harsh comment upon mystical cults, when the fact is that they entered mysticism already suffering from neuroses, or were made worse by the half-baked methods and ridiculous disequilibrium of those cults. A true mysticism, such as forms a part of philosophy, seeks to maintain its balance and retain its common sense, rationality, and practicality, throughout its course. It is much less attractive to the wild neurotics and much more to the sensible or educated people, most of whom are afraid to enter such an apparently doubtful realm of ideas and experiences.

There are four distinct functions of the human personality, four separate activities within the human psyche—thinking, feeling, willing, and intuiting. These four elements of the psyche must become active at their highest levels, and at the same time kept balanced in their activity. Indeed the Quest's entire work will prove a long course in developing and balancing all the three faculties mostly used, and then making them illumined by, as well as obedient to, the intuitive faculty. When only one or two of these functions of being are active and the others are not, there is a lack of balance. If intellect acts without the guidance, check, or control of intuition and emotion, then it will surely mislead itself, make mistakes, and come to wrong conclusions. If emotion ignores reason and is unresponsive to intuition, it will surely become the puppet of its egotism and the victim of its desires. If spiritual teaching is brought into the intellect alone or the emotions alone, and not into the will, it will be to that extent and in that part sterile.

Most aspirants have an unequal development. Some part or other of the psyche is deficient. One may be a very good man, but at the same time a very foolish one. Another may be quite intellectual, but also quite unintuitional. Each enlightenment, each momentary glimpse of the Overself, as it occurs, is a call to repair this inequality and to aim at wholeness. That few people achieve this harmony of the psyche, that most are ill-assorted unions of adult development in some respects with infantile development in others, is all the more reason why the earnest aspirant should make it his business to examine himself honestly from time to time and use the results in purposeful endeavors to educate himself into wholeness.

This need of a developed and balanced personality does not arise only from metaphysical causes, but also from psychological ones. What is the use, for instance, of prescribing meditation to a person who is already too introverted to be able to cope with his personal circumstances? It will only withdraw him still further from the ability to adjust himself to life and to meet its problems both courageously and adequately, and from the willingness to face its external realities. Such a man is already an escapist, and the practice of meditation will only help to make him even more an escapist than he is. Not by escape into further illusion or a fictitious goal can he find a true path for himself.

Philosophy believes in the necessity of integrally developing and harmoniously establishing a reciprocal balance between reason, intuition, emotion, and action in the whole

human personality. Its aim is not one-sided. It refuses to
strengthen character but leave the body weak or to
strengthen reason and leave feeling always at variance. The
philosophic synthesis brings all these different trends together
without interfering with their separate functions. This is done
by reconciling them instead of setting them against each
other, by recognizing the inevitable manifoldness of all manifested existence. The student seeks to correlate his various
tendencies and keep them harmonized, not permitting any
single one to become unruly or to usurp the throne of sovereignty. He must use and unite seeming antitheses.

When he understands the interdependence of all these different sides of his nature, he relaxes the tension of keeping
them in perpetual conflict. No longer is his inner being at
cross purposes with itself. No longer is his will self-shattered
by its own attractions and repulsions. No longer are his emotions torn and divided by conflicting demands. He does not
cling to a pendulum which swings now this way and now
that way. He does not sway over to any particular side
through ignoring the other sides, does not nourish some qualities by neglecting all the others. He achieves a perfectly balanced character which does not sway too much up or down
into intellectual extremes or too far to and fro into emotional
moods, and which discriminatingly keeps a proper sense of
proportion in all actions. All the different parts of his nature,
all the varied faculties of his being, labor unitedly and equili-
bratedly toward achieving this single end of becoming whole.
In this way, he can win gratifying equilibrium from his efforts and actions, even if it comes only with the passage of
the years.

Philosophy does not alter its integral character, but remains
its own self whether it is busy with thoughts or stilling them,
whether it is praying on its knees or working in the fields.
Practicing its preachments, wholeness, and balance are three
essentials which it seeks to cultivate, but they are not the only

ones. To them has to be added some others which are not less but even more important: re-education of the feelings, prayer, relaxation, and meditation. Those who seek by this endeavor to restore their own integrity, remove their own imperfections, and attain their own spiritual awareness, are putting themselves into the best possible position to help others do the same for themselves.

The response of the higher self to the human call is given under the restrictions of wisdom. It does not pander to our sentimentality nor is it willing to reinforce our egotism. Peace that is worth so much cannot be had without producing its equivalent cost. There will necessarily be a self-denying struggle to transfer allegiance from the senses to the soul, and to make personal habits more aligned to the higher laws.

Philosophy is uninterested in flattering a man or in pandering to his vanity. Therefore, it begins the practical side of its re-educative discipline by pointing out his defects, faults, and shortcomings, and by opening his eyes at last to the weaknesses, incapacities, and complexes which hitherto have been unconscious or disguised. To go forward safely on this path, a man needs to be cured of fanatical obsessions and conventional irrationalities. He may think that eradication of personal faults has little to do with finding the true self, but this is not correct. These very faults rise out of the false conception of the "I" which blocks his path to it, a conception which causes him to identify himself with emotions that he has inherited from animal and primitive human reincarnations.

There are followers of mysticism who use it as an escapism, who hope by some magical power to get a transformation of themselves and their lives without having to make any hard effort or to undergo any hard discipline. Three mystical doctrines particularly appeal to them and are constantly taken advantage of to avoid this effort and discipline, this necessary work upon themselves. A fatalistic view of the law of recompense (karma) is taken to justify their stagnation or failure. An infantile view of the relationship with a master is taken to thrust on his shoulders the entire responsibility for their worldly life or problems, and spiritual progress. A too personal view of the doctrine of grace is taken to seek God's favoritism and to support the ego.

Too many would-be yogis, whose imagination easily borders on wild fantasy and whose vanity makes them think they are more advanced than they really are, sit like spiders in a web, spinning a tissue of wholly self-centered thoughts and then enveloping themselves completely in it. They fall into hallucinatory experiences and false visions or become the recipients of deceptive messages from imaginary sources—all arising through unwarranted preconceptions, unjustified expectations and egoistic suggestions derived from misapplying their reading of books or their attendance of lectures. They retrograde into careless slovenly habits, becoming less alert and less intelligent, less factual and less useful, less responsible and less practical. They pack their heads with worthless or misleading information got by some "psychic" or pseudo-intuitive means. The necessity of using caution and feeling responsibility when attempting meditation is thus not to be ignored or forgotten. It can bring many blessings if properly approached and at the proper time, but not otherwise. Therefore, those persons who practice the mystical meditation as a habit, must practice rightly or not at all. Those who do its exercises wrongly or before they are morally prepared or psychologically balanced for it, may receive some benefits but more harm. They devitalize the physical body and disrupt the physical life. It is better to wait until feeling and reason, imagination and discrimination, are brought into healthy equilibrium. All persons are not suited for meditation and the unsuited ones will always find enough to develop in other directions to make them ready for it eventually; meanwhile the practice of simple relaxation offers a useful substitute.

If the divine image is always there within us, the light it

sheds and the warmth it emits are often largely or wholly obstructed by intervening walls from reaching our surface consciousness. What are these walls? They are materialistic tendencies, excessive attachments, excessive extraversion, unbalanced nature, violent feelings, evil thoughts, clogged and poisoned bodies, unruled passions, and above all, the unruled ego. Therefore, to become conscious of this light, the aspirant must refine emotions, govern instincts, and thus fortify character. He should start the practice of mystical introspection exercises, begin the study of the metaphysics of truth, and by this self-education acquire a knowledge of the deeper meanings of self and life, the divine and universal laws of human evolution and destiny. He must cultivate the religious feelings and the mystical intuitions by regular effort through prayer and meditation. The purpose of all this arduous purification is to take chains off the feet of the will and the mind and thus give them a chance to move freely into the realm of the Overself. If he is patient and willing to wait, the answer to all questions within the seeker's heart will be found one day, provided he works at this self-purification while he is waiting.

Regenerating the Body. The Sphinx—that remnant of Atlantean knowledge—stretched itself out in the desert to warn all candidates for illumination who passed beneath and between its forepaws that they had to overcome their lower nature. They could not leave the outer precincts of the hidden temple and gain entry into its "Chambers of Power" until this had been sufficiently done. But the lower nature and lower mind will not relinquish their grip in any other way than by fighting a way out of it. This requires a training of the will, a denial of the appetites, and a discipline of the body which, while not pleasant in the beginning, becomes so in the end.

No man has absolute freedom of will and choice in his outward conduct. No man can do just as he pleases. This is as true of the philosopher as of the fool. All men are limited by some circumstance and conditioned by some situation outside themselves. But if there is no real full and perfect freedom of will and choice for any man, no decision of the mind or act of the body for which he alone is wholly responsible, yet two different forms of submission are nevertheless open to him. He is free to be either a servant of his higher self or a slave of his lower nature. Where is the freedom of will for a man who has let himself become enslaved by petty hates, angers and lusts often born through the body's disorders or toxemias? Men who are not themselves free from these enslaving passions and spiritual unconsciousness will nevertheless proudly boast of their liberty merely because they have a citizen's rights.

To free the will from enslavement to the lower nature leads of itself to enough mental illumination to show the aspirant how false is the freedom which seems to accompany obedience to those passions. It is intolerable to the thinking man that he should let himself be enslaved by appetites that are no longer natural and by passions that are peace-wrecking.

No man who aims at a goal superior to himself is likely to avoid failures in will. He may let them pass for a time but he cannot afford to do so for a long time, for then the habit of inertia or of defeatism may imperceptibly be bred within him and stultify fresh efforts. At a certain point he needs to stop being indulgent toward his frustrations and to start being determined to follow a course of discipline. The smug acceptance of his own shirking of physical and emotional self-discipline, is one reason why he fails to make noticeable progress. If he, and all those other seekers who complain of making little or no progress, would arouse themselves out of their sloth and undertake some real discipline of the body and training of the emotions, they would understand that the first practical step is to *do* something in the direction of reforming themselves; they would then have less to lament. Moreover, it is often necessary for them to initiate vigorous physical changes if they wish to make their intuitive receptiveness more active and more accurate. Such a discipline must include purification of the body and alteration of its habits along so-called ascetic lines for a time, either as a preliminary or as an accompaniment to whatever mental work is attempted. Without it, the latter loses itself in mere dreaming, or sometimes even delusion.

It will be seen that there is a place for asceticism in the philosophic life, but it is a serene and sane place. Instead of being used to hurt or to destroy the body, it is here used to develop and perfect it. Instead of endangering its health, it here promotes the highest state of good health. This work of physical betterment and emotional and passional purification is required most often as a preparation.

We need a new view on austerity and penance, a fresh appraisal of asceticism and self-denial. We must inquire why they have held their place in the spiritual life so long and so widely. The mystical ideal has always been historically associated with asceticism.

The proper purpose of asceticism has often been misunderstood both by its blind adherents and its superficial critics. It is not a dismissal of the body as illusory by neglect and indifference, it is not a despising of the body as inimical by a slow torture; it is an attempt to put the body in its intended place as a servant of the whole of man's being, including his spiritual being.

Although there is much to be said in favor of the rigid disciplines, systems, and routines of most monastic institutions, as devices to detach men from worldly life and to unite them with a holy one; although they may suit the generality of religious-minded aspirants very well, they do not comfortably suit the philosophic-minded. The latter need to grow as the plant and flower grow, with the sun drawing their leaves and petals to spread themselves out. They need a freer air, a less organized and more individual approach. They require fewer rules and easier regulations, less enclosure and less community life.

Ascetic disciplines, when intelligently and properly applied, are turned against the senses' domination of the mind so that the latter may be free to turn its attention inward, exploring its own purer recesses. But unfortunately they have come to mean not only man's denial of the senses by his will, but also his self-tormenting flagellation of them. Philosophy does not give any commendation to an asceticism which seeks to make life as unpleasant as possible under the belief that it is thereby making life as righteous as possible.

The direct aim of a regime of philosophic discipline is to prepare the way for spiritual rebirth, to make penance for the sensuality and selfishness of bygone conduct, and to prepare the body, the emotions, and the mind for the influx of higher forces and holier currents. Its indirect aim is to get rid of disease and give health and vigor to the body. It ought to be recognized that the so-called normal state of civilized man is really unnatural and unhealthy; that the re-education of the mind and training of the body which the Quest brings about are really therapeutic processes; and that this attempt to achieve harmony with the Overself is really a healing effort. Whoever violates the hygienic laws of his body and being is eventually asked by Nature to suffer the consequences.

Whoever remains uninterested in human life and indifferent to the human body, naturally makes no attempt to understand the world, of which the body is a part, and which he regards either as evil or as illusory. Consequently, he has no revelation or insight which will explain their nature, laws, and evolutionary developments. The problem of how to live peacefully in the body and cope with its diseases and passions, is not solved by declaiming the illusoriness of its character.

The student who is seeking this higher knowledge will not only not be able to assimilate it beyond his personal capacity, but also will not be able to make more of it than his short-comings allow. For instance, his unbalance or his insensitivity, his bodily bad habits or unruly emotional conditions will enter into what he learns and deform it. Some degree of mental-emotional self-correction and physical purification is usually laid down as a prerequisite before it can be fully imparted to him. This work upon himself calls for a certain amount of severity toward himself. Therefore, disciplinary practices are quite rightly a part of the earlier stages of the mystical method. Philosophy itself incorporates and does not object to them. It objects only to the exaggerated importance laid upon them, and to the pursuit of them into ascetic extremes.

Typical instances of exaggerated and unreasonable asceticism which it utterly rejects are: the Curé d'Ars's refusal to smell a rose; Suso inflicting horrible tortures on his body with iron instruments, hair shirts, and even sharp nails; the Mohammedan fakir dwelling, eating, and sleeping among the gravestones of a cemetery; Madame Guyon putting sharp flints and pebbles inside her shoes when about to go for a walk!

It is the hardest of struggles for the aspirant to overcome his passions, rule his desires, and control his thoughts. Buddha said that the man who conquered himself was greater than the conqueror of cities. The effort involved is indeed so great that it must necessarily extend over many, many reincarnations. There are some practical ways in which the aspirant can make the struggle shorter, the triumph easier. The first purification to which he is called is that of the body. The practice of this ancient technique unveils the true instincts of the body, and to some extent even of the feelings, instincts which have been deeply buried beneath the conventional materialism of society, civilization, and tradition. It serves a threefold purpose: penance, purification, and healing. The reduction or even elimination of gluttony in flesh-food eating, alcohol-drinking, and tobacco-smoking are signs of such advance.

Gluttony is a mistake in bodily hygiene more than a sin in moral conduct. It consists either in taking into the mouth food and drink in excess of the body's actual needs to maintain health and strength, or in taking such articles of diet as are harmful to it. Such a violation of its laws must inevitably lead with the efflux of time by cumulative effects, to a disturbance of its proper functioning or a manifestation of disease. The accumulation of this unwanted or discordant material ultimately affects health, nerves, emotions, and mind in an obstructive or debasing way. One effective way of reducing this accumulation is fasting, done occasionally and for short periods only.

It is not at all necessary for man to deprive any living creature of its body in order to sustain his own flesh. Nature has provided him with all he needs in grains, vegetables, fruits, and dairy products.

As late as the fourth century, when St. John Chrysostom was writing, he said that "we (the Christian leaders) practice abstinence from the flesh of animals to subdue our bodies . . . the unnatural eating of flesh-meat is of demoniacal origin . . . the eating of flesh is polluting." Let us remember that the writer of this argument for vegetarianism was, in the opinion of St. Augustine, the most authentic and eloquent Christian literary advocate of his time.

The so-called normal man fills his body with toxic waste products by wrong eating and lack of inside cleansing. These in turn fill him with morbid appetites and continuous desires. The really normal man will thoroughly enjoy his meals, yet will never eat for the sake of eating, taking no more food than is needed by the body to sustain its functions.

He may enter into the sex relation, but he will not enter it *solely* at the body's unrestricted bidding, nor *only* under the impulsion of inflamed senses, nor merely at the suggestion of another person who is the victim of such bidding and senses. He will not allow the precious distillation of his vital essence to be wasted continually in weakening self-indulgence nor the precious freedom of his heart and mind to be surrendered to sexual slavery. He will not let himself be blinded by the physical ecstasy produced by sexual intercourse to the metaphysical reflection that it is only a brief, costly and shifting counterfeit of the ecstasy produced by spiritual elevation. Brief—because in a few minutes it is gone. Costly—because its effects are often so disproportionate to its value. Shifting—because those in whom it originates may come to tire, dislike, or even hate one another. It is more immediate and perhaps more enthralling than the ecstasies produced by artistic and intellectual creation or appreciation, but they are less costly and more lasting.

Nevertheless the energy which shows itself in the sexual impulse is a manifestation, in the lowest and most limited form, of the holy, fundamental, and creative energy of the World-Mind. This is why all creatures seek its satisfaction, however blindly and however wrongly, for the joy it yields is a muffled echo whose original sound belongs to a divine region.

The aspirant should not let the morbid, the negative, and the toxic come into his body or his mind. The purpose of ascetic regimes is multifold, but its primary ones are to purify the body and the emotions and to restore them to true health. He who voluntarily reforms his habits of living, introducing certain stretching, tensing, pressing, and breathing exercises, changing the day's routine and diet at the bidding of principle and in defiance of appetite, gains physical fitness and strengthens moral force as a higher result.

It is necessary to cleanse the body of its impurities and cure it of its malfunctionings to some extent, along with emotional and mental cleansing, so that the personality may open up to the forces of the Overself without further obstruction than that which is always present and always the most formidable of all—the ego. Some purification must precede, and make possible, regeneration. The failure to understand this may be one reason why those who practice meditation but neglect balance and purification often fail to make the expected progress toward glimpses of the Overself.

Only out of the growth of his experience and the ripeness of his understanding will man come to question his desire-nature, and to limit it in the interests of the Quest. For only then will he perceive that it is no longer enough to evaluate things from the point of view of their pleasurableness or painfulness alone. By the growth which time and experience, reflection and reason bring to him, he begins to empty his heart of the gluttonous appetites and morbid desires which the body's toxicity creates for him. Although the strengthening of the will and the cleansing of the intestinal tract are needed to carry the process to an advanced stage, grace—magical and sweet and holy—is still needed to finish it and make the heart quite free.

In the reform, uplift, and perfection of his moral and emotional life he may take advantage of certain physical aids which could make his endeavor markedly easier. This re-education of the body's instincts and appetites, passions and nerves, is helped by the use of pressures, tensions, abstentions, cleansings, and even violence constructively directed against them. It is quickest done by an arousal of the will as an act of sacred devotion, by the determined and regular practice of creative psycho-physical exercises which channel the force behind them into health, virtue, and mastery.

From this purifying of the fleshly body, as a part of the total effort to open a way for the entry of the intuitive element, it will be an easier passage to the purifying of the feeling-nature. To find inward tranquillity and outward health of the body is to lay the firmest foundation for whatever other happiness life may bring.

Re-educating the Emotions. In the past, the seeker's emotional life was largely an instinctive response to the senses, a blind process in which he was often carried away to his own harm. There was no real freedom of will in it, only an imaginary one. But now some light falls upon the whole scene. Henceforth, the emotions are to be freed from their enslavement to the senses, are to be guided to move for his best interests by his own higher will, are to be ennobled, refined, and spiritualized.

The petulant childish person who is adolescent in emotional attitude must develop into a more mature, balanced, and self-disciplined adult before the mystical exercises can be profitably pursued. The neurotic whose emotions are still at an infantile level, who gives way to panic and tantrums, who storms into hysterics at the slightest provocation, should realize that his immediate task is not to develop mystical powers, but rather to develop moral virtues. The Overself will refuse him a glimpse of Itself until he does develop them. It is more important for him to build up character than to sit down and meditate in quest of psychic sensations. Otherwise, it is all too easy for the ego to surround him with an emotional mirage, formed of so-called love, hate, indignation, sentimentality, fear, bliss, or whatever else suits its purpose at the time, and thus impede his progress or throw him back.

He who nurses a grievance, for instance, who cultivates a sense of being injured and feels resentment against the person he deems responsible for it, interrupts his own spiritual progress. He cannot manage the trying situation without yielding to its provocation, expressing his lower emotions, or displaying his unworthy attributes. He blames the lack of spiritual development in others for this result when he should blame himself. This evasion of responsibility is an old trick of the ego. But nobody is more responsible for its fortunes and misfortunes than itself.

The ego masks itself so thoroughly and so speciously that he is unaware of how it is harming him. Let him not make the mistake of hiding his faults from himself. It is negative emotions like meanness, dread, malevolence, enmity, malice, intolerance, bigotry, sulkiness, and quarrelsomeness which make up the ego's strength when it stubbornly refuses to yield to the Overself's silent voice. This foolishness of bolstering up the ego instead of acknowledging its guilt, puts unnecessary obstacles in his way and keeps the soul's grace at a distance. His judgments will be wrong, his goals will turn out to be phantoms, and his life will be haunted by misfortunes when he insists on defending the ego instead of censuring it. He will do better to transfer the object of resentment to his own ego for the life-long deception it has played on him and for the life-long injury it has done him. The more it makes itself conscious of its faults, the more it may expect from life. The quicker it recognizes its blunders, the better its future will compare with its past. The less it is anxious to improve its neighbors and the more to improve itself, the greater the likelihood of doing both. While others are wasting their time and harming themselves by searching for excuses for their defects, the earnest philosophical student improves his time and helps himself by searching for constructive ways of amendment. He will need humility to recognize his own deficiencies instead of being engrossed in other people's, but the reward will be commensurate.

Every provocation by the faults, sins, or errors of other persons offers him the chance to practice the casting out of negative reactions to it. The more irritating it is, the more he should smile because of the greater opportunity thus given him. He may regard it also as a test. A provocative situation should be recognized as a profitable chance to start the inner work on it without allowing the common negative reaction to start first. Thus, impatience and irritability at being kept waiting on an appointment can be kept out by immediately declaring his possession of infinite patience, and by remembering the Eternal Now, with its infinite acceptance of Life.

Nevertheless, prudence counsels him to avoid places and persons and situations which are likely to arouse the lower nature. These things are better faced by the strong than by the weak, by the mature and purified than by the young, ungrown, and unseasoned. If he knows for instance that proneness to anger is one of his failings then, until he wins some rulership of the empire of self, it would be prudent to avoid those situations which may provoke his anger.

It is an important part of the disciple's task, this conquest of personal emotion. Life itself will present him with opportunities to test how far he has gone in this direction. They are opportunities to desert a lower point of view for a higher, opportunities to raise, purify, or depersonalize his feelings when they are of a negative egocentric character. This self-denial brings commensurate spiritual rewards in terms of enduring advancement. Such opportunities will show themselves most conspicuously in connection with his relation with other persons. Differences, frictions, and disharmonies which might otherwise rise on both sides can now be limited to one side, and that not his own. He can remain cool, collected, unresentful, and unagitated where the temptation might be to behave in an opposite way. Let him think deeply and calmly for a little and he will see that many of these so-called human feelings and human attitudes are really undesirable; and that he should not submit to their tyranny or excuse himself on their account merely because they are so common and so widespread. Let him reflect that it is in spite of their faults and weaknesses that he likes his friends or loves those near and dear to him. He would not like or love them any the less if those faults and weaknesses were to disappear. On the contrary, he would like or love them all the more. And if this is true of merely human faults and weaknesses, how much truer still must it be of those baser faults and weaknesses, those gross animalities and harsh feelings which bring out what is worst in humanity.

That part of him which changes with the emotional tides, which fears, desires, desponds, and jubilates by turns, cannot be eternally preserved, either in life or after death. Nature will still subject it to the evolutionary law, will still put him into experiences which, by making him aware of his unsatisfactory limitations, will not allow him to find peace until he turns away from resting self-complacently in them.

Is it not inhuman, if not even somewhat insane, many will object, to ask a man to adopt an attitude toward his own personal life somewhat like that of a chemist observing elements in the laboratory? Can anyone ever become so totally detached, so utterly cold, so wholly unmoved and so impassively analytical toward the experiences and events that matter most to him? But such questions show a misconception of the philosophic discipline. To help clear this up, let us ask ourselves a further question. Why is it so much easier to examine the past rather than the present if we want to see where we go wrong, or to discern the true opportunity from the deceptive one, or to recognize real friends as against false ones? Mentalism answers it is because the personal ego interferes more easily when we are actually involved in any situation than when we can look at it in long-range perspective. And this in turn happens because emotion is uppermost in us at the time of any happening, because we excitedly take it to be a material reality. Whereas, after it has receded into a memory, that is a thought, we unconsciously begin coolly and unexcitedly to accept it as having been such even originally. Looking upon it as a thought, we are able to adopt a calmer, more detached attitude toward it now. The calmness with which we are able to view the past is deliberately cultivated by the philosopher as he views the present. Tranquil impersonal feeling is the very essence of his attitude. Feeling is too strong a motive in human life ever to be killed, but when it is egoistic, it ought to be tamed. That is all philosophy asks of a man.

Human feeling is not called upon to eliminate itself, but to elevate itself. Human emotion is not to be destroyed, but to be understood and guided. Nobody can afford to ignore feeling, but must certainly come to terms with it. For it provides the heat which shall energize his life. It gives driving force, but he needs also to see where he is being driven. Its strength is no substitute for the safety of right direction. To gain this protective sight, both the guidance of reason and the prompting of intuition are required. He needs the light of intelligence also, and he needs it even more than heat. It tells him in which direction to move. If he moves in a wrong direction, then the more dangerous will his situation become. It is better if he generates the heat out of his light; then he will both walk aright and walk well. Therefore, emotional faith must be bridled by reasoned thinking. It is enough for most to follow their feelings blindly, but the student, remembering that philosophy can make no room for any mystification, must question his own. If they turn out to be leading him in a right direction, then he will follow them just as eagerly as the others do. But he will have the additional satisfaction of seeing where he is going. It is not that he must cast out all feelings from his heart. It is rather that he casts out what is unworthy and unlovely from feeling, what is low, negative, base, destructive, egoistic, agitated, false, and neurotically self-pitying or sentimental.

Yes, feeling remains, but it is purified, ennobled, exalted, calmed, and made philosophically truthful. Indeed, unless his feelings are aroused, the aspirant will never know the Overself, but those feelings are to be the lofty ones of devotion, reverence, veneration, and love of a kind to which earthly love can only point but never parallel. The Quest must arouse his intensive emotion, his deepest feeling. They must mingle with his intellect, his intuition, and his will in their service of it. Consequently, it cannot be a cold affair or a lifeless one. The true philosopher is not made of stone, nor is he without a heart, but all this feeling is not scattered in a hundred different directions. It is given up to the one thing that attracts it most, to the Overself. He is not unfeeling, cold, and inhuman, but he expresses only the highest emotions, or better still, he is emotionally free. To understand the desirability of such a state, we have only to contrast his durable serenity with the tumultuous emotionality of the neurotic, the hysteric, and the psychopath.

Emotion is so powerful a factor in human life and so valuable a one in human action, that it would be foolish to ask anyone to dispense with it. Philosophy does not ask for such a thing. But it does ask for a proper balance between emotion and reason and a sensible co-ordination between emotion and intuition. What most men do not see is that their real enemy is more often inside themselves than outside. For it is noticeably harder to reason out a situation calmly than to feel about it emotionally. Emotion in itself is neutral. It is not an evil to be overcome. It may ally itself with an evil idea, but it may also ally itself with a good one. The philosophic discipline calls for its conquest when it is joined to a false or evil idea, for it then chains the man to it. Therefore, the disciple, who must live more carefully than most people, will have to make a distinction between the lower and the higher emotions. He will have to discourage the one group and encourage the other. The lower emotions are to be firmly ruled by reason, the higher ones are to be harmoniously allied with it. All must be brought under control by a persistent self-imposed discipline. Refined by intuition, exalted by moral purpose, they are a powerful asset in his spiritual endeavor, but left to sway unchecked hither and thither or to overpower his thinking and will, they are a lamentable debit. He must not be easily moved.

Three practical methods for cleansing and calming the emotions may be profitably included in every regime. The first is to take advantage of the power of habit. Thus, the habit of dwelling inordinately on woman's beauty leads in the end to the desire for woman, whereas the habit of dwelling often on the soul's beauty leads in the end to the desire for the soul.

The second method is to make use of the opposite thought, the contrasting idea. He should take a moral quality which represents the very contrary of the weakness which is troubling him. In his daily meditation he should bring this desired quality or trait before his mind's eye and picture himself possessing it, identify his character with it. The creative power of such concentration will emerge in the course of time, for it will percolate down into those idle moments when the mind instinctively flies back to its desires and passions at the sight of some external stimulant.

The firm decision to cleanse his mind followed by the practical endeavor to nip every wrong thought in the bud is the third method which has helped many an aspirant. If he keeps to the method it will produce definite results. Even within a few months, the improved condition of his mind will be quite noticeable, but the success of the method depends upon catching each thought at its very birth and not waiting for it to grow up into a sturdy plant before attacking it.

He should learn to cherish right emotion, but spurn false emotionalism. This done, the emotional will no longer be the foolish while the intellectual will no longer be the ineffectual.

To curb spendthrift emotions, or even to put them into rational strait jackets, becomes desirable whenever they draw an aspirant away from pursuit of the Ideal. Something of the Stoic has indeed to be cultivated. When passion is finally brought to heel by intelligence and emotion eventually guided by impersonality, in both cases through the channel of the will, he is set free from many needless anxieties and safeguarded from many avoidable perils. His outward life will then run its course more quietly and more surely as his inward life will enjoy more serenity and more freedom than other men's.

There are many to whom such life of inward independence

is terrifying and repulsive. They do not see that their own uncriticized enslavement to bitterness and desire, to hatred and ignorance, to greed and prejudice, their own complacent crucifixion of the Ideal is what is really terrifying and repulsive. Or they declare it inhuman, thus standardizing man by what is base in him instead of by what is best. The weakling who yields at once to a sensual impulse, who does not think of entering into conflict with it, merely lives for the moment. He never cares to pause and consider what it is he is living for. That the best of life can be had only by a discipline of life is something known to more people than to philosophers. There is a pleasure from the results of such discipline which is unknown to those who float with the instincts and the senses. When the Quest enjoins the cultivation of a firmer will in certain directions, it would be a foolish thing to do it in a spirit of sullen obedience. The end of such cultivation can only be a truer enjoyment as well as a newer enjoyment.

To make such a stand against the common and constant identification of himself with the impulses and emotions in his ego, is sooner or later a necessary act on the part of an aspirant to spiritual light. If he repeats this act, a sufficient number of times, there will come to birth within his inner life a kind of fissure. There will be an observing self and an observed one. This may not be evident all the time, but it will be clearly evident at critical times and in important situations. In short, he will be coming under the guidance of, and sensing the outermost aura of, his Overself. The difficulties he formerly encountered in separating himself from his lower nature and the dread of unbinding himself from his ego may have discouraged him from even beginning on the Quest, but as against this he can now reckon the joy of following its obviously wise injunctions, the fascination of studying its history, background, and ramifications, and the reward of edging little by little toward the supremely desirable condition of self-mastery.

CHAPTER XIII

THE SILENT CALL OF THE OVERSELF

TWENTIETH-CENTURY MAN lives in an astounding age which too often prefers the blaring call of the saxophone to the silent call of the spirit. He spends the major part of his days in agitated pursuit of minor things. He wanders eagerly in quest of crowds but is unable to spare a second in quest of that stillness wherein, the *Old Testament* tells us, he can find God.

By inclination and education the Westerner is an extravert. His thoughts are constantly being drawn hither and thither, his feeling worked up by environment and events. He even becomes so intoxicated by his own deeds that he cannot stop doing something or other. This unbalanced extraversion, this continuous preoccupation with the physical aspect of life which is modern human existence is with the masses too often largely necessity, but with the more fortunate classes, deliberate choice. This impetuous desire to keep active, this eagerness to submit to a constant round of activities or engagements, this terrific pace of today which keeps either the bodies or the minds of people continually on the move is aggravated by the harsh pressure and raucous noise of contemporary city life.

The intensification of physical living obsesses modern energies and intoxicates modern minds. When added to the macerating wartime experiences through which so many millions of people have passed during this decade, it hardens the nerves and produces an insensitive materialism. It fills the atmosphere with unending strains. The resulting traumas have inevitably produced a crop of unpleasant psychoses and tormenting neuroses, of unhappy mental disorientations and discouraging nervous exhaustions. Neurotic people are more plentiful than at any previous time in human history. They are the inevitable by-product not only of a devastating war, but also of twentieth-century machine environments and complicated pressures of living. If serenity ever had any worth, surely it is today when violence, destruction, turmoil, change, chaos, and flux heave their troubled waters. Life is now so agitated that there is real need for a remedy for war neuroses and peace anxieties, for an antidote to the unprecedented strains and psychological stresses of the world crisis.

It is common enough to see the unrelaxed man hasten to accomplish his daily programs as soon as possible and remain nervously tense until he has done so. It would seem as if he were engaged in an endless hurried chase, entering on it anew each morning with impatience at the time it takes and in a rush to get through the immediate tasks. He gives clock-ruled time, and not intuitive rightness, the greater importance. The turbulence of his inner life and the triviality of his worldly interests waste his limited years and show either common insanity or personal inanity. He uses his self-created programs of activities as an excuse for postponing spiritual repose and in most cases the postponement is protracted for the rest of his life. Under existing conditions the mere business of attending to the details of living is so heavy that too much of his strength and day is taken up by its long littleness. It is so complicated that even a simple concentration on the spiritual life is hurdled with artificial obstacles. So he ties himself to the circumference of self and never takes or finds time to get at its center.

Modern man is rightly occupied with making money, but when his occupation becomes preoccupation, when it becomes so extremely dictatorial that it prevents him from all thinking about the higher goals of living, or when the spending of what he makes prevents it, he is courting trials and troubles from unexpected directions. The business of keeping his body fed, clothed, and sheltered may take up much of his time and most of his energy, but it ought not to prevent him attending to the higher business of finding his soul.

The nervous unrest, hurry, and excitement of our times leave no room for other than a life of fleeting sensations and brief impressions. Under such conditions, the deep and enduring things begin to disappear, the shallow and sensual begin to rise prominently above them. Love is replaced by lust, thoughtful reflection by mere curiosity, and men follow treacherous will-o'-the-wisps which lead them into marshes where they sink and suffer. On every side there is the spectacle of man fleeing from true life and hugging the mere illusory appearance of it, because that is easier than submission to its demands and acceptance of its readjustments. Yet he does not seem to realize that he is the real escapist.

It is a noticeable trend of this century, more undoubtedly in the modern West than in other areas, that seeks to crowd the utmost number of sensations into the day's experience. The trend has developed to a fantastic degree and has certainly contributed to the phenomenal increase in our times in medical cases of high blood pressure and premature heart failure. The relentless pressures of the twentieth-century man's daily program cause him to race through it and thus wear himself down. He who foolishly starts his activities or movements in such a desperate rush to finish them, such a fierce endeavor to exhaust himself sooner than is necessary, does not realize that he has to pay sooner or later for his foolishness. We must regret the fact but good intentions do not carry with them any guarantee against such error in living and its consequential suffering. Just as the introvert's desperate need is not more thoughts but more deeds, so the extravert's is not something he can do but something that will help him refrain from deeds.

When sickness forces an extreme extravert to take to his bed, do nothing, and be still, it may confer a real benefit on him by allowing his powers of reflection and intuition to become more active and useful to him. This forced confinement between bed sheets affects not only the invalid's body but also his mind. He is granted an opportunity to get some fresh perspective on his life's course and some fresh balance in its judgments. He finds himself in possession of an invaluable gift—an opportunity to revalue those judgments, a pause in this course, and a chance to see more deeply into the meanings of its past happenings and present circumstances no less than its future possibilities. Pressures then begin to lose something of their weight and urgencies to lose something of their speed. Here beneath these blankets he really relaxes—perhaps for the first time in many years—and the Overself, which could not bring him to meditation on his life purposes by pleasanter ways, now gains its end by unpleasant illness.

How many people find illness a time when relaxation, reflection, or prayer is enforced upon them, with results which beneficially influence the remaining years of their lives! How many times does the rest demanded by illness allow unrestricted play to Nature's healing forces to remedy what has been brought on by disobedience to the hygienic laws of the body! Thus Nature balances its physical injury to it.

If the body falls sick because its own proper hygiene is not being obeyed, because the laws governing its healthy functioning are being broken, then the sickness may prove useful to the extent that it arouses the sufferer to the need for living rightly and warns him to reform his physical habits. This should prompt the physician—who, incidentally, is recommended by Hippocrates, the founder of European medicine, to be also a philosopher—to reflect on the large number of illnesses which are really the seeking for refuge from the self's own imbalance, carelessness, or self-poisoning. He should further reflect on the large proportion which can be prevented if the persons concerned can be made to understand the danger signals which the intuition flashes to them, warning them to withdraw for a while into simple repose or spiritual retreat from the excessive tensions of work, passion, worry, and negative emotion, or from faulty habits of eating and drinking.

Where failure to recognize the correct nature of these signals leads to illness and the compulsory repose of, and retreat into bed, the patients have then the opportunity for possibly long-neglected and much overdue reconsideration of the basis of their life and the standards which govern it. If they refuse to accept it, if they are too hurt by their physical suffering or too ego-centered by their emotions to examine themselves and their conduct, then of course the sickness does nothing but harm to them.

Nevertheless it is a paradoxical fact that the same ill health which promotes relaxation and reflection and thus may lead indirectly to a brief spiritual illumination, may also in another person obstruct such an illumination. The general law governing this manifestation is that the body ought to be in a healthy condition if the mind is to receive the illumination correctly and without hindrance.

As if so much turmoil, agitation, and pressure were not enough, too many become and remain isolated from Nature through artificial circumstances of contemporary city life, as well as through wrong thinking and faulty living regimes. None need be surprised that all this has serious and harmful results from the philosophic point of view. Under its rule men tend to lose what religious faith they have or else never come to know mystical intuition. It prevents them finding the time to think for themselves about their life, its inner problems, higher goals, and deeper significance. It destroys the capacity to think for themselves as individuals, and largely lessens the ability to bring their thinking into a concentrated state. It works destructively against the leisurely deliberate quietness of the spiritual attitude.

Even many a spiritual aspirant tends to accept the suggestions of these massed numbers of people who constitute the society around him and who are not interested in nor engaged upon this same quest as himself. He creates fictitious duties for himself as the result. He finds himself without the time to study and think, to pause in the silence or meditate, and without the energy to divert his attention from the external course of events. Thus there is no escape for him unless he becomes an individualist.

Western man has explored and subdued most of the planet's surface; he has yet to explore even one-tenth of his own inner self. Because he has made an ever moving, impatiently energetic, and ambitious life the ideal one, he, more than others, needs to correct his one-sidedness. His agitations and activities may be virtues in his own eyes but are smiled at by those among the Orientals who still keep faithful to their inner heritage and leave themselves enough time for worship, meditation, silence, and solitude every day, and who thus keep an inner life as the core of the outer one. The Western habit of trying to keep occupied all the time leads to frayed nerves and moral confusion. The redress exists in making a place in the daily routine for learning the art of mental quiet. Intervals of the fullest mental and physical repose need to be inserted in this routine. The Occidental's repressed longing for inward peace has itself prepared him for the advent of these psychologic doctrines and mystical methods which can now help him to help himself. That there is an unconscious recognition of this need to secure better balance by taking to relaxational practices is evidenced by the steadily growing popularity of cults advocating such practices.

How different is the attitude of the relaxed man who attends to each step and lives each moment tranquilly and concentratedly! He possesses a serene feeling of leisure, a feeling incredible to those whose attitude is that every hour must be a busy one. He lives at his own pace, not at that of an unbalanced and frenetic society. His whole life moves to a different tempo, one without haste, peaceful and pleasant. There are even aimless hours in it which would be a madness to the modern Westerner. Yet he is neither a drifter nor a loafer. The general direction of his life has a well-defined purpose, his attitudes and actions have an undersurface meaning.

The exercise of unruffled calmness under all circumstances is a definite aid in every way. Out of it there comes naturally an accurate discernment of values and a balanced judgment. There are moments in most lives of great tribulation or of great temptation when controls may be easily shattered, but this is much less true when calmness has been cultivated. The relaxed man never permits himself to get so angry about anything that he loses self-control. His judgments will naturally be dispassionate and disinterested—not conditioned by his desires. His appraisals of the most hotly disputed issues will then be balanced and fair, and more likely to be correct and reasonable. He will not make a negative criticism without at the same time making a positive suggestion.

How can modern man dissolve his unrest and find such a desirable inward peace? He can do it by finding himself. He must begin with an antidote to his excessive extraversion. He can find this most effectively in the deliberate practice of introversion in either relaxation or meditation, or both, as a daily exercise. How few people have such a mystical life today! The present generation, war-weary and surfeited with extraversion, may be ready to welcome philosophic truth and mystical practice. It has tried long enough to live without a higher purpose. This has always failed in the past, as it is failing today. The prolonged immersion in externals has be-

gun to produce in more sensitive individuals a mutual recoil
upon the spiritual life.

Yet modern living holds too many distractions to permit
the easy attainment of inner peace without making a self-
denying struggle for it. What can be done by those who are
forced to take their share of the cares and pressures of everyday life? The idea of calling a sudden if temporary halt to
all this feverish activity is to some people an unpleasant and
irritating one. Yet that is precisely what philosophy bids them
do. They are apt to get so sunk in worldly interests and social
pleasures, in personal activities, that a passivity which with-
draws them utterly from it all appears as something trivial,
empty, useless, and irksome. It is necessary for the aspiring to
withdraw from time to time from their ordinary duties, and
during such periods to observe whether they are making mistakes or condoning weaknesses, to take stock of past experiences and present ideas and to inquire into the best course
of future development. This can most effectively be done in
quiet countryside retreats or by peaceful seaside shores. It is
not easily done in large noisy cities.

Most men need this spell of retreat because they need at
times a respite from the difficulties and struggles of life, so
that they may collect their forces before continuing the effort
to cope with them. They need to seek out places of secret
retreat from the city's noise, intervals of peaceful remoteness
from the city's bustle. This is to be done not as an escape
from the life of the world but as a preparation for it. They
are to withdraw when the inner prompting bids them do so,
when the inner need for such refuge becomes pressing, and
when the outer circumstances allow it.

All aspirants should use these intervals to learn more about
what they really are and what life really is. Then they are to
return to worldly duty, plunge into worldly activity, and
there test their knowledge, practice their discrimination, and
express their ideals. They need to retire from time to time,

whether for a half-hour or a month, to strengthen their forces and concentrate their feelings on the Quest. In these retreats they need solitude to create their own mental atmosphere; freedom to obey the inner promptings of their spirit nature; and aspiration to relax, purify, and ennoble their feelings.

Periodical retirement from the uncertainties of worldly affairs to the certitudes of spiritual ones, from the distractions of city life to the peace of Nature's solitudes, is an excellent rule. It is true that all feel at times the need of escape when overwork or overworry presses too much upon them or when too many contacts and too much bustle in cities make them look yearningly toward the country and toward solitude. At such times a respite from agitation is beneficial, indeed necessary. But, philosophy says, be reasonable with your retreat. Make it occasional in frequency and limited in duration. Go away from time to time but go away for a limited period only. Although philosophy approves of occasional retreats into quietist idleness as a temporary means to a wider end, it does not approve of quietist idleness as an end in itself. It never says find a permanent escape and remain a permanent escapist. A well-balanced life calls for a balanced form of retreat. It is just as effective to seek this and remain a layman as to spend all your life in escapist institutions and become a monk.

It is not necessary to flee to monasteries for this self-training; anyone can practice it in his own home. Sometimes he can even practice it better, for the opposition overcome, the difficulties mastered, will give him a tested strength which no monastery can give. Lecturing to Anathapindika, a multi-millionaire of his time who wanted to renounce the world, the Buddha, archapostle of world renunciation though he was, said: "I say unto thee, remain in thy station of life and apply thyself with diligence to thy enterprise. It is not life, wealth, and power that enslave men, but the *cleaving* to life, wealth, and power." When a man is concerned about lifelong retreat from the world, he may be obedient to a genuine inner need which at that particular stage will make for his true progress. But he may also be obedient, not to genuine need, but to a timid fear of becoming entangled in the affairs of troubled mankind. In that case, he has merely transferred his selfishness from a positive to a negative state. His virtue, having had no strain upon it, becomes a cloistered and enfeebled thing.

Where occasional withdrawal into retreat for longer periods is quite impossible, withdrawal every day into retreat for shorter periods is seldom impossible. They may be anything from fifteen minutes up to a whole day. They offer a chance to take a beneficent vacation away from everyday routines and worldly distractions.

The Adventure of Meditation. In this energetic era anyone who places a high or higher value on the practice of relaxation and meditation, is likely to be thought either a fool or a fanatic. It is one of the chief delusions of modern men, caught in urban maelstroms, that if they were to make these daily pauses in life, they would lose something because of the time lost from their affairs. On the contrary, if the pause is real and sincere, they would gain something in the very sphere in which the supposed loss would occur. Simply to introduce short intervals of the fullest relaxation in the daily regime of personal activity is enough to yield markedly beneficial results. Under the pressures of modern civilization they are a biological need. Any man will do more and better work, will feel less fatigued and conserve more vitality if he replenishes his forces by such rearrangement of his hours. Thus he loses nothing in actuality by losing these few minutes from his labors and pleasures. He needs these oases in the desert of life's journey. Thought and feeling should welcome these brief beautiful deliverances from the burden of common existence. Yet the sad irony is that so many people are too preoccupied with worries to spare time for that which could help them better to bear their worries. It is to their own loss that they have no desire to relax or to meditate. And could they understand the deeper phases of spiritual life, they would understand that the common notion that no activity of the body means nothing done or gained, is falsified by the gratifying results of meditation. The less common notion that no activity of the intellect means the same profitless result is falsified by the unforgettable results of contemplation. Incidentally these two are not the same but lower and higher stages of the same practice.

We may now see what profound wisdom hid behind the ancient religious lawgivers' injunction to keep a weekly sabbatical day of rest. These wise men of antiquity considered ways and means of reminding man of his true purpose on earth. He was apt to become wholly entangled in earthly desires and physical matters, and to forget what should be his supreme desire—the discovery of, and communion with, his divine soul. This is why they instructed him to substitute spiritual affairs and transcendental business for them, why they instituted a special day in the week for the purpose. He was recalled every seventh day to the higher object of all this work, the ultimate end for which it was only a temporary means. He was to be serious and even grave, to put frivolity aside for this one day because death was an ever-present shadow. A day of rest let his depleted surface consciousness lie fallow only to be all the more fruitful later; it gave the deeper levels of mind a chance to present their intuitive knowledge and it turned thought toward the sacred ultimate purpose of all human life.

The same need or duty is even more urgent in this twentieth century of ours. For modern invention, which could be used to bestow more leisure for spiritual pursuits, is actually used to defeat this aim. With the aid of automobiles, trains, and even airplanes, and with the facilities provided by amusement and sports places, the sabbath day is spent in transient pleasures. Such a day should be marked by the re-dedication of life to the loftiest accepted ideal and to the restatement of faith in its essentially spiritual character. It is the proper time to consider the future, to reflect upon the past, and consequently to make advisable changes in thought, plan, and practice. It is the time for a man to reinspire himself with basic attitudes. On that day he is to enter into prayer, think about ultimates, reflect about aims, remember aspirations, read inspired books, and practice meditations. He is to re-estimate his worth as bearing something divine in his heart. He is, finally, to consider and become conscious of the relationship which exists between himself and God.

The flow of everyday living in work or leisure ordinarily distracts the mind from its higher purpose and keeps it moving from subject to subject. This continuous dissipation of the self's psychical energies and vital forces prevents any withdrawal of attention being concentrated in the endeavor to come to itself. The attempt to save a certain number of minutes out of the day's twenty-four hours for the sole purpose of reversing the flow of attention, turning it from restlessness to repose and from the senses to the soul, is the most important any man could engage in. He who excuses himself on the grounds that he cannot find even this short period, should ask his conscience whether all his ordinary activity in both work and leisure is really as necessary as it seems. If his conscience affirms that it is, if he can do no more, then it will be enough to maintain the right attitude toward external affairs and to keep constantly in the background of his mind the thought of the spiritual quest. Yet the truth is that few are really in such an unfortunate situation.

No man may rightly say that he has had a full experience of life if he has not had any spiritual experience during life. If he is to become better balanced, Western man should not only give himself to active life but also to contemplative life. Exercises in meditation should be given a definite and assured place in Euro-American habits. Mystical practices should no longer be confined to a few persons and therefore considered to be abnormal, eccentric, or queer. They should be brought into use by a wider group. Whoever will devote a period of his day to them and will support them by an honest effort to reform his way of life, may one day feel within himself the presence of a purer individuality, a spiritual self. This daily habit of excluding the personal affairs from attention or detaching them from emotion, of holding the mind remote from the trivialities, the temptations, and the frictions of the world, while letting it sink deeper into abstraction, leads it to get and enjoy a tranquilizing respite of freedom from the pressure of life, work, and people.

The man who learns the art of retiring within himself to touch, not the darker strata of the ego's subconscious, but the deepest part of spiritual being, learns to possess both restfulness and happiness at his command. To the extent that he digs more deeply into his mind, he there finds benedictory powers of healing and pacification. A prefatory of such silent contemplation radiates its mood and spirit into the rest of his day.

The more interior degrees of the mind's own being are the degrees nearest to the Overself. It is because of this fact that the value of mystical meditation is unique. For it draws the meditator's consciousness more and more inward, more and more to the divine state that is its kernel. So long as the mind searches in regions alien to it, so long will the world's ultimate secret elude it. For the first step which the primordial cosmic Mind took was outward into world manifestation and this points out the inward direction in which our own last step must go: that is, within the mind itself.

The human mind is everlastingly curious. It wants to know more and more. Yet it can never finally slake this curiosity and satisfy this craving. All that it gathers is finite and limited, incomplete and insufficient—and must remain so. When at last it wakes up to this fact, it will sooner or later put itself upon the Quest. Then, when it finally succeeds in turning around and gazing within, it will be stilled in, and become questionless with, an infinite satisfaction.

We see things around us but not the light which renders the act of seeing possible. We experience the movement of thoughts but not that which renders this movement possible. For just as we must presuppose the existence of light in order to see a thing, so we must presuppose the existence of mind in order to know a thought. So long as the individual consciousness is entirely wrapped up in gazing at this pictorial presentation which it calls the "world," so long will it be unconscious of its own being, so long will it remain an undisclosed mystery to itself. We do not know that the same thoughts which make up the world of our transient experience, at the same time keep us from the world of eternal reality. This is why the need of mystic withdrawal from them is a paramount. The aim of meditation, when culminating in contemplation, is the stilling of all mental activity so that Mind itself, the source and condition of this activity, may be known in its original state. The practice ultimately leads the artist to find beauty and the mystic to find the godlike within himself. This is its highest purpose. Thus it leads them from materialism to mentalism, which teaches the truth about "matter" and unveils the reality behind its manifold appearances.

There is a Mind in man, immeasurably superior to his ordinary mind. If, in quiet moments and still moods, he will patiently wait its promptings and submit to them, if in these utterly relaxed reveries he will wait watchfully yet positively until the Overself reveals its presence to him, he may gain understanding, power, and guidance immeasurably superior to what he ordinarily knows as his own.

Strength runs wild without wisdom and calmness to direct

it; the complementary truth is that knowledge is dumb unless it is put into action. The squatting figure of the yogi seated in tranquil meditation and resting under cooling palm-fronds, silent and motionless as a stone, is fascinating to some harassed Westerners. He is a reflective witness and not an active player in the game of life, his eyes are set, half-closed in a still glance and his mind is held fast in a world where there are no troublesome questions and no worrying problems. But can the yogi bring this same detachment into the busy turbulent kind of life which the average Westerner must live?

That man comes nearer to sanity and a full-balanced life who begins or punctuates or ends his day by sitting erect with folded palms or hands upon his knees, with quiet ordered breathing and with eyes half-open or closed, and who fixes his thoughts for as long as he can spare upon the Mind which is at once the sublime source and mysterious sustainer of his being; and who then, deliberately draws moral strength and far-seeing vision from his moments of meditation in order to go about his daily business, whether in office or factory, law court or hospital, farm or ship. If he seeks to do his work with efficient keenness and effective practicality, both he and the world will be gainers. He will have sufficient philosophic detachment to discern in the very midst of his external activities and earthly ambitions that they are as transient as foam. He will try to do his duty amid the world's bustle, and to do it well, but he will not neglect the higher duty which he learns from the stillness mystically hiding behind that bustle. He will discipline himself daily but the source of such discipline being the Overself, it will more and more rise spontaneously and without effort or seeking. By this regime it will eventually be possible for him to reach a state wherein the hurts and harms of everyday life possess but little power to wound. Even mistakes will be immediately converted into opportunities for growth.

Civilization will justify itself only when men of the world become mystics, and when at the same time mystics rediscover the world. In the kind of period in which we live today, dominated as it is by economics and politics, by materialism and by violence, mysticism is inevitably separated from worldly life. The quieter minds react from its noisiness by withdrawal into solitude. The intuitional spirits react from its materialism by withdrawal into study and contemplation. Mysticism can find no standing ground for itself and allies itself with escapism. But although driven now to do this in self-defense, it will eventually be driven to reverse this process, following certain events. When the climax of violence passes, when materialism sinks exhausted, mysticism will have to return to active service, and its leaders will begin to feel the urge and guidance to work in the outer world. Then they will find a place for themselves in a society which, in its old dispensation, had little use for them. Then public life will be inspired by its revelations.

When a fine Spanish contemplative, Ste. Theresa, finally penetrated the enchanting glamour of her own mystical experience, she remarked: "This is the end of that spiritual union, that there may be born of its working, *works.*" What she found in the course of her own development, foreshadowed what will be found eventually in our own century by intelligent mystics, as contrasted with self-centered neurotic ones. They will have to form precise and clear ideas as to the practical implications and social values of mysticism during a time of world upheaval.

The hour will indeed come for the extraverted man to get a fresh understanding of himself, and at the same time to bring inner peace to his disrupted nerves. He has been questioning the whole universe for centuries, it is inevitable that he should also begin to question himself.

It is hard to say, precisely and accurately, how anyone begins to know that this sublime power, the Overself, exists within him: the revelation is a compounded one. It consists of a metaphysical certitude, an intuitive feeling, and a mystical experience—all pointing to an indescribable something which alone, of all things, exists by its own independent right; which has as its very nature, causeless, eternal, and perfect being.

Take Jesus' statement that "The kingdom of heaven is within you." The meaning of his beautiful words is transparent. He who looks for something ecclesiastical behind them is wasting time. They plainly bid each man to listen in silent reverie to the sublime intimations of his hidden being, that is, to practice mental quiet and enter into contemplation. Once he recognizes that the Divine Mind, wherever else it may also be in this infinite universe, is certainly within himself too, he ceases to wander in darkness and starts walking in light. God is then no longer an alien and remote Being to be propitiated in abject fear or flattered in wheedling mendicancy but a sublime ever-presence to be sought in his own heart—and to be sought nobly in joy, reverence, humility, and love. In the end, religious teachings about the soul must not only be founded on authentic personal experience of the leaders but must also lead to personal experience of the followers, or they will prove insufficient.

The soul, this mysterious entity who is wholly nonexistent to many people and whose quest is a chimera to most people, will eventually prove to be the only one who remains when all others pass away. If a man's thought is always directed toward the objects of his experience and never diverted toward the consciousness which makes that experience possible, then it is inevitable that those objects shall assume a significance and reality in and for themselves alone. That is to say, he will become a materialist. Yet the Overself is that out of which his own consciousness has come. Ought he not to give himself the daily spiritual chance to come in contact with it, with his most intimate self?

He may travel the entire length and breadth of the five continents to commune with their cleverest scientists, but if he does not also travel within and commune with his own divine self, then the secret of life will still elude him. He misses what is most important if he misses going into the invisible temple of his own heart. There the soul abides, there the ray of God strikes the individual, and there alone the satisfying discovery of what he really is may be made. This is the fundamental task—to become aware of the divine that is in him. All others are secondary and tertiary. He must establish himself in the consciousness of the Overself by and for himself. No other man can do it for him. And the Quest's labor in purification and meditation is indispensable for this purpose.

A Practical Exercise. The meditation practices have been described in some of this writer's earlier books—*The Secret Path*, *The Quest of the Overself*, and *The Wisdom of the Overself*—and those descriptions need not be duplicated here.

But it has become advisable to remind readers again of the warning given in those works. They should make clear to themselves that spiritualistic mediumship is not in any way a goal to be sought by philosophic aspirants and that if their meditation practice shows signs of leading to such a result, it should be dropped. They are not ready, and should apply their endeavors in the direction of self-betterment.

The indiscriminate practice of exercises in psychical passivity and negativity and mediumship by people who know little or nothing about the forces they are evoking, is to be deplored. But in a different way the same criticism must be applied to those who dabble in mystical exercises without reference to the moral laws and manifold conditions governing mysticism. Meditation is merely a part of the total approach needed in the quest of the Overself. The work upon proper balancing up of the psyche, upon strengthening character and eliminating negative traits, is even more important. For it is both a safeguard to ensure correct results and a means to avoid needless sufferings.

When intelligence, common sense, judgment and discrimination are lacking while neurotic emotions, hysterical tendencies, and personal egoism are strongly present, when little or no attempt is made to discipline character, to cast out destructive feelings like anger and hate, the powers which may be unfolded by meditation may prove more harmful than beneficial. Such perils are then courted as nervous breakdowns, hallucinations, inflated self-esteem and insanity. Hence it was laid down in the ancient yoga manuals that purification should precede or accompany meditation.

The practical techniques of the relaxation practices have not been given out before and the core of them may now be briefly pictured. The student can begin them by adopting a more restful attitude toward people and events generally. This is a matter of imbibing a little philosophy. Then he can go on to the exercise proper, throwing his body flat on its back in a supine posture, closing its eyes and conserving all its muscular and nervous energy. The body and mind mutually interact. A relaxed body tends to induce a relaxed mind just as an excited mind tends to induce restlessness of body.

Relaxation will give him the tonic he needs and the repose he requires, but to put the body into a more receptive state, the exercise should be prefaced by deep and rhythmical breathing, done as soon as the student lies down on his back. His hands should lie loosely interlocked on the solar plexus. The air is a carrier of life force and a change in the manner of its intake affects the body and removes fatigue very quickly. This rhythmic exercise requires an inhalation to be made silently and very slowly, counting one, two, three, four, five. As he exhales, he should mentally repeat the same count. It is this consistency of measured balanced rhythm which draws vitality from the air into the body and harmonizes its functions. He should saturate the mind itself in this rhythm. In time the lungs will follow it automatically and attention will be so immersed as to become unified with it. The breaths should be long, deep, slow, and even, not jerky and not strained. The slowing down of respiration should result in a lessening of tension. A few minutes of this preliminary practice should spread the vitality in a rippling pattern through the whole body. He should think of the One Life-Force pervading the entire universe, existing everywhere, filling all space, containing and permeating all creatures, including himself and all humanity. He should then imagine it being drawn in from space around the head, then flowing evenly and rhythmically down the right side and back to the head again. This circular flow should be repeated a few times, letting the current rest in the head for a while at the end of each circuit. No part of the body is to be left out of the beneficial flow. All this is done with closed eyes.

The next step is to lift both arms and let them flop down abruptly by their own weight as if they have suddenly gone dead. This is to be repeated with the legs. Then he is mentally to examine the whole body, from head to foot. He will find that some muscles are unconsciously contracted and tensed. He should free them from such contraction wherever found and from tenseness of nerves wherever felt. The limbs should be comfortably slack. He should take special care to loosen any tightness in the hands and spine, and to relax the knot of muscles between the shoulders and the nape of the neck.

The perfect human example of repose is the sleeping babe. Civilized habits of living have brought artificiality. Modern clothes, furniture, and methods of work have interfered with and even perverted the natural ways of reposing self. They contract the muscles when there is absolutely no need to do so, thus wasting energy and running down the bodily battery.

A useful supplementary practice for anyone engaged in

continuous labor, or mental activity, is suddenly and deliberately to take a minute or two out of each hour, if he is free
to do so, and to spend them in the supine posture, utterly
limp and completely withdrawn from whatever he happens
to be doing. When this is impossible, a brief midmorning and
midafternoon break of the same motionless kind will be the
next best help. The amount of energy conserved by reverting
to this relaxed state between working efforts may be infinitesimal at any given moment but it becomes quite considerable when measured on the scale of months and years. What
the undisciplined man unwittingly wastes in unnecessary or
excessive contractions of certain muscles, and in exaggerated
movements of the whole body, let alone in unconscious fidg-
eting of the hands or feet, shows how greatly he is victimized
by bad habits.

The exercises in relaxation may also be used when faced
with many kinds of problems. A mind overwrought by some
troubling event or by nervous fatigue may gain a better approach if it resorts to this limp and lifeless posture and at the
same time makes the body's breathing rhythmic and slow,
or if it takes these short stimulating periods of respite from
such oppression. If he runs into any of life's manifold difficulties, causing anxiety, fear, or distress, the student should
practice the physical technique whenever that is possible, or
the mental technique of relaxing into complete calmness,
when it is not. He should suspend all judgment upon the situation and remember that to manifest fear, for instance, is
really to pass judgment. He must pause from all consideration of the matter and let it go mentally until he can grasp
the first emotional fruit of the successful practice of relaxation, which is a large reduction in moods of fear, worry, or
anger.

The application of these techniques to a difficult or threat-
ening situation is not a form of escape. That a man should
look its facts squarely in the face, is an obvious philosophic

counsel. But he should not look at them while he is panicky, terrified, or too upset to see the best way out. Rather ought he to look at them after the relaxation practice has calmed down his nerves and feelings, restored his poise, shaken off his tensions, and strengthened his judgment. He will then certainly be stronger and serener, hence better able to deal with them. He may even be wiser, in which case, he will be more confident and more courageous too. Nothing will be lost in regard to time, for with such an approach he will be able to make decisions more quickly and begin necessary actions more rapidly.

In the case of that prolonged relaxation which is sleep itself, it would do every man nothing but good if he surveyed his day's activity at its nightly end and asked himself, as Pythagoras advised his disciples to ask: "What have I done? What have I left undone that I ought to have done?" The results of this interrogation should be made use of in renewed attempts at self-discipline. It is an equally useful practice to use the first few minutes after wakening for self-examination or self-preparation. It is a good time to give a little thought— however little—to putting himself into harmony before starting again and carrying on with the routines of the day.

All that has been written heretofore about the freeing of emotion and thought from negative qualities and about their training in meditation and relaxation, has been intended to lead to a spiritual result. This preliminary process is inescapable in most cases for the attainment of such a result. Just as the farmer must spend a long time carefully preparing the earth and properly sowing the seeds if he wants a good crop, so the aspirant must prepare the right conditions and develop the right qualities if he wants an authentic mystical experience. But it would be unfair to the Quest to remain totally silent about its physical result. Medical science has begun, somewhat belatedly, to inquire into the psychosomatic origin of disease and is being forced to yield, somewhat reluctantly, to the conclusion that physical disease can have a psychological cause.

Physical health is something that we can only partly control by obedience to the laws of physical hygiene. For the body's state is inseparably linked up with the mind's. Both interact and influence each other. Wrong thinking, ugly feeling, or disordered passion may not at once but ultimately can find expression in fleshly ill health or untoward accident.

Thoughts can benefit health or harm it, can help the body's functions or hinder them. A man who feels the force of a bereavement to the point of intolerable anguish, may eat food and yet not digest it, may remain unnourished, become weak and thin. "The body is affected by mental agony like the water in a jar by the red-hot iron thrust into it," was pointed out at least five thousand years ago by the sages of India's *Mahabharata*. There are those who would attribute Hamlet's melancholy to the disordered state of his liver, but they should also inquire whether the disordered state of his liver was not due to his melancholy.

Wrong thinking may reproduce itself in diseased tissue. Emotional upset may be the hidden cause of physical sickness. Moral attitudes are not without practical values. Mental processes may have bodily results. The relation between thought or feeling and sickness or disease is a traceable one—the pairs cannot be separated. A man who holds a negative emotional mood, for a sufficient length of time will, sooner or later, find it reflected in a negative physical condition. If it is a mood of excessive criticism of others, it may cause him to secrete bile excessively: the consequence will be the creation of a bilious condition. If this is prolonged long enough, his liver may be permanently disordered. And if hate is added to the criticism, forever filling his mind, then it is a direct operation of Nature's law that poison shall eventually fill his blood. Other negative feelings like anger and bitterness, frustration and hatred, jealousy and greediness, if strong enough and sustained enough, can become translated in time into bodily sickness.

The corruption of man's thoughts and feelings—a long slow process—led in time to the corruption of his body and organs. In the bringing defilement into the one, he brought disease into the other. In his earlier days healing agencies were unknown because they were unnecessary.

If it is possible for negative thoughts and emotions to disturb the functioning of the body, should it not be possible for positive ones to promote it? If the mind can unwittingly create illness should it not be able consciously to create good health? Logic calls for an affirmative answer. Nevertheless if it is a little known but much-needed truth that many sicknesses can be traced to defects in character and errors in thinking, it is quite fantastic to assert that all sicknesses are so traceable. Physical hygiene has its own place and importance, its own laws and principles.

Moments of Illumination. Mystical and religious worship differ. In the former there is an effort to unite through meditation with the higher power, whereas in the latter there is an effort to commune through prayer with it. The separateness from it is therein acknowledged and maintained whereas the mystic seeks to overcome that feeling. Each kind of worship is necessary to, and has its own place in, the spiritual life. The conviction that there is an "Other," a power different from and higher than his own possesses the religious devotee. The conviction that this "Other" is identical with his innermost self, possesses the mystical meditator. Meditation leads in the end to a sense of great strength because the meditator approaches union with his higher self, some of whose strength thereupon begins to enter into him. Prayer on the other hand, because of the sense of distance between the devotee and God, keeps him humble and weak. Indeed, prayer will fail to achieve its purpose if it is uttered by one who feels conscious of his strength and wisdom, his self-reliance and self-importance. If it is to have any effectiveness at all, it must be uttered in a feeling of contrition, weakness, dependence, and humility.

Religious devotion is a correct attitude for all human beings. As rays of the spiritual sun, they should adore their source; as the imperfect, they should love the perfect being.

All meditations should be prefaced by intense devotion, fervent aspiration, loving worship, and humble prayer. The emotions must get deeply involved in this quest. Self-developing thought is necessary but self-humbling prayer is not less necessary. The chief value of any kind of religious worship is the extent to which it abruptly recalls the mind from pre-occupation with worldly affairs to self-humbling recognition of its own relation to the divine source. Every man has the right to pray to his Overself. When he bends himself mentally in its humble silent worship, he is obeying a sound instinct and claiming his own.

Sometimes within the periods of relaxation, prayer, or meditation but sometimes outside them, the aspirant will experience moments, moods, hours, or even days of great uplift, serene exaltation, or ecstatic inspiration. These are really glimpses, either from near or from afar, either clear or ego-colored, of the Overself. Such moments with their rich feeling and deep understanding endure in memory and can never be forgotten. They give another dimension to his life. He will come to esteem these infrequent glimpses, these brief illuminations, as holding the best of all values in life for him.

Linked with these glimpses is all that the more inspired workers in every art are trying to find and express. It is the pure spirit of beauty. It speaks to their intuition and through them to the intuition of mankind, whose higher development is thereby helped.

The felicitous experience of the Overself may or may not

come briefly but it always comes abruptly. At one moment the student is his ordinary egoistic self, struggling with his restless thoughts and turbulent feelings, at the next the ego suddenly subsides, and every faculty becomes quiescent. All he has to do is to be nonresistant to the divinity which is taking possession of him, to receive lovingly and not strive laboriously. The change catches him unawares because of its suddenness. It may be preceded by a curious happy premonition. It may also be precipitated, marked, or helped by an important external event or series of such events. But whether or not this happens he will be fully aware of a movement away from the habitual center of his feeling, thinking, and doing into a new one upon a totally different and superior level.

The oncoming of this experience will be marked by various other signs. The intellect becomes suspended; will, judgment, memory, and reasoning slip gently into mild abeyance. A deep serenity unknown before takes possession of him, and an exquisite calm settles over him. In these moments of joyous beauty, the bitterest past is blotted out, and the ugliest history redeemed. With the mind deep-held by the Overself in an atmosphere of exaltation, the harassments and burdens of life beat but faintly at the portals of attention; the troubles of a lifetime recede to nothingness, the fears of the future decline into triviality. The outlook on the world becomes enlarged, ennobled, and illumined, and is no longer bounded wholly by commonplace interests. Some of the veils hiding truth are lifted for a time. The idea that he has a higher self, the conviction that he is fundamentally a soul, breaks in upon his little existence with great revelatory force, and he feels he is emerging into glorious light after a dreary journey through a long dark tunnel.

For the Overself to give itself wholly and perpetually to a man, is a rare and wonderful event. Most often it gives itself only for a short time. It is a common complaint that exalted experiences of its presence are not continuous, are indeed utterly beyond the aspirant's control. The Overself seems to leave him and the loss brings him back to his ordinary self. These phenomena are not subject to his will. He has no power of himself to repeat them. The heavenly visitations come he knows not how, and just as mysteriously they depart. He will never be able to observe precisely the mechanics of this movement of grace.

The glimpses are fleeting ones because he is still too unprepared to remain abidingly in such a lofty order of being. The glowing experiences are glorious and memorable, but he falls back from them because he is dazzled by their brightness and cannot retain them precisely because he is too unequipped to do so. They are not able to remain for a longer time because the nature is still too undeveloped to be able to hold them forever, because the lower tendencies are too strong to let the Overself abide in the mind and heart without disturbance and because there is lack of balance between the different parts, especially between the feelings and the intellect. Until he conquers his defective nature and attains the required standard of disciplined character, the full and lasting illumination must wait its time.

Because they are so exceptional it is folly to demand their return, but wisdom to work for it. He who has once seen the goal, felt its sublimity, discerned its reality, enjoyed its beauty, and known its security, should draw from the experience the strength needed for the hard upward climb. He should regard the short glimpse afforded him in the glow of these, his best moments, as a working blueprint. He has to make himself over again according to the mental picture thus placed before him. The difference between the idea and the actuality should shame him constantly into renewed endeavor, should call him to more serious, more frequent and sterner efforts, and should arouse in him increased ardors of moral self-improvement. It has shown him his finest potentialities of virtue; now he has to realize them. All elements of personality must be adjusted to the ideal shown by the glimpse, as the whole personality itself has to be surrendered to it. A work lasting several years may be rooted in a flash lasting only a few minutes.

The development should not only be balanced but also broad. It must accept the fact that the human being has four sides needing attention and cultivation. Only when this all-round development is thus brought together and harmonized, do the proper conditions exist for a lasting enlightenment. The temporary illuminations are incomplete and imperfect; they lack the full extent and greater knowledge which comes with the final and permanent illumination. They are minor; it is major.

The delight of each exalted moment and the fragrance of its heavenly visitation will linger in memory for years after it has itself vanished. The influence on after life and thought is as long and beneficent as it itself is short and beautiful. The experience will soon slip away, but the memory of its certitude will remain. It serves to intensify and enlarge his love of, and attraction to, the Overself, and to provide him with beautiful memories to support and sustain him in faithfulness to the Quest during the fatiguing long-drawn years of struggle and darkness. To that diviner self thus glimpsed he must henceforth address all his prayers, through its remembrance he must seek succor, in its reliance he must perform all his endeavors, by its light he must move along the roads of life, and of its compassion he must plead for grace.

It is often asked why it is that this inner self is so cunningly hidden, so utterly elusive, so completely withdrawn from human sight and search. Why have we been put at such pains to find it? The answer is that the greatest treasures are the most carefully guarded. But it is also that the Overself cannot wear clothes of egoistic thoughts and wear animalistic forms without falsifying its real character. It is we who must shed such limitations and thus attain the capacity to approach it.

God has no intention of hiding forever from the children whose very existence is the result of God's own activity. Little by little, and as they learn to use their natural endowments while they grow, they will inevitably come closer to the Overself, God's deputy on earth to them. Nothing is withheld from them except what does not belong to the particular phase they are passing through. They will have to unfold all their faculties of feeling, thought and will, later of intuition, discipline and balance them under the intuition's rule. This done, the revelation will certainly be made and the Overself will then of its own accord bestow its light quite spontaneously, at first through glimpses but in the end fully and finally.

The Overself is the soul of man, his connection with the Absolute Power. One part of him lives, suffers, and enjoys in time and space. Another part, mysterious, almost unknown, transcends it utterly and dwells serenely free from its mutations. Every man in the depths of his essential being is an emanation of the World-Mind. Therefore he is diviner than he knows, holier than he seems, and wiser than he thinks. His self-effort does not bring the transcendental consciousness into being, does not create it. Eternal and undying, it was always there in the deepest layer of his mind. What he does is to penetrate to it, and realize it. His finite ego is not so completely sundered from the infinite World-Mind that there is not even the most indirect relation between them. There exists this holy link of the Overself through which and in which the ego may enter the divine presence. It is the higher individuality, the permanent self in him.

But the Overself's immortality, although ageless by our earthly standards, is still subject to the opening and closing of the cosmic cycle. It is still a part of the World-Mind's manifested cosmos, whose merger in Mind marks its own merger too. It is impossible for human imagination to conceive the duration of a cosmic aeon. So vast is it that it may be taken as a synonym for eternity. The Overself lives throughout such an aeon and then, with the withdrawal of the World-Mind and its entire cosmos of all things and all beings, into utter latency, merges into the ultimate Void. It will manifest again only after the dawn of a new cosmic day.

When we experience Mind through the senses we call it *matter*. When we experience it through imagination or thinking we call it *idea*. When we experience it as it is in its own pure being, we call it *Spirit*, or better, Overself. This is insight, this spontaneous realization that Mind forever is, whether as Void or world. After a beautiful intuition, an ecstatic mystical meditation, the mystic believes that he has had a visitation by the Overself. But it can never really visit him because it has never really departed from him. It is an ever-presence, always with him. That which changes, that which moves is thinking. Whether he listens or not and whether he hears it or not, the Overself, however, perpetually and silently says "I AM!"

There only, in the consciousness which is completely self-sufficing because completely real, is it possible truly to pronounce the words: "I am!" For in all lesser states man may only say: "I am this body" or "I am these thoughts" or "I am these emotions." This is why what the unillumined man calls *I* is really something else. And this is why he must learn the art of abstracting himself from the not-self, if he wants the peace of true fulfillment.

What all this has to do with the critical state of present-day world affairs should be plain enough by now. The connection depends both upon the truth of man's nature and the purpose of his incarnation. The assemblage of men and women called society is no less subject to the necessity of shaping its life by that truth and that purpose than is any single individual. Socrates wept over the corruption and ignorance of Athens as Jesus wept over the corruption and ignorance of Jerusalem. Men pass their whole lives in error when they might pass them in truth. They do wrong when they might do good. The result is suffering when it might be peace. When all the chief decisions of their life are made in a condition of spiritual ignorance, what other results may be expected than unfortunate ones? It is a bitter moment—and the consciousness of their error falls painfully upon them—when they discover that the aims pursued have led them up a blind alley and that the ambitions nurtured have yielded only ashes for their hands.

Materialism is inevitable but can be only a temporary phase of man's endeavor to comprehend the facts of life. To those who wish to escape from the pressures and tyrannies of contemporary materialism, philosophy offers the most effective way and the safest road. It helps to understand the true relationship between the divine and the human. It will enable them to realize their spiritual potentialities.

Every nation's most important problem is human ignorance of divine laws. That crime and sordidness and the remnants of animality expressed in brutality and violence, exist in human life who may deny? But we need not dwell on them. The evil in human nature is a fact for all practical purposes, however relative and ideational it may be for metaphysical purposes. Although the sage on his mental pinnacle may tolerantly see divine goodness everywhere, the sage in his physical relations with men may not overlook the dark elements of their ethical make-up. So philosophy's aspirants must judge how far it is right to flow with the currents of their time and at what point they are to resist them. If others behave wrongly, let them have the pleasure of behaving rightly. If others are foolish and selfish, let them have the satisfaction of being wise and altruistic. If humanity is going downhill, let them start going uphill.

INDEX